McGovern: A Biography

McGovern

A BIOGRAPHY

by Robert Sam Anson

Holt, Rinehart and Winston
NEW YORK · SAN FRANCISCO · CHICAGO

Published simultaneously in Canada by Holt, Rinehart
and Winston of Canada, Limited.
ISBN: 0–03–091345–4 (Hardbound)
ISBN: 0–03–004751–X (Paperback)
Library of Congress Catalog Card Number: 72–183538

Designer: Christine Aulicino
Printed in the United States of America

For Hoa, Thua, Tieu, Huong, Ti,
and the old man

Contents

Preface   ix

1. NIGHT FLIGHT   1
2. A SON OF THE MIDDLE BORDER   12
3. THE *Dakota Queen*   37
4. THE CHANGELING   49
5. AGAINST THE ODDS   68
6. WAR AGAINST WANT   99
7. RETURN OF THE NATIVE   119
8. MAGNIFICENT OBSESSION   149
9. A TIME TO KEEP   186
10. THEIR DAILY BREAD   218
11. TOWARD 1972   243
12. THE POLITICS OF BELIEF   278

Index   293

Preface

In the ultimate sense, this book had its beginnings in the small Cambodian village of Kompong Phloeung, where for twenty-one days in August 1970 I was a prisoner of a mixed force of North Vietnamese and Cambodian guerrillas. Our little town was as remote as any place could be. The last time a white man chanced that way, I was told, was during the first Indochinese war. But isolated as Kompong Phloeung was, its people had heard of George McGovern. One day, during a conversation with an English-speaking Vietnamese officer, Nguyen Cao Ky's name came up, and I started to repeat McGovern's famous characterization of the South Vietnamese Vice President. The soldier cut me off. "Ah, yes," he said, "Senator McGovern called him a 'tin-horn dictator.' Tell me, what is this 'tin horn' of which the Senator speaks?" In the days that followed, McGovern's name arose in our conversations a number of times. It was obvious that both the Vietnamese and the Cambodians regarded him as their one clear hope for peace. "If you see him," one Vietnamese told me, "please tell him that here we remember him." I vowed that I would.

I kept that promise a few months later during a lengthy luncheon with McGovern in the Senate dining room. We talked about the war, the determination of the Vietnamese, and the moral costs, both at home and abroad. Finally, we turned to the inevitable subject, his presidential ambitions. It was still two months until his formal announcement, but McGovern was very candid about it. "I've got to announce now," he said, with surprising force. "I can't pretend that I don't want to be President. I just can't bullshit people about it." A strange politician, I thought; someone who can't stand to bullshit the people. We talked on, and I repeated all the familiar clichés about his supposed lack of charisma. At last I blurted out: "Do you ever get mad about anything?" "You're damn right I do," he shot back. "When it comes to Southeast Asia, I am the angriest man in the Senate." I was beginning to see what the Vietnamese meant.

Some months later McGovern asked if I would take a leave of absence from my job at *Time* magazine, covering the new left, to write his biography. I replied that very few biographies about politicians were credible, and that those that were—I had James MacGregor Burns's excellent study of John Kennedy in mind—usually enraged the subjects. I would undertake the project, I added, only if he would agree to a number of conditions. I sent the letter off, assuming that that would be the end of it. A few days later, McGovern called and said: "Fine, go ahead." I would, he promised, have "carte blanche." "Carte blanche?" I asked skeptically. "Carte blanche," he replied firmly.

McGovern was true to his word. He opened himself up to hours of detailed interviews, covering every aspect of his life, including some intimate incidents that most men—not to mention every politician—would just as soon forget. But McGovern talked freely about everything, as did his staff and family. To supplement the personal interviews, McGovern turned over his files, records, and memoranda, as well as official and personal correspondence—virtually every piece of paper written by him or about him since he entered public life eighteen years ago. The degree of access was remarkable, to say the least. Even more remarkable was McGovern's insistence—which he put into writing —that though this was to be an authorized biography, in the sense that he was cooperating with its writing and benefiting from its publication, he would have no right of censorship or prior approval over the judgments that are rendered in these pages.

This book, then, is in no way the product of a professional image maker. It is, on the contrary, the work of a journalist who started out skeptical and remained so throughout the reporting, writing, and final editing. This is not to say that I have been objective throughout; no journalist ever is. I have, however, endeavored to be fair, including the bad with the good, the criticism with the plaudits; and as I think the reader will discover before he is not too far into this book, there are plenty of both. Whether this effort will fall into the category of most political biographies, whether it will enrage its subject, or whether it will fall somewhere in between is something I have no way of knowing. I have tried to write this book the way George McGovern would have written it, if our roles had been reversed—with his honesty and, I hope, with a measure of his passion.

None of this could have been attempted without the active cooperation of several score of people. Foremost among them is Eleanor McGovern, who is every bit as candid, and in some ways even more remarkable, than her more famous husband. It is one of the failings of biography specifically, and the American system generally, that the wives of the great and near-great tend to be ignored or relegated to the roles of household appliances. Eleanor McGovern is not such a woman. She has done more than hold the McGovern household together while her husband has been off campaigning, though that in itself is no mean achievement. She is, to a considerable degree, responsible for her husband's political success. Without her personal intervention in the closing weeks of the 1962 campaign, it is doubtful that George McGovern would have ever made it to the U.S. Senate. All of which is a way of saying that her role is in major excess of the space she has been granted in this book.

There are several other people deserving of special mention. One of them is Miss Pat Donovan, McGovern's personal secretary, who knows her boss's mind perhaps better than anyone else and has been kind enough to share many of those insights with me. She has also guided me through the labyrinthine passages of the Old Senate Office Building attic, where some of McGovern's most valuable reminiscences are stored. Gordon Weil, executive assistant to the Senator, has also done several tours in the attic and has been of special assistance in promoting and furthering this project. His wit and perception brightened many otherwise dark moments when it seemed doubtful that this book would ever be finished. I confess to having shamelessly stolen from both.

I have also leaned heavily on the published efforts of several other men, including McGovern himself, whose *Agricultural Thought in the Twentieth Century* brought at least a dim understanding of the complexities of the farm problem. *War Against Want* provided similar cognition of the workings of Public Law 480 and the Food for Peace program, while *A Time of War, A Time of Peace* was a valuable tool in preparing the chapter on McGovern's experiences in the Senate. McGovern's most useful book, though, is his soon to be published doctoral thesis on the events leading up to the Ludlow Massacre in Colorado in 1914. As a graduate thesis, no less an authority than Woodrow Wilson biographer Arthur Link says it is unmatched. As a roadmap to McGovern's mind in the critical period of the late 1940s and early 1950s, it is similarly priceless. Arthur Schlesinger's *A Thousand Days* provided much of the background to McGovern's unsuccessful bid to become Secretary of Agriculture and his subsequent trips to Latin America and India as director of Food for Peace. Schlesinger himself suggested that McGovern's wartime experiences, which I had been ready to boil down to a few pages, be accorded a chapter of their own. His perception was right on the mark. "Their Daily Bread," the chapter recounting McGovern's work as chairman of the Senate Select Committee on Nutrition and Human Needs, drew on several resource materials, including the Field Foundation's "Children in Mississippi" and the National Citizens Board of Inquiry's *Hunger USA.* The main underpinning for the chapter, however, was Nick Kotz's chilling study *Let Them Eat Promises: The Politics of Hunger in America.* Anyone who reads this book will not fail to see why this country is in serious trouble, or why Nick Kotz has won the Pulitzer Prize. Many of the details of South Dakota's early history came from Herbert Schell's *History of South Dakota.* It was O. E. Rölvaag's classic, *Giants in the Earth,* though, that provided the mood, texture, and fabric that are so much a part of the prairie.

More important than any single book, or even collection of books, have been the reminiscences of nearly a hundred people scattered across the country who answered my questions—as well as posed some of their own—during the summer of 1971. Thus, however inadequately, I would like to thank: Harl Andersen, William Ashlock, Archie Bangs, Richard Barnet, David Beale, Ray Allen Billington, Mildred McGovern Brady, Olive Mc-Govern Briles, Margaret Buckles, Gerald Cassady, Blair Clark, Margaret Conlon, George Cunningham, William Dickson, Owen Donley, William Dougherty, John Douglas, L. Clayton DuBois, Peder Ecker, Robert Eisner, Myer Feldman, Joe Floyd, Stanley Frank, George Gilkey, Hayes Gorey, Sanford Gottlieb, Jeff Gralnick, Charles Guggenheim, Gary Hart, Jay Henderson, John Holum, Kenneth Holum, George Janke, Mrs. Arthur Kendall, Henry Kimmelman, Marjorie Leach, Richard Leone, Arthur Link, Allard Lowenstein, Frank Mankiewicz, Yancey Martin, William McAfee, Patrick McKeever, Edmund Mizel, Gaylord Nelson, Robert Nelson, Fred Nichol, Don O'Brien, Robert Pearson, Sidney Peck, Ila Stegeberg Pennington, Robert Pennington, Don Petersen, Gene Pokorney, Nelson Post, Gordon Rollins, Arthur Schlesinger, Ken Schlossberg, Eli Segal, Jeff Smith, Matthew Smith, Sr., William Smith, John Stacks, Lefton Stavrianos, Peter Stavrianos, Richard Stearns, Andrew Stein, Gloria Steinem, Marilyn Stewart, Bruce Stoner, Ben Stong, James Symington, Lawrence Towner, Jesse Unruh, Ted Van Dyk, Sander Vanocur, Robert Veschoor, Dick Wade, Adam Walinsky, Cora Weiss, William Wendt, Wayne Williamson, and Alfred Young.

Finally, this book depended in great measure on the work of Ann Victoria Phillips, who culled through literally thousands of pages of clippings, speeches, documents, and letters and thus provided a major portion of the research background. In addition, Miss Phillips, a photographer and designer by instinct if not by profession, selected the photographs that appear within these pages and took the one on the jacket.

And then there are the people whose names I do not know. Wherever they are in Indochina tonight . . . *Hoá Bình*.

R. S. A.

Washington, D.C.
November 1971

McGovern: A Biography

1

Night Flight

SLOWLY, ALMOST SILENTLY, the big plane rose in the reddish August twilight, steadied itself, then headed back for one last pass over the city from which it had come. On board North Central's Flight 705 to Sioux Falls, two men, unnoticed by their fellow passengers, peered through the plexiglas portholes of the first-class section. Three thousand feet below the towers of the city hove into view, jutting defiantly out of the gathering gloom like sabers thrust in the earth. For a few moments the men looked silently on. After the mad, surreal rush of the last six days, there was not much to say. Except that Chicago was a good place to be leaving.

The older of the two men settled back into his seat and brought his hands up to rub the weariness from his eyes. Twelve hours and several hundred miles ahead, another day awaited. A day of shaking hands and nodding hellos, of pleasantries offered, received, and forgotten, until the next day, when they would be remembered again, along with the price of wheat and whether it had rained much the past year. Because in South Dakota that was what getting elected was all about.

There were many people, he knew, who felt that he had forgotten about these things, who doubted frankly whether the hands would be there to shake. The polls showed it, his aides confirmed it, and most important he sensed it. George McGovern was in trouble. And all because of Chicago.

So as the land raced by beneath him, changing now from city to suburb, suburb to farm, and farm to prairie, it was Chicago that weighed on him—the blood, the violence, the 146½ votes cast for him in open convention, and most heavily the visitor who had come to him that afternoon. "John," he said suddenly, addressing John Holum, his trusted young legislative assistant and companion that night. "You know who came to see me this afternoon as I was getting ready to leave the hotel? Teddy White. He said to me: 'How does it feel to be the guy that booted away the presidency of the United States?' Now isn't that something to say? And from Teddy White." Holum agreed that indeed it was, and the talk turned to South Dakota and the state fair in Huron the next day, where McGovern would begin to undo the damage that had been done by Chicago. But the memory of White's visit persisted. Because deep in his gut McGovern suspected that what Teddy White, the chronicler of Presidents, had said so casually that afternoon, more in flattery perhaps than anything else, was in fact terribly, tragically true.

Almost a year ago to the day Allard Lowenstein, the political gadfly, who had taken it upon himself to "dump Johnson," had come to visit him in his office, the same office John Kennedy had worked in as a Senator. Talking fast and brashly to make up for lost logic, Lowenstein had laid out his proposal. He, George McGovern, should run for the presidency. It was his obligation, his moral duty. The odds were long, probably impossible. But on this war someone had to take a stand. Because someone had to challenge Lyndon Johnson. And McGovern was the man to do it. Lowenstein went through his spiel with the practiced ease of a carnival pitchman. By now he had had practice. Bob Kennedy had heard him out in a combination of personal anguish and amusement. His second choice, retired general and former Ambassador to France, James Gavin, author of the enclave strategy, had regarded him as something of a madman and made no secret about it. It was Kennedy who had recommended McGovern. "George," he said, "is the most decent man in the Senate." Then, pausing for a moment, he added wryly: "As a matter of fact, he's the only one."

Decent or not, Lowenstein had his doubts. Besides Kennedy's kudos, there was little to recommend McGovern. Lowenstein had already met McGovern briefly, but that was years before. Like so many people who have been introduced to McGovern before and since, Lowenstein had come away with no sharp impression of the man, simply a vague feeling of integrity and soft-spokenness. Of course, there was his opposition to the war, a nearly unbroken trail of dissent tracing back to 1963, almost four years ago, before even Morse and Gruening had spoken against the war.

Against this was McGovern's heritage. He appeared something of a hick, from South Dakota—or was it North? Whichever it was, McGovern surely looked the part: a slow-talking, stiff-jointed rube in a shiny Sears Roebuck suit. But behind that image, Lowenstein knew, a shrewd, well-developed intelligence was at work. Those farmers might not be slick, but they rarely bought a pig in a poke either. Especially when the porker was a likely promise of political oblivion. Thus one fine morning in August Lowenstein made his pitch, then held his breath, waiting for McGovern to throw him out of his office. Instead, to the New York liberal's wonderment, McGovern leaned back in his green leather chair and listened as Lowenstein talked on, filling in the details of his improbable scheme to dump Johnson. "McGovern was the first man I talked to," Lowenstein recalled later, "to whom I did not have to prove my sanity."

Their first meeting lasted the better part of an hour. When it was over, McGovern had not said yes, but more important he had not said no. What Lowenstein told him, he admitted, was flattering, even intriguing, and certainly worth pursuing. They met twice more, each time McGovern becoming more interested and Lowenstein more hopeful that at last he had found his man, not Bob Kennedy—still and always his first choice—but per-

haps the next best thing: someone Kennedy admired. Lowenstein never promised much; what McGovern could do, he told
him, was to raise the antiwar flag, to present himself symbolically,
almost sacrificially, as a challenge candidate in the primaries.
If all went well, he might gather 20 to 25 percent of the vote in
New Hampshire. And if that happened, Lyndon Johnson might
find reason for pause, might end the bombing or even—and Lowenstein was at his most expansive now—the war itself.

There would be problems, big ones. McGovern lacked not
only the Kennedys' style and élan but their money and organizational base. More critically, like nearly all the leading doves
in the Senate that year—Church, Morse, Fulbright—McGovern
was up for reelection, and the last time around he had squeaked
through by 500 votes. McGovern was torn; instinctively he
longed to answer Lowenstein's call. A deceptively self-assured,
even prideful man, McGovern had had the presidency in the
back of his mind since 1960, when he had run unsuccessfully for
the Senate against Karl Mundt. Casting the office in terms of a
moral summons made the appeal to the son of a Methodist minister, and a man who had once studied for the ministry himself,
all the more irresistible. Out of habit, McGovern began to solicit
opinions. The two or three people he approached on his staff,
all of them South Dakotans, were appalled that he was even considering the notion. Do that, they told him bluntly, and kiss the
Senate seat good-bye. From an overly protective and inevitably
self-interested staff, that reaction was predictable. So McGovern
reached outside Capitol Hill to touch men whose minds he respected. Arthur Schlesinger, whom he had come to know when
they both served as special assistants to John Kennedy, was
among the first he tapped. But Schlesinger was only slightly less
direct than the staff. He was especially impatient with Lowenstein's moral argument. The morality of the situation, he told
McGovern, dictated that the Senator stay out of this "reckless"
effort and continue to speak out responsibly in the Senate. To
throw his seat away on such a quixotic pursuit, Schlesinger said,
would be nothing short of a "disaster."

McGovern next took up the proposal with Marcus Raskin
and Richard Barnet, two former disarmament specialists with

the Kennedy administration now working out of the Institute for Policy Studies. Raskin and Barnet were as tough-minded as Schlesinger, only far more radical in what they were prepared to do (Raskin was a co-defendant in the Doctor Spock conspiracy case and Barnet had been to North Vietnam), as well as urge others to do, to end the war. Weeks before Lowenstein's first visit they had lunched with McGovern in the far corner of the Senate dining room and pressed the same course on him: fight the President head to head. Then McGovern had been flattered, a little shocked, but no more. Now he was more seriously interested as they urged the matter on him again. Should he run, they argued, McGovern could end up far more than a token. He might capture the nomination itself. And Raskin and Barnet were not alone. More establishmentarian figures, like James Wechsler of the *New York Post* and Joe Rauh, a founder of the Americans for Democratic Action, were urging the same course on him. "Run," they said, "run."

Emotionally, the counsel was what McGovern was longing to hear. At the same time, he could not dismiss the more pragmatic counsel of his staff and friends. When Lowenstein visited his office again McGovern did the talking, and Lowenstein the listening. Quickly reviewing the advice he had received, McGovern said that in his own mind the biggest block to running for the presidency was the very practical matter of time. He doubted whether there would be enough of it to campaign both in South Dakota and in the nation at large. Besides, McGovern knew that his running would create a backlash in his home state; already he could visualize talk of George getting too big for his britches. What he proposed, then, was that Lowenstein go out to South Dakota himself, spend some time in the state, talk to the politicians and the people, and when he had done so make his own honest evaluation of what he, McGovern, should do.

Lowenstein went to South Dakota wanting to find reasons for McGovern to run. By now he had removed any doubts in his own mind. McGovern, it seemed to him, was "in a very real way almost too good to be true. He was a centrist. He had been against the war for a very long time. He was a bomber pilot and he was against LBJ." Lowenstein soon discovered that South

Dakotans felt much the same way about their man—as a Senator. As a candidate for the presidency, running on an antiwar ticket— that was something entirely different.

One of the first people Lowenstein talked to when he touched down in Sioux Falls was, Peder Ecker, a former chairman of the state's Young Democrats and soon to become the chairman of the state party. "Pete" Ecker was a Kennedy man, and like his chief he had a keen sense of the possible in American politics. What Lowenstein was proposing about his friend George McGovern seemed not only impossible but preposterous. Before Lowenstein was finished, Ecker was on the phone calling Bill Dougherty, another young Kennedy man who in 1970 would become Lieutenant Governor of the state. "Billy," said Ecker, "you've got to get over here. There's some Jewish guy here from New York saying that he's going to make George McGovern President."

Dougherty was there in a minute, and along with Ecker he spent the next several hours telling Lowenstein what his hare-brained idea would do to George McGovern and to the South Dakota Democratic party, which had been painfully rebuilding itself from the point of virtual extinction in the early 1950s to the verge of a virtual renaissance. If McGovern followed his advice, they told Lowenstein, that work would be undone over-night. The Democratic party would slip back into the contempt held out now only for mad dogs and Socialists, which in South Dakota, one of the most rabidly Republican states in the nation, were regarded as equally dangerous.

In other words and emphases, that was the message Lowenstein heard again and again as he spent the next several days moving across the state. When his trek across "the great vacancies" was finished, so was most of his hope for McGovern as a challenger. He revealed his findings to McGovern during a long meeting at the Sioux Falls airport. Lowenstein did not agree that the logistics and the timing of a presidential and senatorial campaign were incompatible. Nor did he believe that a presidential candidacy would be necessarily fatal to McGovern's senatorial chances, though he conceded that if McGovern did make the run against Johnson, it would cause him more trouble at home than he first imagined. But while these were drawbacks, they were not in Lowenstein's view immovable deterrents. Rather, as he explained it, the problem was one of vocabulary. As a presidential candidate, the Senator "had to talk in New York and Minnesota and even in Wisconsin in terms that would make him seem like a fanatic in South Dakota. How would he talk about cities unraveling in Sioux Falls? The vocabulary, the mood, and the pace are so different. And he could not run except by talking in a way that underscored that things were urgent, that the kids were going to Canada, that there was alienation, that the cities were coming apart, that the people were losing confidence in the government. And if he talked to the people of the country that way, the people of South Dakota would think he was off his rocker."

That was the difficulty, Lowenstein concluded—a clear cleavage in how the people of one country perceived themselves and their land. Perhaps not an unbridgeable gap, but one closed only with extreme doing. While Lowenstein spun out his gloomy tale, McGovern listened, interrupting here and there with a question or an observation. In many ways he was as disappointed as Lowenstein. Even in the face of the evidence, his instincts were pushing him on. He sensed that there was something stirring in the country, a depth of dissatisfaction not even Lowenstein had guessed at, and that if one man could seize this mood it might carry him to the White House itself.

What held him back was an accident of timing: a reelection that came in 1968 instead of 1966 or 1970. Two years either way and he wouldn't have hesitated. But at that moment, he would explain later, "I had become convinced that my own hatred of the war had gotten the better part of my political judgment. I really thought that my staff and my friends were probably right saying that I owed it to the cause of peace and the cause of good government not to throw away this Senate seat. It never occurred to me that I could make the run for the presidency and still run for the Senate in South Dakota. I saw the decision to run for the presidency as synonymous with resigning from the Senate."

That McGovern was not prepared to do. Back in Washington a few days after the Sioux Falls meeting, he talked again

with Lowenstein and, thumbing through his Congressional Direc-
tory, considered other possibilities. Frank Church and Gaylord
Nelson were his first choices, but they faced the same reelection
dilemma in Idaho and Wisconsin. Fulbright, Morse, Gruening,
and Young were out of it, and Bobby was unwilling to risk what
seemed a far surer bet in 1972. That left what McGovern called
the "peripheral doves," the men who had opposed the war, to the
extent that they had signed letters and petitions against it, but
whose personal objection, so far at least, had not driven them to
make a major issue of it on the Senate floor. Two of these men,
McGovern knew, were not up for reelection in 1968: Lee Metcalf
of Montana and Eugene McCarthy of Minnesota. McCarthy
seemed the likelier prospect. McGovern wasn't sure what precisely
it was—perhaps something he said, or merely his manner—but he
felt McCarthy might be the more willing. "Try those two," he
told Lowenstein, "and if they won't do it, come back to me
again."

Three hours after Lowenstein left his office McGovern
bumped into McCarthy on the Senate floor. "I sent a guy to talk
to you," he began. "Yeah," McCarthy said sardonically. "We
talked about it, and I think I'm going to do it." McGovern walked
away stunned. McCarthy's instincts had been the same. There
was only one difference: McCarthy had relied on his.

The next time McGovern and Lowenstein talked at length
was on June 8, 1968, as they rode back together from Robert
Kennedy's funeral. McGovern was stricken. Superficially, it was
hard to imagine two men more nearly opposite in background
and personality than Robert Francis Kennedy and George Stanley
McGovern—Kennedy the handsome young scion of one of
America's richest and most powerful families, McGovern the
balding, awkward-looking son of a rural fundamentalist preacher;
Kennedy aggressive to the point of ruthlessness, McGovern shy
to the point of introversion; Kennedy a man who could drive
thousands to a frenzy, McGovern a man who could lose himself in a crowd of half a dozen. Yet the two men had grown
remarkably close since their first meeting, in the late 1950s, when
McGovern was a young Congressman and Bobby was on the
staff of the Senate Rackets Committee. Their attraction was im-

mediate, and it was that closeness to the Kennedys, many said, that brought George McGovern under in 1960, when John Kennedy was losing to Richard Nixon in South Dakota by 50,000 votes and George was losing to Karl Mundt by a mere 15,000. Bobby called McGovern at 4 A.M. on election night with personal apologies of the Kennedys. Later Bobby served as McGovern's champion, first in the unsuccessful effort to have him named Secretary of Agriculture and then in landing him the Food for Peace job in the White House. They kept in contact during the Kennedy years, and when Bobby entered the Senate the relationship deepened. Though never one of the Hickory Hill regulars, McGovern made frequent appearances at the Kennedy estate seminars, and by 1966, according to McGovern's own account, "I was urging everybody I would talk to to get behind Bob Kennedy for the presidential nomination." One of the people he failed to convince was Kennedy himself, who said on a number of occasions, both public and private, that if it had been George McGovern rather than Gene McCarthy who had emerged from New Hampshire as the standard bearer of the New Politics, he, Kennedy, would never have run.

That knowledge had preyed on McGovern since the phone call that had roused him from sleep four nights before, when the sobbing voice of his South Dakota field representative told him that "Bob had been shot." McGovern's first reaction had been irritation at his aide's emotion. Kennedy was tough; a bullet couldn't bring him down easily. But of course it could, and it did. In the days that followed, Eleanor McGovern saw her husband cry for the first time since she had met him as a high school senior. "You know, Al," McGovern said a few nights later as he and Lowenstein rode through the darkened Washington streets, "if I had taken your advice back in August, I don't think we would have been here today."

And now, less than three months later, Teddy White had confirmed it. McGovern's mind drifted back to the hotel suite in Chicago and fixed on what White had said. "If you had run, Bobby would never have gotten into it. Johnson would still have withdrawn. Humphrey would have been no more electable than he is today. And so the convention would have turned to you, because, unlike McCarthy, you were respectable to the regulars. And if you rather than Humphrey were the nominee, with Bob Kennedy alive and campaigning for you, then. . . ."

McGovern was uncomfortable second-guessing history, and even more uncomfortable since the second-guessing seemed all too true. White's scenario was a bit facile and perhaps too pat, but it was hard denying the fundamental logic that underlay it. He himself had reached the same conclusion long before White. Now, there was nothing to do. History had run its course and for that moment at least had passed him by, a footnote in a presidential scholar's tome. He could reflect on it, dwell on it, even feel guilty about it, all of which he was doing this August night as the jet raced him back to the land of his past, but there was nothing he could do to alter it. His strength was his instinct. It had carried him from a rude parsonage to the U.S. Senate. When the safe course seemed caution, when his friends advised going slow or not at all, instinct had always demanded the boldest course, whether it was challenging a supposedly unbeatable incumbent for Congress or saying that the war was filthy and immoral long before most people knew where it was being fought. And he always followed his instincts—except once: the one time when it really counted.

In the long sweep of history, McGovern knew, opportunity and personality converged only rarely. Now he knew he was ready; the debate with Humphrey and McCarthy before the California delegation had told him that. If this was the competition, he had decided at that moment, he could handle it. And there were others who sensed it too. After Humphrey had been nominated, and Muskie acclaimed the vice presidential choice, he had met secretly with Mayor Daley of Chicago, and Daley, even if metaphorical, could hardly have been more explicit. "My dear mother, God rest her soul, always told me, 'Richard, as one door closes, another door opens.'" From Dick Daley such words did not come lightly, and McGovern did not take them so. Now all he could do was wait and plan, and most of all hope that history would come again.

Slowly the big jet began its long descent toward the Dakota flatlands. The land loomed up, a sea of unbroken blackness. The

balding figure in the first-class cabin stared out the window.
Whatever happened tomorrow and the days after, McGovern
knew one thing: he had missed once. And he would not miss
again.

2

A Son of the Middle Border

THEY CAME FOR the simplest of reasons: there was nowhere else to go.

To the east the land seemed fairly to teem with humanity, fed by a transatlantic stream of flesh whose source was ever changing: now England, now Germany, now Ireland, now Scandinavia, now Poland, now Italy, now Ireland again, and on and on. The first cities of the seaboard were already well on their way to becoming vast urban slums, and at midcontinent Chicago was bursting to follow their lead.

So they had rushed west, looking for new land, clear out to California and Oregon, where men told tales of gold and valleys rich beyond imagination and trees rising up out of the ground to challenge the very sky. And so they came, all through the 1940s and 1950s and into the 1960s, until in time that land too seemed to fill up. Which left one last space: Dakota, the land of the middle border.

For the first seventy years of the nineteenth century the pioneers had hurried by and around Dakota, and for good reason. Dakota was the land of the Sioux, mightiest of all the Indian nations. The Indians called themselves *Dakota,* which meant friend. But Dakota was anything but friendly for whites who ventured onto its prairies. For decades, the very name Dakota was a synonym for trouble to the neighboring homesteaders in Iowa and Minnesota.

It was the discovery of gold in August 1874 that finally pushed the first tide of settlers across the territory and into the Black Hills. In one five-month period between 1875 and 1876, more than 10,000 people swarmed into the rugged foothills of the western part of the state. Tough, ornery, wildcatters to a man, they were a little larger than life, and they provided the West with some of its most famous legends: like Calamity Jane and Wild Bill Hickok, who was shot dead on August 2, 1876, in a Black Hills gambling saloon holding a winning hand of aces and eights. They made their unofficial capital at Deadwood, which boasted that it was the wildest town in the wild, wild West. From there they struck out with pick-axes and pans, up into the hills and down along the gulches and creeks, searching for the fortune that few of them ever found.

But the real wealth of Dakota lay in its land, a veritable ocean of prairie, an expanse so vast and flat it seemed a man could lay a blade in the earth and plow a furrow, straight and true, all the way to the horizon. Until the 1870s, however, the homesteaders clung to the eastern rim of the territory, huddling together in the comfort of their numbers. Only a brave and reckless few ventured further into the vacancy, following the Big Sioux, Vermillion, and James valleys. These, O. E. Rölvaag wrote, were "Giants in the Earth."

They came in the spring, staked out the 160 acres the law allowed them, dug their wells, and worked maniacally through the summer, tearing strips of sod from the prairie, piling them one atop the other, painstakingly fashioning the rudest kind of

huts. Because in September the winds would blow and then there
would be no mercy save that which man himself provided. The
land, said Rölvaag, was

> endless . . . beginningless. A grey waste . . . an empty silence
> . . . a boundless cold. Snow fell; snow flew; a universe of
> nothing but dead whiteness. Blizzards from out of the North-
> west raged, swooped down, and stirred a greyish-white fury,
> impenetrable to human eyes. As soon as these monsters tired,
> storms from the Northeast were sure to come, bringing more
> snow. . . . "The Lord have mercy! This is awful!" said the
> folk, for lack of anything else to say. Monsterlike the Plain lay
> there—sucked in her breath one week, and the next week blew
> it out again. Man she scorned; his works she would not brook.
> . . . She would know, when the time came, how to guard her
> own and herself against him!

And there was more than cold or snow or even ice. There
was loneliness, a sense of desolation that could drive a man
mad for the sound of another man's voice. And if they survived
till spring, they could look forward to dust storms that could
block out the sun and plagues of grasshoppers that could strip
a field of newly risen wheat with the suddenness of a spring
shower. Yet they pushed on, a few more of them each day,
defying what at times seemed an almost biblical injunction to
move no farther west.

Then came the railroad and the rush was on. They called it
"Dakota fever" and there were times when the swarm for land
genuinely seemed like a sickness. The affliction took its heaviest
toll in the neighboring states—Iowa, Wisconsin, Illinois, Minnesota—and cut a fearsome swath through those of Scandinavian
and German descent. One of the victims was a young man named
Hamlin Garland, whose family in the space of two generations
had moved halfway across the continent from their home in
Maine, settling first in Wisconsin, then moving on to northwestern Iowa, until finally they were swept along in the invasion of
the Dakota territory. "I bought a ticket for Aberdeen and
entered a train crammed with movers who had found the 'prairie
schooner' all too slow," Garland recorded in his classic, *A Son*

of the Middle Border. "The epoch of the canvas-covered wagon had passed. The era of the locomotive, the day of the chartered car, had arrived. Free land was receding at railroad speed, the borderline could be overtaken only by steam, and every man was in haste to arrive."

Half a step behind the pioneers came the priests and ministers, Lutherans mostly, reflecting the heavily Germanic and Scandinavian cast of the new arrivals. But Methodism was growing fast, borne in the saddlebags of John Wesley's ubiquitous circuit riders, who sowed the word of God in the farthest reaches of the territory. And where the Gospel took root, churches sprang up, nurtured by a second wave of ministers, the builder-priests. Unannounced, like a sudden storm blowing across the prairie, they would sweep into a town and rally the Christians to raise high the roof beams for God. Where none would help, they would build themselves, nail on nail, board on board, and slowly a steeple would rise. Then, when the work was done, the roof caulked, the pews in, they would move on, searching for a new town and another supply of lumber and Christians.

In the late 1800s one such preacher made the long rail journey to the Dakotas from New York, where he had recently been ordained a minister of Wesleyan Methodism. His name was Joseph McGovern. He was a strong, powerfully built man, his body reflecting a boyhood in the rough-and-tumble coalfield communities of Pennsylvania, Illinois, and later Iowa. At the age of nine he was down in the mines, scooping loose coal into hoppers for a penny a bucket. His father, an alcoholic, died when Joe was a boy, and when his mother passed away five years later it left Joe, at the age of thirteen, as breadwinner for five other brothers and sisters. The baby of the family, named George —after whom Joe would one day name his own first son—was eventually put up for adoption. With the help of relatives Joe saw that the rest of the children got into school. Then, still a teenager, he struck out to make the family's fortune, as another preacher named Billy Sunday had done, in the big leagues of professional baseball.

Joseph never made it to the majors. He wound up playing second base for Des Moines, a farm club for the St. Louis

Cardinals in the old Western League. The experience was not
devoid of profit. Without it, Joseph might never have seen the
loose-living, painted women he so zealously railed against in later
years. Because baseball in those days was not a gentleman's sport,
not in the minors, and certainly not in the Midwest. For a raw-
boned rookie like McGovern, the game was endless days in
crackerbox ballparks and endless nights in fleabag hotels, where
the team's most loyal followers—the hookers and the gamblers—
competed for the ear and affection of young ballplayers.

If McGovern ever gave in to either, it is not recorded. In
later years, after he was a man of God and a respected member of
the community, he carried a sense of embarrassment, almost
guilt, over ever having been part of such a sinful atmosphere.
When his own sons were growing to manhood, he discouraged
them from any kind of organized athletics; such pursuits, he
advised, were a waste of time. The boys never understood the
reason for their father's feelings until the day they were playing
ball at a tent revival. As they passed the ball back and forth, a
mouse stuck its nose in under the tent. The Reverend McGovern,
then nearing sixty, called for the ball and with a mighty wind-up
dispatched the unfortunate rodent with a single pitch.

The circumstances of Joseph McGovern's conversion—if,
indeed, a conversion was necessary—have long since been forgotten. But before too many years had gone by, the idea of
fame on the diamond had been pushed aside by a call to the
cross. He returned east and entered Houghton College, a four-
year liberal arts school run by the Methodist Church in upstate
New York. Following his graduation and theological studies, he
once again headed west, this time an ordained minister of
Wesleyan Methodism.

The church whose word Joseph McGovern would spread
had come into being when a fundamentalist hard core in the
parent church decided that orthodox Methodism was, in those
fast-changing modern times, drifting dangerously away from
the precepts of personal salvation laid down by John Wesley
himself. Wesleyan Methodism had little use for the social gospel
that then was coming so strongly into vogue. Instead, it laid
great emphasis on personal evangelism, a literal reading of the

Bible, and a life filled with personal striving and good works, which in the Wesleyan view clearly excluded such things as card-playing, dancing, gambling, drinking, smoking, and going to the flickers, or as they are known today, the movies. It was a hard credo, but as McGovern would argue to doubters so were the times and the people. And so especially was South Dakota.

The proof of McGovern's words was his success. In twenty years' time he found enough believers to warrant the building of half a dozen churches. He also took a wife. But within the year she was to die, leaving him childless. He lived alone for two years; then in 1919 he married again, this time to a slender strawberry blonde named Frances McLean. They met in Aberdeen, where Joseph was building yet another of his churches and Frances had recently arrived from her home in Canada to find work as a secretary. At the time of their marriage Joseph was forty-eight and Frances, as serene and quiet as her husband was forceful and strong, twenty years his junior. But though she was a woman of twenty-eight and in her own soft-spoken way an uncommonly strong woman at that, he treated her as a child. If there was a decision to be made, he made it. If there was something to be bought, he bought it. If there was a meal to be planned, he planned it. She was left to care for the children, who came in quick succession: first a girl, Olive; then a year and a half later a boy, George; two and a half years after that another girl, Mildred; and finally another boy, Larry, the most handsome and outgoing of all the children, and on whom the parents lavished the most attention.

At the time of George's birth the Reverend McGovern was serving as minister for a tiny church he had built in Avon, a rural hamlet of a few hundred souls tucked away in the southeastern corner of the state, a hundred miles or so from Sioux Falls. There in the parsonage on July 19, 1922, a first son was born. At his father's direction, he was christened George Stanley. The infant was barely beginning to walk when the family was on the move again, heading north to Calgary in Alberta, Canada, so that Frances could be close to her aging mother. Shortly before Mrs. McLean died, they returned to South Dakota and settled in Mitchell, a railhead seventy miles west of Sioux Falls,

where on a plot of new ground in the center of town Joseph
McGovern was destined to erect his last church. At the time, his
oldest boy had just turned six.

Mitchell, South Dakota, during the 1920s and 1930s was much
like Mitchell is today, a town of straight-lined streets and straight-
thinking people, a place where the grass is as well attended as
the churches. The 15,000 or so people who comprise the town
tend to be plain and Protestant, slow of speech and short of
words, and a little suspicious of anyone who isn't. Mitchell was
Middle American long before it got to be fashionable, and it
hasn't changed—nor for that matter has it really much noticed.
Saturday mornings the farmers still drive into town in their
pick-up trucks, the Chevys and the Fords with the rack for the
thirty-ought-six in the rear window. They stay the day, filling
up the back with feed grain and supplies, while their wives shop
at Penney's or Newberry's. If there is something to celebrate,
then maybe they'll have dinner down at Margaret Conlon's
Lawler Café, where George McGovern used to eat rhubarb pie
at the end of a day's campaigning. If the occasion is extraspecial,
they'll go over to the Paramount to take in the latest movie, and
finally, after a soda at the Dairy Queen, move out onto the
highway for the long drive through the night back to the farm
and the wait for next week.

Except at harvest. Then for one week Mitchell comes alive.
Main Street is blocked off, and the tourists pour in from all over
the state, lugging their campers and kids behind them. A carnival
comes to town, brightening the night sky with its glittering ferris
wheel. While the children enjoy the rides, the adults crowd
toward what brought them there in the first place, the thing,
some say, that keeps the town alive: the Mitchell Corn Palace—
"The World's Only Corn Palace," as the brochures boast. It is a
garish structure, topped by turrets and battlements, decked out
in a confusion of browns and yellows, blues and reds and greens.
Functionally, it is the town auditorium cum souvenir shop. Only
it is much more than that. It is a monument to corn and to the
men who sweat to coax it out of the ground. It is a billboard for
the works of Oscar Howe, the Indian artisan who each year
directs the construction of huge murals on its outer walls, made

only of corn cobs and grain. It is, the town fathers proclaim, "one of the great masterworks of the Western world." And it is even more. Mitchell's Corn Palace is perhaps the only place in the entire state where Dakotans have indulged themselves in an orgy of frivolousness. All the rest is practical, deadeningly functional, as everything must be on a land that is hard. The Corn Palace is the solitary exception. And that is its triumph.

It was to this place that Joseph McGovern, now nearing sixty, brought his bride and brood. They settled in a rambling white house on the south side of town, a few blocks from where his church was slowly rising. Ever practical, McGovern selected the house not only for its location but for its size, a far bigger space, he figured, than his family would ever need and perfect, once a little work was done, for two rental apartments. McGovern kept his eye out for other good buys around town. His minister's salary was small enough. Some weeks instead of money in the collection plate there would be an offer of a bushel of corn, a chicken, and on at least one occasion a quarter section of a newly slaughtered hog. If he were to die, the income for his young family would disappear entirely. While the Lord still provided, he must lay away for the future. And lay away he did, buying a few parcels here and there, carefully building the base of a sustaining income, neither knowing nor suspecting that in a few years the Depression would virtually erase his efforts.

In the evenings after supper, while Joe retired to the study to work on the church accounts and Frances sat sewing in the darkening parlor, the children would bound out of the house to the corner, where their playmates from the neighborhood were gathering to "kick the can." They would play just as long as the light and the tolerance of their parents allowed them. When one or the other finally gave way, it would be one last kick and then a steady, if sullen retreat back to the piles of homework that awaited them inside.

George played as hard as anyone. Already, though, the dark, good-looking boy seemed serious and quiet beyond his years. In many ways he was his father's son: strong, sober, slow-speaking, straight-out in what he said or believed. But the similarity did not extend entirely. On occasion the Reverend McGovern was capable of explosive anger, and even at his calmest there was aggressive dynamism that never lingered too far beneath the surface of his personality. In this respect the son tended to be like the mother. Frances McGovern recoiled from violence or behavior that even suggested it. She was serene, self-possessed. It was almost as if she was incapable of obvious display. And so it was with her son, who when his study was through would come into the parlor and perhaps play the piano, as he did every week for the children in Sunday school; or if the mood moved him, he would quietly work on the stamp and coin collections he amassed with such laborious care. Finally, when the lights were snapped off and it was time for bed, he would go to his room and the stack of books he had brought back that week from Mitchell's Carnegie Library. Then for the next hour or two he would go down the river with Tom Sawyer and Huck Finn or out West with the Indian scouts and pioneers of the Altenscheller series for boys. He explored the Dakota territory with Rölvaag, Nebraska with Cather, the middle border with Garland, and of course Treasure Island with Robert Louis Stevenson. More than once he would get so carried away with the mythical adventuring that he would forget about the time completely, until the first light of sun-up crept into his window. Then he would force himself to sleep, because in an hour or so would come the call for breakfast and chores, and after that the daily morning prayer. And one was never late for prayer—not in the McGovern house.

Like his brother and sisters, George owned his own Bible and learned to read aloud from it before he entered school. There was not much choice in the matter; his father insisted on it. Joseph McGovern impressed on his children that they were, as Olive puts it, "not quite the same as other children. We were expected to be a standard for the community. Everything that other Christians did, we had to do double." In the morning the family would gather for the daily reading of Scriptures. "It only lasted five or ten minutes," Mildred remembers, "but of course it seemed like five or ten hours to us."

The most exacting worship was reserved for the Sabbath, when the children were packed off for morning Sunday school, followed by the regular worship service, to be succeeded in the

afternoon by another special children's service and finally by an
extended prayer meeting in the evening. In addition, traveling
revivalists were permitted to come into town three weeks out of
every year, one week at the Wesleyan church and two more
weeks just outside of town in a tent erected for the annual inter-
denominational meeting.

In matters of faith and morals Joseph McGovern was a stern
disciplinarian. His children missed a revival service at their own
peril. But his oratory, unlike that of the evangelists whose platform he shared, was not of the hellfire and brimstone variety.
He could quote the Bible as loud and as long as the best of them,
but his was not a message of fear or a gospel of retribution.
McGovern dwelled instead on the meaning of faith. He saw faith
as a builder of character. Fear and temptation, he told his children,
were the same; both could be overcome by faith and discipline.
The more one overcame fear, the stronger one became. "There
was a phrase he always used," says his older son, " 'making the
best use of your time.' He said you couldn't make the best use
of your time if you were going to live by fear. That was his
message to me: I couldn't be the kind of person who would let
fear get me down."

There was one point where the parents and their children
parted, and that was Wesleyan Methodism's prohibition against
movies. The children were careful lest their defiance seem apparent, if for no other reason than their father's reputation for
wielding a heavy hand when his word was challenged. They
snuck out to the show and alibied for one another. "It was an
unspoken thing between us," says one of the girls. "We were
never tattletales." For George, going to the movies was more than
just entertainment; it seemed sometimes like an act of personal
liberation. He went as often as his money would let him, and
it seemed—then as now—to matter little what was playing. He
had his favorites, of course; Westerns mostly. But long before
Marshall McLuhan he discovered that it was the medium that
was the massage. To slip into a theater unnoticed, to sit there
alone in the cool and the dark as fantasy flickered across the
screen—that was the one time, perhaps the only time, that he
could let down a little.

As the years went by, George would gradually break all his church's archaic strictures; he would take a drink or two, and when at special ease he would lean back with a good cigar. On occasion he was even known to dance. But by that time he felt neither the guilt nor the exhilaration that might have come from defying the law when it meant something. He had long since become skeptical of the worth of petty abstinence, and for that matter dubious of the value of organized religion itself. The faith of their father, says a friend, "was something the children never really thought about. It was just something they accepted."

Still George would never, not even as a Senator, lose entirely the legacy of his fundamentalist upbringing. The most obvious totem of the experience, and the one he treasures most deeply, is a love of the Bible, not only as an ethical blueprint but as a masterwork of literature. In his office, amid the clutter and memorabilia of the years, hangs a small framed card engraved with his five favorite passages from Scripture:

> Whosoever shall save his life shall lose it, and whosoever shall lose his life for my sake shall find it.

> What doth the Lord require of thee, but to do justly, and to love mercy, and to walk kindly with thy God.

> Inasmuch as you have done it unto the least of my brethren, ye have done it unto me.

> He who is without sin among you, let him cast the first stone.

> And as you would that men should do to you, do ye also to them likewise.

These are but five of the literally thousands of verses that have been indelibly marked on his consciousness by a repetition that began at his mother's knee and ended only when, as a young man, he went off to war.

In the meantime, George McGovern grew up. As a boy, he did the things that boys are still doing in Mitchell: going for long walks in the country, collecting Indian head pennies, making slingshots, building treehouses, and telling stories to brothers and sisters until sundown. One special project that consumed fully three summers was the construction of a great "cave" in a nearby lot. It was an elaborate, two-chambered affair, shored up with timbers and covered over with dirt. From the way he talks about it today, meticulously re-creating every detail, it must have been a magical place, not unlike the movie theaters he loved so well: dark, cool, lonely, fantastic.

He was a shy boy, almost withdrawn. He very nearly failed the first grade because his teacher interpreted his reluctance to read aloud in class as lack of intelligence. In fact, George had learned to read, and read well, long before entering school; it was shyness that was holding him back. The explanation did not impress his teacher, however, and she promoted him to second grade only "on condition." Outside the classroom George had as many friends as any retiring son of a minister could expect. In short, not many. But there was really not much time for fun-making. When George was not in school or in his room studying, he was apt to be out earning spending money cutting lawns in the neighborhood at fifteen cents an hour. One of his customers was an old woman who lived across the street in a three-story red brick house. The building fascinated George. He could sit on the porch of his own house and stare at it for hours, unable to imagine anything so graceful or fine as the vision in front of him. One day, he told himself, he would own that house. He didn't know how or when, but one day it would be his. Twenty years later, when he returned to Mitchell as a bright young history professor with a family of his own, he didn't have to look for a house. He knew the one he wanted.

They were not a close family, the McGoverns, especially not the father and his children. "It was a very businesslike relationship," says Mildred. "He was not what you'd call a buddy-buddy type." Now and again Joseph would take his son along on a pheasant hunt. But there was always a distance, a sense of reserve about the man that discouraged warmth. Instead, he inspired respect. Partially it was a simple matter of age. By the time George was a teenager, his father was sixty-five and retired. Partially too it was the matter of his office. But mostly it was the matter of the man himself. Joe took an interest in his children, was proud of George's straight "A" record and forensic prowess, and was always solicitous of their troubles, corporal and spiritual. But the distance remained. Of all the children, none was more intimate with—or influenced by—the man than George, and it is George who says: "I admired him and respected him and liked him, but, no, I was not close to him. He was not the kind of man you got close to." Nor did Joseph McGovern try to persuade his sons to follow him into the ministry. Indeed, the only occasion that his older son's future was mentioned was in reply to a rather offhand question from George about what he should do with his life. Joseph thought for a moment, then said, almost noncommittally, that doctors performed an essential service. More than that, "they always have people's respect."

The McGovern family had respect, both in Mitchell and wherever else Joseph had built a church. But it was not the kind of respect that brought with it money or even social esteem. Wesleyan Methodism, with its Bible-banging emotionalism, was distinctly of and for the lower middle class. "It was not," says one Mitchell-bred minister, himself an Episcopalian, "a religion that the silent majority looked upon with great favor." If Joseph McGovern had chosen regular Methodism, his life and that of his family might well have been different; he might even, according to some predictions, have become a bishop. What difference that would have made in the career of his son can only be guessed at. As it was, the family grew up steeped in the sternest tenets of the Puritan ethic: discipline, sacrifice, hard work.

McGovern's instructions to his family were in many ways a credo for the time—and a harsh time it was. Following the boom of the war years, the bottom suddenly dropped out of farm prices. As the prices plummeted, farmers fell behind on loans; banks foreclosed. Within a few years there was a glut of farmland, and it was the banks themselves—175 in South Dakota alone by 1924—that were closing their doors. By the time the Depression descended on the rest of the country, rural America, and particularly the Plains States, had been suffering through it for nearly a decade—and the worst was still to come. Between 1920 and 1930 real estate values in the state declined

58 percent; farmland fell from $71.39 an acre in 1921 to $35.24 in 1930 and within five years dropped to a low of almost half again that figure. Total cash income from South Dakota crops decreased from $17 million in 1929 to $6 million in 1932. Wheat was selling from fifty to fifty-five cents a bushel, while oats and corn sold at twenty-two and twenty-nine cents respectively. By the time George McGovern entered high school, nearly one farmer in five had lost his land to foreclosure.

Inevitably, the McGoverns felt the crunch. Never well-off to start with, the family teetered on the poverty line all through the 1920s and 1930s and nearly fell off when Reverend McGovern's modest real estate holdings were sucked under. It was not, however, the kind of penury that kept food out of their mouths. It was a poverty of a far less detectable kind, camouflaged by plain clothes and donated shoes, kept in the background by afternoons of grass-cutting for George and nights of babysitting for his sisters. It was, in sum, like most poverty: unseen and invisible, even to the poor themselves.

But it was never totally out of mind, either then or later. "I remember seeing a dry, parched topsoil swept into the air by blowing winds that sometimes made the noonday sun as black as midnight," McGovern wrote in a letter twenty years later. "I shall never forget the ditches filled with fine dirt over the tops of fence posts. I remember too the grasshopper invasions that stripped the fields clean. I remember the anxious faces of the farmers scanning the sky for rain that did not come." There were months when it was cheaper for a farmer to let his labor rot in the earth. "The first day I knew that big men cried," McGovern recalled, "was the day my father and I arrived to hunt pheasants at the home of one of my boyhood heroes south of Mitchell. Art Kendall, a fine farmer, was the man. We arrived to find his eyes filled with tears. In his hand he held a check he had just received in payment for all his hogs. It was barely enough to pay the trucker who took them to market."

As they grew up, the McGovern children paired off by age: George and Olive were closer to one another than they were to the younger Mildred and Larry, who formed a special bond of their own. Within this loose arrangement all the children came to look to, and in large measure depend on, George, whose serious, quiet mien two of the three children were to reflect in later life. The exception was Larry. Four years younger than his brother, Larry was, almost from infancy, unlike the other children. Where George was retiring and responsible, Larry was outgoing and carefree, or so at least it seemed. The trouble started off small enough, no more than the petty annoyances that were to be expected from any child so full of life. But it soon escalated. The disciplinary reports from school all came back bad, which was hardly a surprise at home, where Larry and his father were enmeshed in a series of increasingly fearsome rows. On one occasion Larry stole the tires from his father's car and sold them. And there was worse. In Mitchell friends of the McGovern family still haven't forgotten. "Larry was their cross," says one of them. "He was a real hell raiser, that kid." When he was sixteen Larry dropped out of high school to marry a girl he had made pregnant. Divorce and another marriage quickly followed. Then alcohol, intermittent commitment to a veterans' hospital, and finally painful, drawn-out recovery.

For the less tormented Mitchell offered the unbroken, perhaps unthinking, serenity of small town America. Even today McGovern can conjure up the familiar images. "There is a wholesomeness about life in a rural state that is a meaningful factor," he says. "It doesn't guarantee you are going to be a good guy simply because you grow up in an agricultural area, but I think the chances of it are better, because of the sense of well-being, the confidence in the decency of life that comes from working not only with the land but also with the kinds of people who live on the land. Life tends to be more authentic and less artificial than in urban areas. You have a sense of belonging to a community. You're closer to nature and you see the changing seasons—you're more aware of man as a part of the universe. You're more aware of the simple values of life like weather, sunshine, and rain. The dependence upon nature . . . a sense of belonging to a particular place and knowing your part in it . . . the importance of the family—all of those things are virtues that are given a very high priority in rural America. . . . It's become a cliché now," he says, a little wistfully. "Life was so much easier, so much simpler, in that kind of atmosphere."

To some, though, the simplicity could be cloying, sometimes even suffocating. Father William Wendt, who grew up in Mitchell and knew McGovern through high school before going on to become a well-known, as well as radical, Episcopal minister in Washington's black ghetto, remembers the town of his boyhood as "a walled city." Through these defenses few alien—which often meant new—ideas penetrated. It was as if Mitchell was still a frontier town, protecting itself against the ancient enemies of the Plains. Only now the enemy came from the city, and its name was change.

A boy could live and grow up in Mitchell, as George Mc-Govern did, not really knowing, or for that matter needing to know, what lay beyond the walls. "Mitchell," as McGovern gently puts it, "tended to be a self-contained community." The radio made the most serious breaches in the wall, but they were only that. To see and feel what lay in the land beyond one had to venture forth, like Rölvaag's pioneers had done, outside the warmth and security of the past. For McGovern, the discovery came in stages, each a little more bold. At first there were the overland visits to his father's relatives in Milwaukee and Des Moines. Later came political talk at the family dinner table, where Democrats were damned like the devil and Republicans canonized like the saints. The exception was Roosevelt; in the face of the country's economic recovery, the Reverend McGovern had to admit a grudging respect for the man—not that he would ever vote for him, of course. The penultimate, and in many ways most important, step in the process was as simple a thing as joining the high school debate team.

Debate in South Dakota was and remains not simply debate. Within the state it holds a place roughly equivalent to basket-ball in Indiana or football in Ohio. How this got to be so is not certain, though the heavy influence of the circuit riders, as well as speakers from the Chautauqua Movement, which flourished in the state long after it lost popularity in the East, no doubt had a lot to do with it. In any case, the preeminence of the state in things forensic is incontestable. During one period, twenty-seven of the one hundred national titleholders in speech and debate hailed from South Dakota. For years South Dakota Senator Karl Mundt served as chairman of the National Forensic Society. (In an irony not lost on anyone in the state, Mundt, who is twenty-two years McGovern's senior, often judged his future rival in high school and college tournaments.) Perhaps the best known of South Dakota's orators, of course, was the son of a Huron druggist who later moved over to Minnesota and into some political renown of his own. And perhaps just as well, because according to old-timers Hubert Humphrey "talked too fast" to get elected to much of anything in South Dakota.

At first glance, McGovern seemed hardly the ideal candidate for a debate squad, much less the nationally ranked champion he would later become. While he was reading aloud now, thanks to a second-grade teacher who would brook no nonsense about shyness, he was in many ways still the withdrawn young man he had always been. Ironically, it was that very shyness, which McGovern came to regard as a fault, and like all faults in need of being overcome, that veritably "forced" him into public speaking. He got his chance when as a high school sophomore he attracted the attention of Rose Hofner, his English teacher and the school librarian. There was nothing terribly unusual about the young man who spent so many hours in the library reading and studying, only the "sweetness" of his disposition, but for the kindly Miss Hofner that was enough to recommend him. She encouraged him to try out for the school debate team; for a young man of his intelligence and application, it was the academically wise thing to do.

George took her advice and approached Bob Pearson, an American history teacher who doubled as Mitchell High's debate coach. A recent addition to the faculty, Pearson by his own account was "the first teacher less than a hundred years of age" to walk the corridors of the school in some years. Pearson's relative youth made him enormously popular with his students, the best of whom—George McGovern included—would continue to seek his advice and approval decades after graduation. But there was far more to Pearson than the accident of his age.

From the testimony of his former students, he seems to have been one of those rare men who are as charismatic as they are gifted. And Pearson's gifts were extraordinary. His intelligence was broad and deep-rooted and no less keen than his wit. There was a grace to the man in the way he said and did things and a genuine love of learning for its own sake. But what stood out most about Pearson, what marked him above the merely great teachers, was his evident concern, both for ideas and for the people they influenced. Pearson's own ideas tended toward the conservative, and on certain issues decidedly so. It was not that Pearson was against change. On the contrary, he was all for it, as long as it was not "change for the sake of change" but harkened back to what Pearson described as "Jeffersonian democracy," which in plainest terms meant the old way of doing things. At the time, that argument was very much in line with McGovern's thinking, and not surprisingly the coach and his new charge hit it off immediately.

McGovern, says Pearson, displayed "a natural talent for speech. He had a personal presence and a rare ability to organize facts and express them effectively. He was always very keen in his insights and in picking out inconsistencies in his opponents' arguments. He caught illogical thinking, and it would turn him on when he did. He would be very joyful in picking it out, then standing up to point out where they had gone wrong logically. In that sense, George was the best debater on the team." What McGovern lacked was personal flamboyance. Though Pearson worked with him for hours every day after school, trying to coax him to do something, almost anything, with his hands, the effort failed. "I couldn't get him to throw his whole being into something," Pearson confesses. "It was as if there was some kind of block." The block was nothing less than McGovern's personality, a character that shied away not only from personal assertiveness but from what was perceived as any gross display of emotion. As Pearson explains it: "The thing about George, though—he didn't excel for the sake of being ahead of everyone else. He had great curiosity. He wanted to do well. To him, that was his duty: to fulfill himself. He never saw any kind of obligation to place himself in the forefront for the sake of honor.

Rather God gave you certain talents and you were expected to make the most of them." George Janke, McGovern's high school principal, agrees. "Some kids go out and they are automatically the leader. People just naturally say: 'Let's elect him president.' George was not one of these. George wasn't the pusher type. He was a plugger. He did a little bit at a time. But he didn't leave many stones unturned."

"George's colorfulness," concludes Pearson, "was his colorlessness."

No one ever really got close to George; his personality never encouraged it. To most people he came off merely as the fulfillment of what a minister's son should be: quiet, serious, bookish, as well starched as the clean shirt he wore to school every day. Everything about him seemed to enhance the image: the pale skin, the plain clothes, the thin smile, even the slicked-down hair. "For a debater, he's a nice kid," recorded the 1940 edition of the high school yearbook, and left it at that. Truly it was hard to think otherwise of someone who would favor debate, drama, and glee club over football, baseball, and basketball. He seemed then, as he would to many later, "almost too nice," to quote the impression of one of his friends.

McGovern could be sweet, but he could also be pitiless in flaying the pretenses of his opponent. He could seem unathletic and unassertive, but in his own peculiar way he could be almost savagely competitive. Debate became an obsession. For hours each day after school and sometimes late into the night, he would work with his partner, Eddie Mizel, honing and preparing his arguments, gathering data and statistics, cramming quotations and yet more facts on endless reams of 3×5 cards, and when they proved inadequate for the purpose, 4×5s. Mizel was as quick and clever as McGovern was deliberate and meticulous, and together they made a devastating team, arguing for what always seemed to be the affirmative position, whether it was unicameral legislatures or government ownership of the railroads or a permanent alliance with Great Britain. They began winning as sophomores, and they continued winning as juniors. By the time they were seniors debating excellence had gained them regional renown and had won for McGovern a forensic scholarship to Dakota Wesleyan University in Mitchell.

But for McGovern the scholarship and trophies were the least of debate's rewards. Its real worth was far more elusive: the opportunity to pursue what at the time seemed radical ideas to their logical ends; a sense of the ebb and flow of history and in time a fascination and a love for it; the instinct for competition and the delicious sensuality of winning; and finally a glance outside the wall, even if the gaze extended no farther than Rapid City or Aberdeen or Brookings or Sioux Falls or anywhere their weekend trips in Bob Pearson's car would take them. The point was not so much the destination as the going, and gradually, almost imperceptibly, it drew McGovern out. "It really changed my life, no question about it," he reflected later. "If I had not gone out for debate, there is not a chance in the world, in my opinion, that I would have ever come to the United States Senate. It was the one thing that I could do well. It really became the only instrument of personal and social power that I had."

One of the places the debaters went, and suspiciously often from their coach's point of view, was the little town of Woonsocket (population: 800), a farm hamlet thirty miles northwest of Mitchell. To the casual eye, Woonsocket High had little to commend it as an opponent for the forensic powerhouse from Mitchell, who seemed by comparison the essence of urban sophistication. But then the casual eye is not the same as the eye of a high school boy and might not have noticed the presence on Woonsocket's squad of the Stegeberg twins, Ila and Eleanor. Certainly the boys didn't miss it, and small wonder. By any measure the Stegeberg sisters were striking girls, and according to more than one witness of the day the petite brunettes were downright beautiful.

They had been born on a farm eight miles outside of Woonsocket at the onset of the Great Farm Depression. The day of their birth the house had been warmed by heaping feeder corn into the pot-bellied stove; prices were so low that it was cheaper to burn corn than to sell it. The girls' mother died when they were young, and they were raised by their grandfather and father, who at the height of the Depression took off a year to work in a CCC camp. The banks were foreclosing on farms all around them; a family of homesteaders across the way lost everything. Many of their neighbors stood in bread lines. Somehow, though, the Stegebergs held on. "I remember my father listening to the radio for the price reports from Chicago, trying to decide when to sell," says Eleanor. "Sometimes he guessed right and sometimes he guessed wrong. He was at the mercy of the market. Few people thought much about why prices went up and down. It was just something that happened." Earl Stegeberg, however, did think about prices, and when he did he became a Democrat and eventually Democratic county chairman. "I grew up," says Eleanor, "thinking that the only way one spent a Sunday afternoon was discussing and debating politics." Those Sunday sessions were not without their profit. By the time the girls were in high school they were well versed in the ins and outs of male argument; so well versed in fact that when the boys from Mitchell came swaggering into Woonsocket, a couple of overconfident males named Mizel and McGovern barely knew what hit them. Returning home, George sheepishly reported to his parents that he and Eddie had won all their debates save one—and that had been lost only because "a couple of girls flirted with the judges."

For the remainder of high school the memory of the "little girls" was never to move far from McGovern's mind. He had several more cracks at debating them, and happily for his wounded ego he eventually managed to beat them. But by then McGovern was interested in pursuing a less academic relationship, though with which of the identical twins seemed an insolvable dilemma. There was no need to make up his mind quickly, though, because other than engaging in the most casual conversation, he couldn't make much headway with either twin; Woonsocket was still thirty miles away, and far more to the point, George was still deathly afraid of girls.

His chance finally came as a college freshman, and as it worked out McGovern had little to do with it. He was attending Dakota Wesleyan University, a small (enrollment: 500), conservative liberal arts college not many blocks from the family home on the west side of town. With his grades (top 10 percent of the class) and his forensic skills, McGovern undoubtedly could have won a scholarship to a larger and more prestigious school. That, however, would have deprived him of the free room and board he enjoyed at home. Even as it was, he had to supplement his scholarship with a variety of odd jobs, from candling eggs at forty cents an hour to touring the state in a borrowed car as a recruiter for the college. Eleanor and Ila Stegeberg had chosen DWU too, Eleanor as a business student and Ila as a candidate in nursing. A skating party in their freshman year brought all three of them together at the Mitchell Roller Rink. Still shy, McGovern glided around the rink alone in long, lonely strides, casting a furtive eye now and then in the direction of the two girls. They didn't miss it. When the first ladies' choice was announced Ila skated over to George, and at that moment it seemed that the choice had been made for him. But later, when George mustered the courage to ask Ila for a date, he discovered to his considerable chagrin that she was already spoken for, and by no less than one of his own friends. If George still wanted to go, that left Eleanor. George did, so Eleanor it was, and as Eleanor McGovern puts it today: "After that there was really no one else."

He courted her in the style of the day: slowly, romantically, and with a lingering touch of embarrassment. They went to movies at the Rex and drank sodas at the college inn. There were parties at friends' homes and regular outings to the skating rink. DWU, which insisted on thrice-weekly chapel attendance for its students, wasn't about to let them dance, instead, while the band played sedately in the background, they were permitted to "stroll" about the gymnasium floor. Dates like these, though, were the exception. Most of the time they did nothing more grand than take a walk in the light of the harvest moon. More quickly than they both realized, they were drawing very close together. When it came time for George to bring Eleanor home to meet his parents, she fretted for days about whether to wear her customary coating of lipstick—a Wesleyan taboo. Finally, she decided not to, at least not the first time. Her decision paid off. The McGoverns, usually very reserved people, warmed to her immediately.

George had no such problem with Earl Stegeberg. The first time he was supposed to pick up Eleanor at her house, he showed up late, only to find that Eleanor had already left with another couple for the dance. George sat down to pass what he assumed would be a few minutes of polite conversation with Mr. Stegeberg, stumbled into politics, and didn't emerge from the house until two hours later. "He had a better time," Eleanor says, "than he would have had at the dance." As 1941 slipped by, the young couple daydreamed and mused about the future. George was set on becoming a history teacher, something he had decided almost the day he met Bob Pearson. Eleanor guessed that when her business training was complete, she'd get a job as a secretary in Mitchell. It seemed an idyllic time. The gathering war in Europe was, literally as well as figuratively, still far over the horizon. They talked about politics and world affairs, but only in the most academic way. George warned Eleanor to be wary of such "left wing" influences as Walter Reuther and the CIO. Then, one Sunday in December, George was at home listening to a radio broadcast of the New York Philharmonic for an assignment in a course in music appreciation. The orchestra was still warming up when John Daly's voice broke in with a bulletin. Suddenly, the horizon was upon them.

The war had a way of pushing personal plans to the background. For George and Eleanor, who were planning on marriage in the not too distant future, it meant a delay of at least several years. George, ever practical, had pointed out that it was hardly much use being married if he was on one side of the ocean and Eleanor on the other. What didn't need saying was the chance that he might not be coming back at all.

McGovern could only hope that the call, when it did come, would be late enough to let him finish college. At the time of Pearl Harbor, he was nineteen and in the midst of his sophomore year. His class had just elected him president (as it would for the next two years), and his work was beginning to attract the attention of a number of men on the faculty. One day, not far off, he would have to begin considering graduate school. And of course there was speech, still his overriding passion. In 1942 he won the South Dakota Peace Oratory Contest with a speech called "My Brother's Keeper." (Later the National Council of Churches selected McGovern's oration as one of the twelve best in the United States during 1942.) Eddie Mizel had gone off to Northwestern, but with his new debate partner, Matt Smith, Jr., the son of the college's president, McGovern had reached into the upper ranks of national competition. Even after proving himself in competition, however, McGovern lacked complete self-confidence, as evidenced by a letter he wrote Pearson during a speech tournament in Minneapolis. "I guess I was pretty lucky winning the Peace Oratory Contest," wrote McGovern, "but I certainly feel insignificant speaking against some of these smooth fellows here in the national. It is taking all the courage that I've got to hold my head up and dish it out to some of these polished veterans. I really get a lot of satisfaction out of it, however."

In February 1943, coming home to Mitchell on a bus from Moorhead, Minnesota, McGovern's spirits could not have been higher. He had just been named "best debater" in a five-state tournament, and Eleanor had been there to see him take the honor. Now, heading home, they laughed and joked with Matt, who had come in second, and tried to guess what they would all be doing next year. They didn't have to wait long to find out. When the bus pulled in to Mitchell, President Smith was there to meet them, one hand extended in congratulation and the other hand clutching the induction notice that had arrived that day for George.

McGovern was crushed. Shortly after Pearl Harbor, he had gone off with a group of his friends to the recruiting station in Omaha. They had talked with representatives of both the Navy and the Army and had finally decided on the Army because it was handing out free lunch passes and the Navy was not. McGovern had assumed that he would have ample time to finish at least his junior year. Now, in midterm, he was suddenly being uprooted and ordered only God knew where. But if he had to go, he wanted to go the best way, and for him that left only one choice. Early in his college days he had consented, as a favor to his friend Norman Ray, a fanatic about flying, to sign up in a Civil Air Patrol flight instruction course at the college.

McGovern didn't think much about it until the first time he got up in the air. Then he hated it. The very thought of flying, he confessed to Eleanor, "scares me silly." He suffered through the lessons, soloed, flew all the required hours and not one minute more. The day he won his license, he said to Eleanor, was one of the happiest moments of his life. It meant he would never have to fly again. From then on, McGovern's phobia about flying had been a standing joke. George laughed about it with the rest, but deep down it troubled him. His exposure to new people and new ideas had not expunged the Calvinist streak in him. It remained very much a part of him, along with his father's admonition that character was built by overcoming fear. "Make the best use of your time, George," his father had said. "You can't make the best use of your time if you are going to live by fear." Fear hung in the air, and so it was to the air that McGovern must go.

Mildred remembers the day that they went down to the depot to see George off. "All the kids were there, and father and mother and George's girl, Eleanor. Everyone seemed to be crying except Dad and George. They just stood there talking gravely for a while, until finally Dad shook his hand and it was time to go. George got on the train and we didn't see him any more. It was like the bottom had dropped out of everything. We thought the whole world was ending."

3

The
Dakota Queen

MUSKOGEE, OKLAHOMA, might have been remote, even a little God-forsaken, but it was not quite the end of the world. Nor, after the initial bouts with airsickness that seemed to accompany every rollout and spin, was flying quite the terror McGovern remembered it to be. The one thing that was worse than he imagined was his loneliness for Eleanor, who had gone to wait out the war with his parents in Mitchell. Primary flight training was barely half completed when he wrote her, asking her to forget the good wisdom about waiting until after the war and marry him now. Eleanor didn't need convincing. On his first leave they were married in Woonsocket by the Reverend McGovern.

It was hardly the ideal start to a new marriage. Army regulations forbade flight cadets from living off base, so Eleanor had to settle alone into a tiny apartment near the field, waiting for George's infrequent passes and trying not to wonder whether her husband was involved in any of the constant crashes that rattled her kitchen windows. Economically, they were living at the subsistence level. When a flying cadet got married, half his $100-a-month salary was automatically deducted and set aside for his wife. In typically bureaucratic fashion, the Army remembered to deduct the $50 but neglected to pass it along to Eleanor. It was months before the administrative snafu was unscrambled, and in the meantime Eleanor and George were making do on half a hundred a month, plus whatever Eleanor could bring in from part-time jobs.

Things started looking up when George won his wings. Now, at least, they could live together. But they were constantly on the move, shuttling from one flight school to another, and even faster than usual, since by this time McGovern had conquered, or at least put aside, his fear of flying and had been moved into the accelerated course. "I became a camp follower," says Eleanor. "Ten weeks here, twelve weeks somewhere else." The final stop for bomber pilots was Liberal, Kansas, where George's instructor was flight-happy Norman Ray, the man who had gotten him into all this trouble in the first place. On a cold, crisp Kansas day in February 1944 George shipped overseas. Eleanor went back to South Dakota, to wait out the war—and the birth of their first child.

By the fall of 1944 the war in Europe was almost over. The Allies had been on the Continent since June, and with each day the breach they had forced into fortress Europe opened a crack wider. Paris had already been liberated, and now the armies were racing for the Rhine. After years of battering by round-the-clock bombing—the Americans by day, the English by night—the Nazi war machine was slowly crumbling under its own weight. To the south the Allies, after clearing North Africa and seizing Sicily, were slowly inching their way up the Italian boot. A miracle had saved Mussolini, but only for the moment. There remained for the Axis one last, convulsive shudder—the Battle of the Bulge—and then the denouement.

A key element in the Allied strategy during the closing months of the war was the systematic pulverization of the Axis' southern defenses—northern Italy, Yugoslavia, and Austria, and on into southern Germany. There, especially in Austria, lay some of the enemy's last lines of supply, marshaling yards, ammunition dumps, munitions factories, and oil storage dumps. From bases scattered throughout southern Italy American planes rose every day at dawn, circled like gathering birds of prey, then headed north and east with their heavy cargoes of death.

They flew mainly in B-24s, or as the Convair Company, which rolled more than 18,000 of them off the assembly line, liked to call them, "Liberators." The pilots who flew them had their own names for the ships, of which two of the more polite were "the flying coffin" and "the liquidator." By any name, the big four-engine bomber was an impressive and for its day awesome weapon. Faster (180–220 m.p.h. combat cruise speed, and up to 300 m.p.h. in a pinch) and better armed (twelve fifty-caliber Browning machine guns, with some models carrying cannon as well) than its predecessor, the B-17, the B-24 could bear a heavier bomb load (up to six tons of high explosives) and bear it farther (2,500 miles and more) and higher (25,000 to 30,000 feet). From San Giovanni, Italy, where the 15th Air Force's 455th Bomb Group was based, Liberators could reach to within a hairbreadth of Berlin.

All of which, from a strategist's point of view, made it the ideal aircraft. "The B-24 has *guts*," beamed the Air Force instruction manual for pilots. "It can take it and dish it out. It can carry a bigger bomb load farther and faster, day in and day out, than any airplane that has passed the flaming test of combat. At present, it is the heavyweight champion of the world. When the super-bombers capture the title, the B-24 will still be the middleweight champ and a tough baby to beat."

To the men who had to fly, fight, and too often die in them, it was a somewhat different story. The ship was not a "forgiving" airplane; mistakes that a pilot might get away with in a B-17 could well be fatal aboard a B-24. For all its speed, the B-24 was a surprisingly sluggish aircraft. As one of the men who flew them says: "That plane took its own good time to do whatever it was going to do." Worst of all, the Liberator lacked the sturdiness of a Flying Fortress, which could, and often did, limp back from missions riddled with holes and with only one of its propellers still turning. If even a single engine were lost on a Liberator, says one airman, "you were right now in trouble." Of course, it was the flak that the men feared most. The Liberator could survive a few hits, but not many. In particular, its newly designed Davis wing displayed a distressing tendency to fold up and break off when hit by a large shell. When the antiaircraft fire was intense and well directed, as it was over the oilfields of Ploesti, Rumania, in August 1943, the result could be a slaughter. In one day over Ploesti fifty-four B-24s were blasted from the sky.

When the newly commissioned Lieutenant McGovern reported to the headquarters of the 15th Air Force's 455th Bomb Group at Cherignola, a small, rural town halfway up the Italian peninsula, he had heard all the horror stories and more. But there was nothing he could do about them, and even if there were he lacked the time. Because like any young pilot he had to move fast, get his bearings, gather his crew, and when that was done set up housekeeping with the two other officers on his ship in a tent on the edge of an olive orchard from which the base had been cut. His roommates were Bill Rounds, the co-pilot, and Sam Adams, the navigator-bombardier. Both were within a year or two of McGovern, but the three of them could not have been more different. Rounds was a bouncy, wisecracking prankster from Kansas, the very image of the devil-may-care flyboy. "I don't know how he ever ended up in bombers," says one of his friends. "Everything about that guy said fighter pilot." Adams, by contrast, was a gentle, easygoing, somewhat reclusive figure from Milwaukee who planned on becoming a Presbyterian minister after the war. He was also possessed of a tough, well-developed intelligence, which soon attracted McGovern to him. "I was very close to him," McGovern says. "He was a very deep guy. I could really talk to him."

The rest of the crew was a varied lot. There was Bill McAfee, of Michigan, the ball turret gunner, popular with his buddies, happy-go-lucky by nature, but when pushed likely to push back —and hard. Ken Higgins, the radio operator from Texas, was at most moments serious beyond his years. Except when he detected pomposity; then could come a quip that would deflate its victim

in a second. The tail gunner, Nebraskan Isadore Siegal, was a
bizarre figure, given to sleeping with a loaded .45 under his pillow
and walking around his tent nude, save for a bayonet strapped
around his middle. Before the tour was out, the other enlisted men
would "vote" him off the crew and Siegal would transfer to another ship. Whether it was more than coincidence that Siegal was
the only Jew on the plane could never be proven. The gambler
of the crew was Bob O'Connell of Brattleboro, Vermont, who
could be just as cool sitting behind a straight flush as behind the
twin fifties in the nose. "Bob wasn't any older than any of us,"
says one of the taken. "But when he played poker, you would have
thought he was thirty." Bill Ashlock, the softly drawling waist
gunner, was the second Texan on the ship and the only one to be
cursed with the inevitable nickname that heritage brought. That
left Valko, the flight engineer and the oldest man aboard by almost ten years. Michael J. Valko, who stood less than five-
five, was also the shortest member of the crew, and he never
forgot it. He was a tough-talking kid from the slums of Bridge-
port, Connecticut who had had it hard all the way up. He could
have had it better, he always claimed, if he had only been taller.
So instead Valko did what, in wartime, came easy: he drank.

For all their apparent disparity, the men of the *Dakota Queen*,
as their ship had been christened, were alike in one respect.
And that was their regard for their leader. They addressed
him as "Captain" or "Sir." By rank of course such courtesy
was due him, though he never mentioned it. The respect, according to Ashlock, was something that flowed naturally: "He
was just a damn good pilot." One of the best, said the ground
crews, who claimed that the mark of McGovern's flying was
that he invariably came back to base with more gas in his tanks
than 99 percent of the other pilots. He knew his ship inside and
out, not only his own job but all the others. He flew formation
by the book: in tight and close, where there was less chance
of being jumped by fighters. He prided himself on never missing
a mission, not even on that December day in 1944 when word
reached him that his father had died of a heart attack while
hunting pheasants.

The 455th Bomb Group had drawn a tough target, and the CO told McGovern that he could pass it up with no disgrace. But McGovern flew his mission, just as he flew each of the thirty-five: calmly, methodically, unemotionally. "If he ever panicked, I never knew about it," says one of his crew. "Whatever happened, that sort of nasal twang of his came over the radio as clear and flat as it was on the ground." "I don't know how you describe a good pilot," says McAfee. "I do know George, though, and as far as I was concerned, he was the best. Because he always got us back on the ground."

There were moments, however, when even McGovern must have wondered. Once the *Dakota Queen* blew a tire on takeoff, a seemingly minor happening which on a B-24 could have disastrous consequences. McGovern continued on with the mission, completed it, and on return gently eased the big ship onto the runway, revving up the engines in the opposite wing to keep as little pressure on the damaged wheel as possible. One miscalculation and the *Queen* would have ground-looped as other less fortunate planes within the group had done, killing their crews. But McGovern brought the *Queen* to a halt without incident. They were not so lucky on what turned out to be the *Queen*'s final mission, a massive raid on the marshaling yards at Linz, Austria. Over the target the flak had never been thicker. Black smoke covered the sky, laced with red fireballs of exploding shells. Buffeted by the concussions, the *Queen* pitched back and forth, thrown like a cork on a rising swell. Suddenly there was a tremendous explosion and the ship gave a fearful shudder. A near-direct hit had blown out most of the nose, carrying away the brakes and the hydraulic system. Another loud report and the plane shook again, and this time Tex was screaming into the radio: "I'm hit! I'm hit!" A red-hot sliver of shrapnel from another shell had burst, punching a gaping hole in the flaps and gouging out a deep canal in Ashlock's thigh.

McGovern surveyed the damage. Luckily, the flaps still worked. If they hadn't, with the brakes gone too the crew might as well have bailed out there. As it was, they had to crank the landing gear into place by hand and ready parachutes near the rear hatches for use as drogues to slow the ship down. The *Queen* came in low over the base and dropped a flare, signaling that she had a wounded man aboard. On the next pass McGovern put the wheels down at the very end of the runway, and braced himself. The runway hurtled by beneath him; there wouldn't be enough. The chutes popped out, and slowly—too slowly—the plane began to ease its mad rush down the runway.

But not quite in time. The *Queen* rolled off the end of the runway and up the side of a dirt embankment. For a moment it seemed to poise there, as if deciding whether to continue on; if it had, the results could have been grim. For the other side of the embankment sloped steeply into a deep creek. Finally, with a groan the *Queen* slipped back down the hill, giving the tail section, where most of the crew had taken refuge, a heavy whack. Shaken, bruised, but except for Ashlock unhurt seriously, the crew scrambled out. "Once we were down and on the ground," said one of them, "it seemed sort of funny." It had never really been funny, of course, and certainly the Air Force didn't see McGovern's nifty piece of flying that way. For bringing the *Queen* in and saving the lives of his crew, he was awarded the Air Medal.

On the ground they never talked about medals or heroics. As much as possible they tried not to even mention flying. By the end of a mission, which could go ten hours—and when they probed into Germany or Poland, even longer—they were physically and emotionally exhausted. A quick shower, some hot food, maybe a drink at the bar, and they would collapse in their bunks, sleeping away a good portion of the next day until it was time to fly again. They spent most of their waking hours playing cards and gabbing about what they would do after their twenty-fifth mission, when they came up for ten days of R & R on the Isle of Capri. McGovern spent much of his free time in his tent, writing to Eleanor (always being sure to include somewhere in his letter a number signifying how many missions he had to go) and plowing through the stack of history and philosophy texts he had brought with him from South Dakota. To those who asked, he explained that he was boning up so that he could finish his studies after the war. But there was also a deeper, unspoken purpose, which they all shared, whether they read or talked or drank or played cards. It took them away. It made them forget, if only for a moment, the war that was intent on killing them.

There was one mission they could never forget: the 400-bomber raid on Pilsen, Czechoslovakia, site of the mammoth Škoda ammunition works. They were cruising at 25,000 feet, an hour away from target, when the number-two inboard engine quit. McGovern feathered the prop and increased power on the remaining three to keep up with the formation. At that point he could have broken off and returned to base without incident; in the same situation many other pilots would—and had. Instead, the *Queen* flew on. "So we're minus an engine," he said to Rounds. "Let's go." On they went. Then, thirty seconds shy of the drop point, a cylinder blew out in the number-three engine and the prop began spinning wildly. Adams sent the bombs away on target, and McGovern pulled hard on the controls to wheel the crippled craft toward home, 600 miles away. If they were to have a chance of reaching base, McGovern had to stop the runaway prop, which, if it kept turning, could tear the wing off in five minutes. He pushed at the feather button once; no response. He tried again; still no response. "Prepare to bail out," he radioed over the intercom. In the rear of the aircraft Ashlock sat poised over the escape hatch, waiting for the final word. Meanwhile, in the cockpit McGovern tried to bring the prop under control one last time. He pushed the feather button again; this time it worked. "Resume your stations," McGovern signaled. "We're going to try to bring her home."

If it had been a B-17, they might have had a chance; but with a Liberator it was well-nigh hopeless. As they headed back over Yugoslavia on a new course that Adams plotted to keep them away from the heaviest flak concentrations, they were losing altitude at the rate of a hundred feet a minute. As they passed through the 8,000-foot level, McGovern asked once again if anyone wanted to jump; no one did. Like a balloon with a slow leak, the *Queen* continued its sickening descent. By the time the blue-green waters of the Adriatic hove into view, they were at 600 feet and still falling. Desperate now, they jettisoned anything that would lighten the ship. Out went chart tables, oxygen masks, flak jackets, even guns and ammunition.

Suddenly the tiny island of Vis appeared on the horizon. Mc-Govern knew from his briefings that the British had built an emergency dirt strip for Spitfires on the island. At 2,200 feet in length, the runway hardly provided enough margin for a fighter, much less a four-engine bomber, but at that moment it was either Vis or the Adriatic. McGovern took dead aim and headed in. "There was a mountain at the end of the landing strip," McGovern said later. "You either made it the first time or you were all through. I knew if I came in short, I couldn't pull up and go around. You only had one shot at it, and I took mine."

As he glided in over the tip of the island, nestling in between the peaks that guarded its approaches on either side, McGovern could see the charred carcasses of other planes that had taken their shots and missed. He set the wheels of the *Queen* down on the very edge of the runway, and stood on the brakes. Tires smoking and brakes screaming, the *Queen* rolled to a halt a few feet away from the end of the strip. Just yards away the mountain face loomed up. McGovern and his crew piled out just in time to see another B-24 try to duplicate the feat. This one was not so lucky. It slammed into one of the peaks by the side of the runway and exploded in a plume of orange fire, killing all on board. In a few hours a DC-3 arrived to ferry McGovern and his crew back to Italy. A repair team came in to put the *Queen* back together, and within days men and machine were back in the air again. A few months later, 15th Army Air Force Headquarters announced that because of his "intrepid spirit, outstanding ability, and rare devotion to duty, . . . First Lieutenant George McGovern, 22, Mitchell, S.D.," had been awarded one of the nations highest medals, the Distinguished Flying Cross.

In the beginning the war seemed "a glorious venture" to Mc-Govern. "My spirits and enthusiasm were high," he recalled later. "It seemed to me that what I was doing was central to the defense of Western civilization. There was a sense of exhilaration in that period, a certain amount of pride in being involved in one of the most important aspects of the war effort. There was none of the torment that is involved in fighting today." Death somehow seemed remote, as detached and laconic as the entries in a flight log:

December 26, 1944: Hit oil refineries at Osweicim, Poland. Flak was very heavy over the target. Also passed over flak at Brataslavia, Austria [sic]. Piece of flak hit windshield between pilot and co-pilot.

January 31, 1945: Hit Moosbierbaum, Austria—bombed through overcast—very light flak. Today Lt. Perry and crew ditched in Atlantic. Hanson and Dodge in hospital.

February 28, 1945: Bombed railroad bridge in Brenner Pass. Flak was moderate but very accurate. Had very large hole beneath cockpit. Saw German fighters on Udine airstrip. Today Lt. Heardman's crew went down.

To survive when, as McGovern puts it, "men flying on my wings were getting blown out of the sky," one had to be detached, had to hide, as McGovern hid, "the feelings of terror, the thoughts that you could never survive." Sometimes there was no place to hide, like the day Sam Adams, anxious to put in extra missions so that he could go home with McGovern, went out with another crew over Vienna and didn't come back. Adams' death hit McGovern hard, harder probably than anything during the war. "I had seen other men killed before," he says, "but never anything like that. When there are just three of you living together so closely for a year in a tent in an olive grove in Italy, a helluva long way from home, you really get to know one another. And then all of a sudden you see the empty bunk, and they come in and get his personal things to ship back to his mother. It really gets to you."

But one could never afford that luxury for long, because with terrible regularity came the missions, one every two or three days. Then the sorrow, even the high purpose and resolve, was suddenly forgotten. Out went the months of learning the theories of high-level strategic bombing. As McGovern told a friend after the war: "You just dropped those damn bombs where you could and got the hell out of there before they shot your ass off." And if somehow one made it, one was never the same again. "War develops a sense of fatalism," McGovern reflects today. "What is to be is to be. The old thing that soldiers talk about: 'the bullet that has your name on it.' In war it's really true. I know it made me fatalistic. It had to. Because when you are up there in a bomber, it's not like being a fighter pilot, when you are flying against another plane and it's sort of a duel. No, when you are up there in a bomber, there is nothing you can do except sit there and hope that the next burst doesn't hit you—and pray to God that it doesn't."

There were times when the war, and what it was doing to all of them, came home with blockbuster force. Once McGovern was at the bar in the base officers' club when a couple of fighter jocks came in bragging about two Italian civilians they had shot off a bridge. "Apparently, they were coming back from a strafing mission and they had some rounds left," McGovern remembers. "So they gave them a burst of fifty caliber. One of them said, 'Did you see the way that son of a bitch hit the water?' I just couldn't believe what they were saying. I still don't know whether it's true or not. It might just have been whiskey talk. I was stunned that anyone could be so barbaric about the taking of a human life."

McGovern was only slightly less incredulous over a similar happening aboard his own ship. The incident involved a substitute navigator, one of several who joined the *Queen* following the death of Adams. Heavy weather had forced the group to abort their mission, and they were heading back to base. Under normal flight procedures, they were to jettison their bomb load before landing, either in the open sea or in a remote, unpopulated area, since landing with a full bomb load could be fatal. The *Queen* was over a rural area in Yugoslavia when the bombardier signaled McGovern to turn into a final approach course. Halfway back in the airplane, Tex Ashlock was watching the scenery go by through the camera hatch. Suddenly he couldn't believe his eyes. The bombs were away, and they were heading dead on a small farmhouse in front of them. In seconds, the ground shook with the roar of six 500 pounders going off at once. The farmhouse Ashlock had been watching disappeared in a rolling cloud of brown smoke. In Ashlock's mind there could be no doubt about it; he had just witnessed cold-blooded murder.

When they got on the ground, Ashlock threw aside all the rules about respect for officers and grabbed hold of the bombardier. "Listen, you son of a bitch," he yelled. "I saw what you did. I'm not going to have anything to do with you again. As far as

I'm concerned, you're a disgrace to humanity." Then Ashlock went to McGovern. The young lieutenant listened grimly. After Ashlock finished his story, he questioned him closely. "There isn't any doubt in your mind it was deliberate?" McGovern asked. "How could it not have been?" Ashlock retorted. McGovern thought for a few moments, then finally said: "You know, if we bring charges, it's going to be your word against his—an enlisted man against an officer. It's going to be hard to make it stick without any other evidence or witnesses. I'll tell you one thing, though. We aren't going to fly with that guy again." McGovern was true to his word; that day the bombardier was kicked off the crew.

McGovern's last mission was on April 25, 1945. Two weeks later the war in Europe was over, and McGovern was heading home, ferrying a Liberator back across the Atlantic. He would say in later years that he never regretted what he had done in the war, that Hitler had to be stopped, as he put it, if Western civilization was to survive. He had learned from the war and had been changed by it. In a perverse yet necessary way, he said, it gave him a strength that he would not otherwise have had. Death now had less terror than before, and as he would soon discover, so did the past. But all this lay ahead. On that April day in 1945, as he walked away from the ugly green bomber for the last time, he felt both exhilarated and sick.

The testing was over. He would never have to fly—or fight —again.

4

The Changeling

IT WAS AS a different man that George McGovern came back to South Dakota. To friends he seemed, if it were possible, even more serious and mature than the college boy who had gone off to enlist in the Great Crusade. He also seemed more sure of himself—"more worldly," some said, as well he should be. Because this time he had been outside the walls too long, gone too far, and seen too much to ever be completely contained. What seemed "worldliness" to some was actually the beginnings of a still undefined restlessness, deep, pervasive, almost existential. Later it would take the form of a particular kind of impatience, a dissatisfaction with some of the ways he had lived in the past. Right now it was merely a vague questioning, and for now that was enough.

The life he had left behind had also changed. The family was beginning to scatter. His father had died the previous December,*

* In one of his last letters to his son, written barely a month before his death, Joseph McGovern said:

You never caused us to loose [sic] any sleep. We always felt that we had one of the best boys in town and we feel that way yet, and I

Larry was married, and Olive had already embarked on a career of high school teaching. Soon even Mildred would be leaving home, and within two years his mother would suffer a stroke that would leave her speechless for the next twenty years, until her death in 1967. In his absence his own family had also undergone a radical transformation: with the birth of his first daughter, Ann, on March 10, while he waited out the weather to raid Austria, it had doubled.

He was a family man now, with major responsibilities. To fulfill them he had to finish his education, which he could just barely afford to do, thanks to the GI Bill. He enrolled almost immediately in Dakota Wesleyan's summer term and as best he could tried to settle down to the routine of being a married civilian. It was not altogether easy, especially at night. Eleanor worried about his nightmares, the visions of planes crashing and men falling through the sky. Gradually his system purged itself, and he could talk about the war. He didn't linger over it or revel in the telling, either then or later. He discussed it in a reflective way, posing a number of questions, more often, it seemed, of himself than of his listeners.

McGovern resumed his studies in history, looking for answers there; then, under the influence of one of his professors, Don McAnich, he probed into philosophy and theology. He was interested, he said, "in the reasons for things and the causes of events," not the least of which was life itself. One of his first discoveries was that the faith of his father did not hold out the answers he was looking for. McGovern had long since become skeptical of Wesleyan Methodism's more fundamentalist tenets and plain disbelieving of its archaic prohibitions. One day, with neither fanfare nor fuss, he simply abandoned it in favor of regular Methodism, which while still conservative was light years closer to his own thinking.

---

know the people of Mitchell feel that way. But my dear boy these are awful times in which we are living and you will need to let Christ have first place in your life and trust Him to help you to fit into all his blessed will for your life. Jesus said John 15:15 "Without me you can do nothing." Read that 15 ch. of St. John and think on those words. Read the 23 Psalm often, and meditate on it.

By now, that thinking had become strikingly similar to the views of Walter Rauschenbusch. McGovern gorged himself with the turn-of-the-century Baptist theologian's works. The more McGovern read, the more appealing the notion of spreading Rauschenbusch's social gospel became. Before his senior year was out, he announced to Eleanor that he planned to become a minister. Eleanor received the news with mixed feelings. Her most vivid memories of religion were of prayer meetings attended as a child, of cowering in her seat when the minister called down hellfire and damnation, thinking that he was speaking directly to her and no one else. "I remember thinking that people were always praying for the right thing, and that maybe instead of praying so much, they ought to be doing some of them," she said later. "There are very few of those people who do. But let there be an issue like whether liquor will be served in a restaurant, and they work with great imagination, diligence, and tenacity. So long as they are not involved or intimately concerned." Now her husband wanted to be a preacher. Well, she would wait and see.

Meanwhile, George continued with his schoolwork and renewed his interest in speech and debate. Not surprisingly his favorite themes were war and peace. What was surprising, at least within the borders of his native state, was McGovern's advocacy of world government as the only hope for peace. In thinking that way, McGovern was not unlike many of the men who came back from Europe and the Pacific; nor were they so dissimilar from the veterans of any war, who always seemed to return home convinced that the war they had fought would surely be the last. "There was a new excitement about the world," McGovern remembers, "a great sentiment that because the United Nations was being born we couldn't have another war. There was a great spirit of hope and a great wave of practical idealism running through the campuses. Coming back from the war, we had a feeling that we had done a damned important thing, and that maybe this time we could start anew." Later, when the Cold War set in, the veterans would be seen as naïve and idealistic, even dupes. But at the same time what they said and the way they said it could seem very tough indeed, as witnessed by the language of one of McGovern's orations.

The speech was called "From Cave to Cave," and it won McGovern first place in the state Peace Oratory Contest, just as "My Brother's Keeper" had done three years before. In tone as well as thought, "From Cave to Cave" was a far stronger document than the earlier, sometimes pietistic effort. It was the work of a mind still formulating a world view, and today much of it seems rough, incomplete, even simplistic. But the essential thrust, the barely controlled rage running through it, is there, pointing the way in which he was heading.

The speech begins with the recitation of some recent abuses of American power. Of a group of Chinese killed in a U.S. atrocity, McGovern asks: "Why did they die? Because American values insisted that even in this minor instance American military pride was of more value than the human life of a foreign village." Of an American steel mill in India that made a profit of 300 percent while its workers earned twelve cents a day: "Why?" McGovern demands. "Because American values insist that maximum financial return is of greater concern than human welfare. It was such a system of values that led Gandhi to tell America: 'Bring your Christ, but leave your Christianity at home.'" There are other sins in the litany, like a Senate proposal to block wheat shipments overseas because they would involve the addition of more dark bread to the American diet. "Why was this proposal to block the feeding of starving people so popular?" McGovern asks. "It is because as Americans we place such a high value on our daintily pampered appetites and pleasures that we sometimes lose sight of people dying of starvation the world over." Or the suggestion that the United States seize whatever Pacific islands it wishes, without regard to the sanction of international law: "What is the basis of these demands that are in such direct contradiction to international cooperation? It is the fact that many of us place a higher value on American military expediency than we do on international cooperation."

McGovern's solution is a return to what he calls "the applied idealism of Christianity." What he proposes sounds strikingly like Wilsonian idealism. To the pragmatic doubters, McGovern responds:

It is this type of practicality, so-called, that has hindered every attempt to better man as an individual and as a member of society. . . . The practical men have had inning after inning in which they have constantly piled up a higher and higher score on the side of war and chaos at home and abroad. . . . As long as men continue to scoff at idealism, at spirituality, at such ideas as international cooperation through the United World Government, and continue to advance the notion of expediency and material gain, just so long will we continue to reap the tragic harvest of so-called practical men. As long as economic and social exploitation of weak and unprotected groups exists, just so long will there continue to be economic and social insecurity, racial and class hatreds and strife—the very hotbeds of depression and warfare.

McGovern graduated the following June. A few months before, he had been accepted at Garrett Theological Seminary, across the street from Northwestern University in Evanston, Illinois. With his admission came an appointment as a student minister at Diamond Lake, a resort and retirement community thirty miles northwest of Chicago. McGovern left to take up his new assignment almost immediately, while Eleanor, now the mother of two (a second daughter, Susan, had been born the previous March), stayed behind in Mitchell for a few weeks to gather up the family belongings.

Diamond Lake suited the young student minister perfectly. In appearance, it had an almost postcard picturesqueness. The "town" was no more than a line of trim, whitewashed cabins strung out around the rim of a cobalt-blue lake like a strand of gleaming white pearls. Diamond Lake was even quieter and smaller than Mitchell, and its people, including several retired millionaires, almost as conservative. From the wooded tranquility of Diamond Lake, Chicago and all the name stood for—the sweat and grime, the toughness and turmoil—seemed remote indeed, a fairy tale of a monster's imagination. McGovern's congregation was a tiny one. He counted himself lucky if more than a few dozen turned up to listen to the sermons he worked hours over.

But the remoteness and inactivity had its advantages. With church business taking little of his time, McGovern could concentrate on his studies in virtually uninterrupted quiet. Best of all, the student minister was given a roomy frame parsonage rent-free, no mean consideration for a father of two supporting himself through school on the GI Bill. It was a spacious house, large enough to shelter not only his own family but Eleanor's sister, Ila, and her husband, Bob Pennington, a graduate student in history at Northwestern.

McGovern swept out the new house and began the rudiments of housekeeping. He also set to work writing his first sermon for the coming Sunday. The routine continued for a few weeks before it dawned on McGovern that the arrival of his family was only days away, and that come Sunday, in the best clerical tradition, he would be standing on the front steps of his church introducing Eleanor to his congregation, men and women whose names he did not know. "Good to see you" and "Glad you could come" simply would not do. Frantically, he began connecting names with faces, asking people he knew who other people were and touring the outlying districts with what seemed evangelical zeal. By Sunday he had made it; with Eleanor at his side, he didn't miss a name or a face—nor in later years, as a politician, would he miss many, thanks to the experience.

On the whole, though, church work seemed neither as pleasant nor as uplifting as it had appeared in the pages of Rauschenbusch's books. Diamond Lake was hardly the ideal setting for preaching of the social gospel. A minister was expected to put less effort into his sermon-writing craft and more into the traditional ministerial duties—which were precisely the opposite of McGovern's priorities. "George was interested in the overall impact," says Pennington. "He would rather write a sermon than sit holding the hand of some person who had just lost her husband." The ministry cast McGovern in a new, less active role, one in which, after the hyperactivity of the war, he did not feel entirely comfortable. There were things, often simple things, that a Methodist minister could not or should not do. Pennington recalls the night when he, Ila, Eleanor, and some friends decided to go bowling. Out they went, leaving George on the front steps of the church waving forlornly after them, wishing for just that once that he could let himself go.

But that was the price of the ministry. In time, McGovern might have been willing to pay it, had it not been for the overweening church bureaucracy. "George was interested in whether the church was getting across to the people, touching their lives," says Pennington. "The hierarchy was interested in whether membership was going up, because if membership went up, that meant there were more contributions coming in. Once George heard a bishop discourage another minister from taking a congregation in Minnesota, because Minnesota, he said, was only at the $5,600 level. That is all they seemed interested in: how much money they could make. It was pretty disillusioning."

Disillusionment does not fully describe McGovern's mood. He was depressed, as low as he would be during any point in his life. He had committed himself to his church. His family was watching him, especially his mother. She had not been happy when George announced his vocation. The call to the ministry, she said, should come from God—not, as it had been for her son, from the logic of the intellect. For several months McGovern debated what to do, hoping for fortune to improve and knowing it never would. The professors in Northwestern's history department, where he had been taking several courses, were urging him to take up academic life. The pressures continued all through the year, pulling him first one way and then the other. Finally, late in 1947 McGovern made up his mind.

It was a decision McGovern never regretted. The thought of teaching had been in the front of his mind for nearly a decade; only the emotional aftermath of the war had pushed it aside. Nothing had changed in the motivation that had originally led him into the ministry. He was still raw-boned and idealistic, full of evangelical fervor and intensity, and anxious as ever to spread the social gospel as well as the good news of world peace. What had altered was his perception of the best way to do it. Clearly, for him at least, the ministry was not the answer.

McGovern's own father's vocation, according to his friends, may have had a lot to do with his decision not only to enter the ministry but to leave it as well. For a young man of his background, home from the trauma of war, the ministry offered a natural refuge, a sort of emotional halfway house, a chance, as it were, to be in the world and not really a part of it. The ministry represented familiarity and comfort, much of the sort that he had enjoyed as a boy. But in time he would discover, as Eleanor puts it, "that being a minister is not the same as being a minister's son." That recognition, while perhaps inevitable, was crucial. In moving away from the ministry, says a minister who grew up with him, McGovern was also moving away from his father, the past, and all they represented.

The transition from clerical to "civilian" life presented certain dislocations. The most pressing were the loss of the minister's salary and parsonage. The latter was replaced by an old converted rooming house at 710 Clark Street, in the very midst of the Northwestern campus. Rented out at $25 a room, the house was truly a horror—cramped, noisy, dirty, and ridden with cockroaches so large, says Pennington, "you didn't know whether to kill them or throw a saddle on them." The McGoverns and the Penningtons rented out most of the third floor, including three bedrooms and a kitchen (separated from the living room by another apartment), bath, and living room that they shared. The space was so small that Eleanor had to do the typing she took in to bolster George's $125-a-month veteran's allowance in a broom closet. One of their biggest worries was fire. Finally, they devised an ingenious means of escape. Under each bed they placed a large board, which when extended to the window of the apartment building next door would provide a crawlway from the flames. They conducted fire drills to be ever on the ready. Fortunately, they never had to employ their contraption under actual operating conditions.

Their money problems, which eased slightly when McGovern secured a teaching fellowship in his second year and a Hearst fellowship in his third, bordered at first on the critical. Broke, when their veterans' checks failed to arrive, McGovern and Pennington began collecting empty soda bottles from the building and around the neighborhood to return for the penny deposit. Eventually, they scrounged enough money to buy some peanut butter, soup, and milk for the children, and on that diet they subsisted for the next two weeks.

The veterans who filled up the graduate schools throughout the last half of the 1940s were a very special breed of student. There are many professors who call them as a group the best students the universities have ever seen. They were older and more mature than the usual run of graduate student, and more committed to learning, not only for its own sake but for what they imagined it could do in—and to—the world. Bright, idealistic, battle-toughened, they were the social activists of their day, certainly far more so than the undergraduates who had not gone off to war, and tended to be, at a place like Northwestern at least, comfortably Republican.

Among the veterans liberalism was riding high. At Northwestern a number of them dropped out to organize for the CIO. "As a cause, trade union militancy was then what the Negro thing is today," recalls one of McGovern's fellow students. Within McGovern's own class, the liberal feeling was partially reflected in the subjects of the graduate dissertations. "We all chose topics that had some social purpose," says Alfred Young, a student with McGovern and now a professor of history at Northern Illinois University. "We wanted to be involved in history that could do something."

McGovern himself embarked on a massive, highly sympathetic study of the bloody Colorado coal strikes of 1913 and 1914, which climaxed on April 20, 1914, in the so-called Ludlow Massacre, in which a number of miners were shot down and eleven women and children burned to death during a fierce pitched battle with the Colorado militia and a private army of thugs and detectives imported to break the strike.

The choice was a remarkable turnabout for a man who a few years before was warning his wife-to-be about the "dangers" of anything so radical as the CIO. But given the context of the times, the maturing of McGovern's mind, and the ideas he was being exposed to, both at Garrett, where his teachers were surprisingly liberal, and at Northwestern, where the professors were even more left-wing, the switch is understandable, even predictable. In the late 1940s the past and everything about it was seriously in question, especially for veterans. One of them, Lawrence Towner, now director of Chicago's Newbury Library and a graduate school friend of McGovern, says in retrospect: "I remember coming back for my first year of graduate school in 1946 and thinking, well, we've really done it. We've licked Hitler, set the world in order, and now we can all live in peace. Then—wham—I turn on the radio and Walter Winchell is predicting that we'll be at war with Russia in four years. They taught us during the war that Russia was our friend. They rationalized their system of government to us as 'an alternate form of democracy.' They did too good a job, because a lot of us came back believing it. Until Churchill's speech of 1946, the image of an iron curtain descending on Europe seemed inconceivable. Churchill shocked us. It turned us all off. We had fought our war. Now they were telling us we probably would have to fight another one. We thought, my God, what can we do now?"

For many of them, the answer seemed to lie in the presidential candidacy of Henry Wallace. "He was the only one of the candidates who presented any sort of alternative to the Cold War ideology," explains Towner. "We were turning to him, as a lot of kids back from the war were turning to him, because we wanted to build a better world, and he seemed the man to do it. It seems corny and naïve now, but that's what we wanted to do." At Northwestern the Wallace candidacy attracted a small but determined following. "There wasn't much progressive thinking on the campus," says Young, "but whatever there was went to Wallace." Wallace himself credited an open letter signed in 1947 by more than sixty Northwestern faculty members, urging him to run, as one of the factors that finally persuaded him to challenge Dewey and Truman on the Progressive party ticket. One of the strongest pockets of Wallace support on the Northwestern campus was the history department, where twenty-three of twenty-six graduate students backed him. So overwhelming was the sentiment for Wallace and so deep the passion about it that, as one of the lonely holdouts put it: "Some students went along because it was the smart thing to do. If you didn't have a Wallace button on in some classes, your grades could suffer."

McGovern's own feelings about Wallace are one of the few

things he does not readily volunteer about his past. One searches his official biography in vain for some mention of the man, or McGovern's regard for him. Likewise, a lengthy biographical summary that McGovern prepared as a Congressman for the editors of *Good Housekeeping* in 1959 makes no reference to the 1948 campaign and deals with the whole Northwestern experience only in passing, not even hinting at the considerable changes in political philosophy he was undergoing. McGovern's campaign propaganda conveys the impression that his beliefs have never been anything except the most regular Democratic kind. McGovern's reluctance to advertise his political affiliation during the 1948 campaign is perhaps understandable. In every race he has run, especially the first two congressional campaigns, it has been the source of some of the most virulent Red-baiting. As one observer of South Dakota politics sums it up: "People out here can forgive George for just about anything, the war, the blacks, even the hippies. But there's one thing they've always found a little hard to swallow."

That "thing" is McGovern's espousal of the Wallace campaign. It was more than ordinary political support. Intellectually, emotionally, politically, McGovern was committed to Wallace and to what he perceived as the cause he stood for. After school, he cranked an ancient mimeograph machine in the teaching assistants' lounge, turning out leaflets for Wallace and for a variety of anti-Cold War causes, including the defeat of the Mundt-Nixon bill, one of the first legislative attempts to register "Communist-front organizations." McGovern also lent a hand in the campaign of Curtis McDougal, a Northwestern journalism professor and perennial liberal runner who was trying that year —unsuccessfully, as always—for the U.S. Senate against incumbent Paul Douglas. (Ironically, more than twenty years later John Douglas, Paul's son, would become chairman of the Citizens for McGovern in the 1972 campaign.)

Back home, McGovern endorsed Wallace in a letter to the editor in the *Mitchell Daily Republic*. "I take off my hat to this much smeared man who has had the fortitude to take his stand against the powerful forces of fear, militarism, nationalism, and greed," he wrote. "I'm tired of listening to the thoughtless jeers and charges of 'crackpot' and 'Communist' being thrown his way. If someone doesn't come to my rescue soon, I'm going to be forced to vote for the 'crackpot' come next November."

Once the campaign was under way, McGovern returned to Mitchell to speak on Wallace's behalf before a polite but none too sympathetic audience of Kiwanians, whose forbearance he later congratulated in another letter to the editor in the *Daily Republic*. "This experience was a heartwarming example of democracy in action—the free exchange of ideas between Americans," he wrote hyperbolically. "It illustrated the superiority of American democracy over Russian authoritarianism. . . . Some people, calling themselves Americans, may resort to egg-throwing, smear charges, witch-hunting, or intimidation of their employees on political grounds. But these Fascist-tinged minds are still a minority. Anyone capable of recognizing the devil must surely view such individuals as the real threat to the United States."

McGovern's feelings about the election were running high enough to strain his relationship with Pennington, a Truman man. (Ila didn't have anything to do with Wallace either; further left than anyone, she voted for the Socialist Norman Thomas on Election Day.) "Personally," says Pennington, "we were as far apart as we have ever been. It got hard to talk. Tempers were a little thin." McGovern, then as later, took his politics in deadly earnestness, especially when they involved what he saw as an overriding moral issue. "I felt then, as I do now," McGovern says today, "that U.S. foreign policy was needlessly exacerbating tensions with the Soviet Union and that we were wrong in our support of Chiang, the French in Indochina, and Bao Dai. I wasn't happy with the direction the Democratic party was taking in those times. I liked what Wallace had to say about foreign policy. I still think he was essentially right."

The great disillusionment set in when McGovern went to Philadelphia as a member of the Illinois delegation to the Progressive Party convention. The Communist influence, which doubters had perceived far earlier and which the faithful, McGovern included, had always dismissed as "smear," came more or less into the open at the convention. McGovern was disappointed and bewildered at the "fanaticism" of some of the people closest to Wallace. Communists or not, their rigidity put him off. McGovern returned to Northwestern subdued and a little sheepish from the experience. As Election Day neared and Wallace appeared, in Towner's words, "more and more a captive," much of his support began to wane within the history department. There were still some, though, who voted for him, taking the trouble to write in his name on the Illinois ballot. McGovern didn't vote at all.

The lessons learned during the Wallace campaign did not sour McGovern on liberalism. It did teach him, however, to be more selective about liberals. Three of the liberals he valued most highly, and who would have an abiding influence on his life, were, not so coincidentally, the three leading professors in the history department: Ray Allen Billington, who called him "one of the three best students I have encountered in twenty years of teaching"; Arthur Link, the renowned Wilson biographer, who directed McGovern's graduate dissertation; and Lefton ("Lefty") Stavrianos, perhaps the country's foremost authority on Greece and the Balkans.

As personalities, the trio could hardly have been more dissimilar. Billington was a former newspaperman, a teller of tales, collector of limericks, and mixer of good drinks, which he would serve in profusion to his students during occasional parties at his home, where they would discuss history, politics, and life late into the night. "We were always talking about politics," says one veteran of the soirées. "We were always looking for new approaches for doing things. I remember George there. He had a good laugh. And he liked jokes, especially if they were a little dirty." Billington was a constant kidder, but beneath the casual affability a penetrating intelligence was at work. It was from Billington that McGovern took the course in intellectual history, a series of lectures that, he later told Billington, help convince him to leave the ministry. McGovern was entranced with the way Billington wove ideas, never missing the opportunity to make liberal points but never being blatant about making them either. If he could teach like that, McGovern told Billington, he could reach "a far wider audience with a liberal point of view" than he might from the pulpit. "George was a very quiet kind of guy," Billington remembers, "but he was extremely forceful about what he believed. He could persuade you gently."

Arthur Link, then only in his twenties and already established as an historian of the first rank, was as intense and serious as Billington was light and gay. Wilsonian in his own way ("He is the only man I know of who could have devoted his entire life to studying Woodrow Wilson," says one of his colleagues), Link brought out, according to one student, "the more serious side of George that was always there." He also called forth his best academic work. "I have seen perhaps one or two students who were as good as McGovern," Link said more than twenty years later, "but I have never, in twenty-six years of graduate teaching, seen any who were better."

Historian Lefton Stavrianos could never devote his life to the study of any single man—or any single country. His interests and curiosity were simply too far-ranging, his person too rambunctious to be long tied down. He conceived of history not as a string of unrelated episodes, each one greater or lesser than the last, but as a grand sweep of men and events, moving in concert—and conflict—with one another. "There was absolutely no crap about the man," says one of his colleagues. "His grasp of the meaning of events was absolutely fantastic. Of all of us, he had the best sense of proportion, of the way things were ordered and the way they ought to be." There was an excitement about Stavrianos that was contagious. He was a vital, passionate man—"truly a Greek," some said—and it showed. His eyes fairly twinkled as he strode back and forth across the room, lecturing young men in the deeper meaning of European history, what it had wrought on the world, how it had changed the temper and the times of where they now stood. Of all the men on the faculty Stavrianos was the furthest left, a down-the-line Wallace man to the end and even after. He was also the man closest to McGovern. The two of them spent hours together, arguing philosophy and politics, bantering back and forth over beer and sandwiches about the United States, the Cold War, and the rest of the world. Stavrianos felt a personal as well as philosophical attraction for the young man: "McGovern was a very idealistic person. His social consciousness was terrific. We always talked about what was going on in the United States, and what needed to be. He felt very strongly that if he could get involved personally, if everyone did, then the world might be turned in a direction other than the Cold War." Late one night, toward the end of one of their talks, Stavrianos asked impulsively: "George, what makes you tick?" Reflectively, McGovern replied that it was his father's philosophy more than anything else. And what was that? Stavrianos pressed. McGovern's answer was a quotation from St. Matthew: "Whosoever shall save his life shall lose it, and whosoever shall lose his life for my sake shall find it."

Friends who dropped by the McGovern house found the couple "as poor as church mice and apparently not caring one whit about it," in the words of one visitor. It was hard to be concerned, when, aside from money, everything seemed to be going so right. They were together at last, with a growing family that now numbered five, and plenty of friends and stimulating talk to go with it. George even managed to solve the chronic space problem by fashioning beds for the two youngest girls in the drawers of a chest in the closet. "In many ways," says Eleanor, "it was the happiest time in our lives." For George, certainly, it was one of the most fruitful. In his own words, he had "come alive to ideas, matured intellectually," during his years at Northwestern. Politically, he had fashioned an ideology that would change little if at all over the course of the next two decades. Perhaps equally important, he had had a taste of practical politics, and he had savored the cynical with the sweet. He was, at its plainest, simply older than when he had come. And now, with his course work completed and the research for his dissertation finished, he was ready to leave.

He went back to Dakota Wesleyan—not for the money certainly (which was less than $4,500) or for the prestige, which was virtually nonexistent, the college being, in the kindly description of Billington, who later tried to get him jobs elsewhere, "hardly the academic Valhalla of the world." What he was seeking was some familiarity, while he tested the still uncertain terrain of college teaching. No other school in the country could offer him a hometown base, and a hometown base would be important if McGovern were ever to run for elective office on his own, something he had been considering since his final year in graduate school. The voting record of South Dakota's politicians, and Karl Mundt especially, appalled him, and if the chance arose to change it he thought he would take it. But in 1951 the possibility seemed a remote one. He was coming back to Dakota, he assured his friends, for only one reason: to teach.

He started out a bit stiffly at first, a little shy despite all the rounds of debate and speech (of which he was now the college's coach), of lecturing to students who were not many years younger than he. The timidity passed quickly, though, and within months the quality of McGovern's lectures established him as a student favorite. His most popular course was human relations, a social-scientific survey of current events. The course was a reflection of McGovern's ideas and those of Dakota Wesleyan's president, Samuel Hilburn. For his time Hilburn, a product of the University of Chicago, was a radical educational reformer. He encouraged his faculty to innovate and fostered the interdisciplinary approach to teaching that later would come so much into vogue. The new-fangled ideas at the university did not escape the notice of the local American Legion post, whose members began to sit in on classes, conspicuously taking notes of anything that might be construed as Communist-influenced; nor did it escape the notice of the FBI, which investigated several faculty members, including Pennington, who had come back to join the History department. Somehow McGovern escaped official scrutiny. "I guess," he says, "that people thought I was a decent young guy who had gone off to Northwestern and been radicalized." There was some grumbling in the community over his rather modest efforts on behalf of the Democratic party, which consisted of some letters to the editor, two radio addresses, and a few speeches around town. But by and large the opposition was underground and muted, if for no other reason than that the McGoverns were too well known and respected in Mitchell. Dakota Wesleyan's ultraconservative board, which finally fired

Hilburn for reforming with what was deemed as too much zeal, never accosted McGovern directly. It was known, though, says one of his colleagues, that "his backing of Wallace was something of a skeleton."

Nor was the board pleased when McGovern endorsed the recognition of Red China and then threatened to sue someone who accused him of following the "Communist party line to do so." By June 1951, he was advocating a cease-fire in Korea, and negotiation of what he called "the Asiatic crisis." "The nonrecognition of China and continued warfare against her is driving the Chinese into the arms of Moscow," he wrote to the editor of the *Mitchell Daily Republic*. "We have weaned the Communist government of Yugoslavia away from the Soviet orbit by patient and peaceful means, including an aid program. I believe that the same possibility is open in the case of China. Our present policy leaves the Chinese with only one place to turn—Moscow."

McGovern spent most of his time finishing his dissertation, which Eleanor laboriously typed out, page by page, footnote by footnote, well into the ninth month of her pregnancy with their fourth child. She was still typing the manuscript only hours before she was taken to the hospital to deliver. Out in the hospital corridor, McGovern paced back and forth and wondered what to name the child. "We had not anticipated having a boy after three successive girls and had no name in mind," he recounted in a letter. "Nineteen fifty-two, however, was the year of Stevenson's campaign, a man whom I greatly admired. I suddenly had a hunch a few hours before the baby's birth that we might have a boy, and at the time a newspaper headline lay near my wife's bed with Stevenson's name prominently displayed. We decided right then and there to name the boy Steven if a miracle should happen and the baby were a boy." It was.

During the fall semester of 1952, some of McGovern's friends at Northwestern told him of a position in the University of Iowa's history department that would fall open the coming year and wondered if he was interested. He was indeed, and the application went out to Iowa City immediately, along with a weighty envelope of glowing recommendations from his Northwestern professors.* Some eighty professors had applied for the job; eventually, the field was narrowed to three, and McGovern was one of them. Then, one day came the word: he had lost out to an Ivy Leaguer. Disappointed and a little hurt, McGovern considered the alternatives: he could continue teaching at Dakota Wesleyan, where he had already gathered a considerable following, or he could seek out an opening at some other school, where Ivy League credentials didn't carry quite the weight they did at Iowa. Finally, and most improbably, there was the offer that Ward Clark, the state Democratic chairman, had made after the 1952 campaign. Clark wanted a full-time organizer to serve as executive secretary of the state party and put the pieces back together again. He had already approached several other possibilities, including Bruce Stoner, editor of the Mitchell *Daily Republic*, and had been turned down by all of them. Then he noticed a series of newspaper articles extolling the Democratic party, written by a young college professor at Dakota Wesleyan. He looked up the professor, who turned out to be George McGovern. Clark

---

* In a letter of application to another school, the University of Denver, McGovern summarized his life and beliefs as follows:

I was born in 1922 as the son of a Methodist minister, a fact which doubtless accounts for my determination to be a minister—until my sixth birthday. After successively considering careers in medicine, law, and crime, I finally decided while a high school sophomore that history was more interesting than any of these. . . . I should perhaps confess that I am troubled with both a sensitive social conscience and a rather wide range of interests. Perhaps these factors will prevent me from becoming the specialized scholar that you would most like to secure. I find myself devoting a considerable amount of time to the study of contemporary social and international problems. . . . There are several other minor, disconnected facts that might be of interest to you. I am married to a beautiful girl who plays the part of research assistant and mother of three little daughters. I am a member of the Methodist Church, although some of the better members will probably dispute the point. In politics my generous friends classify me as an honest-minded, independent liberal, though [others] would not be nearly so kind. Dakota Wesleyan is now paying me $4,600 a year as a full professor—a title which impresses neither me nor my associates considering the small size of the college. This letter seems to be a compilation of self-styled compliments, but perhaps you may learn of an even larger list of faults upon investigation.

laid out his proposal, and McGovern, skeptical, promised to think
about it.

For months he did think about it. McGovern's friends were
horrified that he would even consider it. "If you have a job these
days, George," Pennington told him, "you'd better hold on to it."
Of course, Clark was offering him a job; the trouble was it wasn't
much of one. He would even have to raise his own $6,500 salary.
With four children and a new mortgage, it seemed out of the
question. Still McGovern was undecided. All through the winter
and into the spring he sought out opinions. The verdict was
unanimous. Bradley Young, manager of the local J. C. Penney
store and a lifelong Democrat, said bluntly: "I'd love to see the
Democratic party stronger, but a man would have to be a darned
fool to give up a good job to take on a hopeless venture." Former
U.S. Senator Herbert Hitchcock of South Dakota advised: "It
can't be done, George. Good men have been beating their heads
against this stone wall for as long as I can remember." Nowhere
he turned—to Bob Pearson, to his friends, to his professors at
Northwestern—could he get a positive opinion. Eleanor was
scrupulously neutral. All the evidence and good sense said no.
Only McGovern's instincts kept pushing him on. One day in the
spring, he called Clark and in three words gave him his answer:
"I'll do it."

5

Against the Odds

SMALL WONDER that the job of executive secretary of the South Dakota Democratic party seemed so unattractive to so many. The 1952 Eisenhower sweep had left only two Democrats in the seventy-five-member Assembly and none at all in the thirty-five-member Senate. The debacle was only the final step in a drawn-out decline and fall that had its immediate origins in the 1940 presidential election, when South Dakota went against Roosevelt and New Deal "socialism" by the largest margin of any state in the Union.

With rare exceptions Democrats had never been popular in South Dakota since it gained statehood in 1889. As late as the close of the nineteenth century, Republican orators could still strike a responsive note by blaming the Democrats for all the manifold evils of the Civil War. For their part, party leaders were hardly worthy of anything but scorn. Often more conservative than their Republican opponents, they were generally unsympathetic to any and all reforms, from Prohibition to women's suffrage. The party gained a modicum of power in the 1890s, when the Populist movement swept the Plains States, but only by submerging its principles to those of the Populists. Even then, it took incredible ineptitude on the part of the Republicans to allow the Democrats and their Populist allies into office. Such mistakes, however, were not often repeated, and not until a trauma the magnitude of the Depression did Democrats regain any real foothold in the state. With recovery out went the Democrats.

By the early 1950s, the Democrats had become so dispirited and disorganized (some counties lacked party chairmen, much less a precinct organization), that they naturally expected to be defeated. When the Republicans did disappoint them, it came as something of a shock. "Being a Democrat in South Dakota," says Peder Ecker, a former state party chairman, "was like being a secondclass citizen. One of the biggest problems was credibility. If you were a Democrat, people didn't regard you as a social menace or anything; they just found it hard to take you seriously." That was indisputably true about businessmen and lawyers, many of whom changed their registration to Republican as their first official act after graduating from law school. It was either that or no clients. "If you were blame fool enough to be a Democrat," says someone who was, "there was only one thing you could do about it: keep your mouth shut." The Republicans never held anything less than a three-to-one bulge in registration over the Democrats (who in one rural county, Hutchison, numbered all of three). More telling still was the Republican record in elections; between 1889 and 1967 the GOP won 90 percent of them.

A few, a very few, claimed that the Democratic cause was not as hopeless as it looked. A Democratic lawyer once told Bruce Stoner that if the Democratic party ever got organized the Republicans couldn't win, because there were more people sympathetic to the Democratic cause than to the Republican one. They voted Republican, the lawyer went on, more out of habit than anything else. The story made some sense. Of course, Stoner allowed, the lawyer who told it to him was an old drunk. But in truth there was something to the thesis. As Republican and conservative as South Dakota seemed (especially west of the Missouri, in the sparsely populated ranching area, where legend has it that the concerns of life are three: "wheat, cattle, and communism"), the state had an undeniably Populist heritage stretching back some seventy-five years, to the days when exploitation by the railroads and the banks moved South Dakotans to organize the first Populist party in the country. On occasion, the people were also capable of electing to public office men who fit into neither the Republican nor the Democratic mold. Perhaps the most colorful was Senator Richard Pettigrew, who was elected as a Republican in the late 1800s, switched to the Populists, and finally ended up as the only Marxist in the U.S. Senate. The man who is still recalled as South Dakota's greatest Governor was Peter Norbeck, who after his election in 1916 promptly unfolded a whole array of socialist schemes, including state hail insurance on farm crops, a state coal mine, state-owned grain elevators, and a state cement factory, which is still in operation today.

In short, it was not easy to figure South Dakota out; even South Dakotans had difficulty resolving the seemingly contradictory strains of self-reliance and populism that composed such an essential part of the state's political fiber. By the early 1950s the Democratic party seemed to have forgotten even the rudiments of common political sense. Incredibly, until Ward Clark dreamed up the notion of an executive secretary, there was not a single full-time organizer for the party in the state. If they expected to win, they had to be organized. That is where McGovern came in.

After two years of teaching and four years in graduate school preparing for it, McGovern was not keen on leaving the profession; nor for that matter was the college administration keen on seeing him go. As McGovern tells it: "They begged me to stay. The president of the school practically had tears in his eyes." But McGovern had made up his mind. "I really wanted to see what I could do," he says. "I wanted to move onto a larger platform." His interest was not in political organizing for its own sake but rather in what such organizing could do for the party, its candidates, and specifically himself. He was taking the job, he made clear to Clark, only with the understanding that one day in the not too distant future he would use the organization he meant to build to further his own political career. It was that plan, and that plan only, that finally persuaded McGovern to take the job. As he puts it today: "The principal reason I wanted to move from the classroom into politics [was] that I felt I could influence the course of history more directly by being in the political process."

Those are not the words of an unambitious man. Then, as later, underestimating his own capabilities was one failing McGovern never suffered. There were many, especially in South Dakota, who saw in him, as one friend says, "a certain egotistical bent." The less kindly critics would say that he was simply overreaching himself. The truth of the latter has yet to be proved, but there is no denying the former. In his mild, unassuming way—which makes it all the more startling—George McGovern is a very prideful man.

Even in the early 1950s—before he had either senatorial or presidential ambitions—it was easy to dismiss him as nothing more than an overly ambitious job jumper, someone who in the course of less than a decade would hop from minister to teacher to politician and who fully intended to hop again, when the opportunity availed itself, to the even grander role of statesman. But when examined closely, there is a fundamental logic in each of McGovern's moves. Each time he took a new job, it was for the express purpose of enlarging his platform, widening his audience, and expanding his influence. He came out of graduate school a believer neither in the "great man" school of history nor in the Tolstoian thesis that history is the product of massive social movements. McGovern's view was somewhere in between: "The great man may not be able to create events, but he can perhaps channel them." In assuming the seemingly thankless task of rebuilding the state Democratic party, he was himself entering history at a propitious moment. "It was like Lombardi taking over the Redskins," says McGovern. "Things had to go up." If McGovern was right, the rewards for such a job—as they were for Lombardi—could be bounteous indeed.

Right away, though, there was the more practical consideration of how, with no salary and negligible savings, the McGoverns were to eat. McGovern's answer was to enlist a large group of "supporting" party members, each of whom would contribute up to $10 a month to sustain the party and its new executive secretary. The going was not easy, nor were the contributions always regular. More than one month passed with McGovern collecting no salary at all. Federal Judge Fred Nichol, who had taught both

George and Eleanor at Dakota Wesleyan and was a $10-a-month supporter, says: "If they had a pound of beans then and a hamburger, they were living high." Most of the money McGovern collected went to running the party's organizing machinery, which operated out of a dingy one-room office over White's drugstore in Mitchell and consisted of a desk, an old Underwood, a mimeograph machine on which McGovern ran off his own press releases, and a part-time college girl who came in a few days a week to type out letters. "I remember him when he first came in," says Harl Andersen, the Associated Press's Sioux Falls correspondent. "He had a press release he had just written and he was pretty proud of it. He wasn't the pushy, forward type at all. Just came in, introduced himself, and sat down to chat for a few minutes. It was a surprise when he said he was from the Democratic party, because there practically was no party at all in those days. George, though, he was sure there was."

McGovern spent most of his time on the road seeing to it. His first task, after securing money for gas, was erecting the beginnings of a party structure, which in many counties either did not exist or had ceased functioning some years before. McGovern would usually leave at dawn or a little earlier, so that he could roll into a county seat well before noon. If there were party leaders he would confer with them, briefing himself on the extent of the disaster. What was the registration? Were there any party officeholders in the county? How long since there had been? What were the voters talking about? Who were the precinct captains? What about the ward organization? The questions were endless—if he was lucky enough to have someone to pose them to. Often he would have to start from scratch, poring through voter registration records at the county courthouse, trying to pick from the list of names someone who would be suitable for county chairman—provided, of course, he'd serve. In one county, where the chairman of record ran a general store, McGovern strode in, introduced himself, and said that he understood he was talking to the party chairman. "Shhh," said the man, putting his finger over his mouth. "I'd be out of business if my customers knew," he whispered, and hustled McGovern into the back room to talk. Once McGovern found a chairman, there were precinct officers, treasurers, secretaries, and vice chairmen to appoint, the entire nucleus of a party organization. He recorded all their names down on 3 × 5 cards, just as if he were jotting down facts and quotes for a big debate. The important party people of every county were thus inscribed, along with anyone who would give so much as a dollar a month. Eventually, McGovern amassed 35,000 such cards, and when it came time to run on his own he had an organization —right in his file box.

Some of the old party wheelhorses grumbled about Mc-Govern's tactics, especially those that seemed to leave them out. One of the traditional amenities that went with long service in the Democratic party was the flattery of being consulted by younger party officers, but McGovern ignored it and sometimes seemed purposefully to steer away from the old pols. There were even more raised eyebrows over McGovern's practice of, as he delicately phrased it, "reaching out beyond the party." More plainly, McGovern was spending a lot of his time meeting with Republicans across the state. His usual tactic was to schedule himself into some sort of party function in the evening or, where none was available, a neutral group, such as a church social. That left him free to meet the enemy at noon, over creamed chicken and peas, at the weekly meeting of the Rotary. At these sessions McGovern's message tended to be more philosophical than it was partisan, an instruction on the dangers of one-party government. McGovern was asking them, in short, not so much to register Democratic as to vote that way, if only because fair play and two-party government was the good old American way. The line may seem naïve, but in fact it was shrewdly political. The collapse of the Democratic party, while no doubt deserved, disturbed a significant number of South Dakotans. When McGovern warned against one-party rule, faintly suggesting that there was something antidemocratic and totalitarian about it, he was hitting home, and the results showed in the 1954 elections. Democratic registration did not increase appreciably but the Democrats were able to expand their representation in the South Dakota legislature to twenty-five seats. Miffed as the old wheelhorses might be, it was hard to argue with that kind of success.

Of course, McGovern was not thinking entirely of the party.

He was looking out for his own good as well. As he puts it quite candidly: "If there was to be any possibility for me as a candidate, I had to have Republicans and independents for me. So, really, I was building two organizations: the party's and my own." Not everyone saw it so simply, or so favorably, especially when, after having made up his mind to run for Congress, McGovern began collecting funds for his own campaign while still party secretary, a decision he now admits was one of his biggest political mistakes. "They all say that George McGovern rebuilt the Democratic party in South Dakota," comments a high party official. "Horseshit. George rebuilt the party all right, but it wasn't the Democratic party, it was the McGovern party."

The party man's exaggeration may not be too far off the mark. McGovern, both then and in later years, seemed more interested in building movements than political organizations, as well he had to if he was ever to be elected in a state where Democratic registration chronically trailed Republican figures by 30,000 to 40,000 votes, or around one-third of the total vote. It was no accident that even in 1968, long after the party had gained a measure of respectability, the McGovern billboards that stared out at motorists throughout the state bore the legend "Courageous Prairie Statesman" and said nothing at all about his party affiliation. The one election in which McGovern violated his own rule about staying away from the party was his successful 1962 bid for the Senate. A preelection survey that year showed that Dakotans had overcome nearly all their distaste for John Kennedy's Catholicism, and that the President was actually quite popular. Thus assured, McGovern campaigned on the theme "He can do *more* for South Dakota," meaning that his Democratic affiliation would carry greater sway in Democratic Washington.

By 1968, the tide was running against the Democrats, and McGovern once again adopted a nonaligned position. One of the hallmarks of that and every McGovern campaign has been the ubiquitous presence of Republicans for McGovern clubs. McGovern does his required bit for other Democrats on the ticket, but no more than that. For someone who began his public career in the nitty-gritty of political organization, he does surprisingly poorly in smoke-filled rooms. He stays out of other people's primary fights. "If we got a slate together," explains a party leader and McGovern loyalist, "then every damn one of them would want to become part of the Senator's personal entourage. They'd want him to finance their campaigns. You could never do enough for them because so much always needed to be done." The one time McGovern actively pushed a candidate for state party chairman, in 1964, his man got exactly one vote. Since then he has usually made it a point to be elsewhere when the party gathers. One year he found an excuse to be in London. In the critical year of 1968 he was away addressing the World Council of Churches in Uppsala, Sweden, while the men whom he personally—but quietly—favored were elected state chairman and national committeeman. "He's better off being away," says Peder Ecker, the McGovern man who won the chairman's job. "If McGovern tries to do something openly and doesn't succeed, the Republicans will jump on it. His real problem, though, is that there are people in our party who belong in the other party. They are supercritical of everything he does. They hate him just as much as the right wingers."

By the spring of 1956 McGovern had transformed the once-decrepit party into a going concern. There were party chairmen in every county, with functioning precinct organizations. The groundwork had been laid; he was ready to run on his own. His first thought was to go for the Senate, where Francis Case, a highly respected if colorless figure, seemed vulnerable. But in 1954 McGovern had persuaded Ken Holum, a farmer of enormous energy and savvy who would later become Assistant Secretary of the Interior under Stewart Udall, to run against Karl Mundt. The result was predictable, but Holum had run a tough race and deserved a second shot against a less formidable opponent. "I knew I didn't want to be Governor," McGovern says, "so that left the Congress."

McGovern claims that being elected to the Senate in 1956 looked easier than going for the First Congressional District seat held by Harold Lovre, a four-term incumbent. And on the face of it, so it seemed. In the 1954 elections Lovre had been the top Republican vote getter in the state. He was also a former state party chairman, with presumably his share of IOUs to collect. As a Congressman, he was commonplace, with no great sins or credits to his record. According to the South Dakota poll, if the election had been held that spring, Lovre would have captured 78 percent of the vote. After a public meeting in Sioux Falls, Lovre himself took McGovern aside, told him that he had heard he was considering running against him, and advised him against it. "You're a nice young man, George," Lovre said. "I'd hate to see you get beat your first time out." McGovern smiled, thanked Lovre for the advice, and allowed how he thought he was going to have to run anyway.

Once again it looked like McGovern was job-jumping, and into another lost cause at that. It may have seemed that way to the unpracticed eye, but a few saw what McGovern spotted—that beneath the veneer of Lovre's supposed strength lay a quite glaring vulnerability. After four terms in Congress, Lovre had committed the classic mistake of taking the home front for granted. In his absence fences had gone unmended, friends had been estranged. And while it was true that he had led the ticket the last time around, he had not had an easy time of it against his Democratic challenger, Circuit Court Judge Francis Dunn, who had come within hailing distance of beating him. "Dunn really softened him up," says one Dakota politician. "George came along two years later and picked the cherry."

But not without effort. The First Congressional District in 1954 included all the territory east of the Missouri River, an area of some 38,000 square miles. Topographically, the "East River district," as it is called, is lush, rolling green prairie, dotted here and there, especially to the north, by clear blue lakes. Economically, the district depends on agriculture, and in particular on the small family farm with a few hundred acres of corn and vegetables and perhaps a few dozen head of cows. Ethnically, the East River is heavily German and Norwegian, with a surprising number of Irish Catholics. The bulk of the state's population lies on the East River side, along with the largest city, Sioux Falls (population: 72,000). In the East River district, as in the rest of the state, candidates for public office tend to be judged not so much on what they say (so long as they are dependably *for* agriculture and *against* Communists), as how they handle themselves, so simple a thing as shak-

ing a man's hand, talking to him for a few minutes, and looking
him in the eye while you did. If the process were repeated often
enough, and done each time with evident sincerity, then it was
said, only half in jest, that anyone could win, "even a Democrat."
Which is precisely what McGovern was trying to prove.

He set out each day shortly after 7 A.M., sometimes driving
alone but more often as a passenger in a red and white Rambler
station wagon owned by George Cunningham, his chauffeur and
aide-de-camp. The two made an odd-looking pair: McGovern
lean, tall, and taciturn; Cunningham short, round, and jovial. It was
as if Laurel and Hardy had suddenly gone into the feed and seed
business, peddling their wares from door to door. The reality,
however, was quite something else. Behind Cunningham's determinedly hick pose was a first-class political mind, testing the scent,
alert for danger, constantly glancing over the terrain, like a prairie
dog deciding whether to venture out of his hole. A few years
before, Cunningham had been president of the Young Democrats
at the University of South Dakota, perhaps the loneliest job on
campus. "We used to meet in the phone booth," as he puts it.
After he got his B.A., Cunningham went into the Army, and it
was there, leafing through a dated hometown newspaper, that he
read about a man named McGovern "doing things to the Democratic party that hadn't been done before." Cunningham wrote a
letter of support, and McGovern wrote back, suggesting that
when Cunningham was discharged they get to know one another.
They did, and the friendship took. Later Cunningham would become one of McGovern's most trusted aides, with responsibility
for seeing that his boss did not commit the same mistakes Harold
Lovre had with such fatal consequences.

During the summer of 1956 Cunningham's duties were to get
McGovern from place to place at top speed—which, to Mc-
Govern, meant literally that*—and in good humor. The latter

---

* Then, as later, McGovern displayed a mania about speed and wasted
time. He drove with his foot to the floorboard—"one of the few men I
have ever seen who does it with complete confidence," says a friend—
and expected all others to do likewise. As a Senator, McGovern refused
to leave for National Airport, which is some distance from the Hill
through the thickest Washington traffic, any more than twenty-five minutes

requirement was the least difficult, because during the summer of 1956 there was plenty to laugh about. "Some of the places we went," Cunningham cracks, "if they found a Democrat, they cut his ears off and took him to the county auditor for bounty." Once McGovern and Cunningham journeyed to Pierre, the state capital, for the annual "Texas picnic." The handshaking and campaigning went well enough, but on the way to the next town McGovern reached into his watch pocket to retrieve the $20 bill that was to buy their gas and food for the coming day. It was gone. Somehow the bill had slipped out during the afternoon's politicking. Low on gas, getting hungry, and with no other money between them, they turned the car around and drove back to Pierre. By the time they arrived it was dusk, and on their hands and knees, with a flashlight to guide them, they pored over every inch of the picnic ground, but to no avail. There was only one course open to them now. They went out to Pierre's main street and began hawking "McGovern for Congress" buttons for a dollar apiece. Eventually they managed to sell nine of them, and with the new stake they filled up the tank with gas and headed back toward their next destination, Hidden Wood Lake, where a public meeting was scheduled for that evening.

The scene that greeted them hardly looked promising. The pavilion where the crowd had gathered had been built by the WPA in 1934, only now it was hard to tell, since the plaque that recorded the event had been angrily plastered over lest any trace of socialism remain. Sucking in his breath, McGovern stepped forward to make his pitch, while Cunningham circulated through the crowd passing the hat. McGovern's speech must have been especially eloquent, because by the end of it Cunningham had collected the remarkable total of $274. "That night we really lived it up," Cunningham says, deadpan. "We got a motel room and we both took showers."

The money problem was one that McGovern never overcame. Total expenses for the entire six-month campaign came to exactly

---

in advance of a scheduled departure. Once an aide made the mistake of getting him to the airport ten minutes early. McGovern was plainly put out. "What the hell do you expect me to do for the next ten minutes?" he demanded irritably.

$12,339.95, an absurdly low figure for a congressional race in 1956, even in South Dakota. The campaign literally paid its own way, with McGovern and Cunningham moving from town to town on gasoline bought and paid for with proceeds from the sale of McGovern's outsized campaign buttons. It was a simple proposition: if they sold no buttons, they went no farther. Sometimes, instead of cash McGovern's supporters would contribute a chicken or a bushel of corn or a basket of beans, just as his father had received from the congregation in Mitchell years before. The food was always welcome, because during the campaign the McGovern family was on tight rations. Cunningham, who often ate with the family at the end of the day, remembers a depressingly steady diet of macaroni casseroles and spaghetti. "We usually ate it plain," he says. "If we had a little extra money, Eleanor would make some meat sauce."

But the sacrifice was paying off. All through the summer Lovre had confined his campaigning to a few public appearances and the usual glad-handing with party regulars. "How are things going?" he'd ask. "Fine, Harold, fine," they'd reply. "It's in the bag. Don't you worry about a thing!" And so, until it was too late, he didn't. Meanwhile, McGovern continued the steady, unspectacular task of shaking as many hands and remembering as many names as he could. At first it wasn't easy. He was uncomfortable accosting a stranger on the street, thrusting his hand at him, and in the next breath asking him to buy one of his campaign buttons. The whole thing seemed so contrived, so needlessly ritualistic. "But it seemed to matter to people," he says, "and so I learned to do it. And after a while I got to be quite good at it."

He was at his best in small groups—half a dozen, or even two or three. "Hello," he'd begin. "I'm George McGovern and I'm running for Congress." He'd let his listeners take it up from there. If there were questions on issues, he'd often say, even as he does today: "Gee, you know I've been giving that an awful lot of thought lately. What do you think we ought to do?" McGovern wouldn't be faking. Invariably, he had been considering the issue, and even if he had made up his mind—as usually he had—he was still searching out advice, seeking the one piece of information he might have missed. Of course, being asked for advice, even by only a *prospective* Congressman, could be enormously flattering, especially if the incumbent had never bothered to even stop by and shake hands.

McGovern didn't make that mistake. He traveled the side roads, stopping here and there at a farmhouse to ask for a drink of water. While he was drinking it down in long, purposeful gulps, he would tell the farmer who he was and what he was about. They'd chat for a few minutes, and McGovern would move on, driving down the road a few more miles to another farmhouse and another drink of water. The farmer would talk to his neighbor, and the neighbor to his, and soon word would get around that a young fellow wanted to get elected to Congress so bad that he was talking to anyone who would listen to him, even farmers. The technique worked roughly the same in cities and towns. "We never wasted our time on the guy in the front of the store," says Cunningham. "We knew he'd never vote for us. We went around back, down the alley, to meet with the people who worked for him, the waitresses and mechanics and cooks. They were our people." Taken singly, such encounters were of minor significance; taken together, as they were on Election Day, they provided the margin of victory. "George only builds a stone at a time," marvels Harl Andersen, who covered the campaign for the Associated Press. "After a while, though, it begins to show up."

For a long time, however, Lovre and his organization ignored it. They snidely dismissed the upstart from Mitchell as a "schoolteacher," counting on the rural prejudice against education to do the rest. It did precisely the opposite. "George's being a schoolteacher didn't hurt him," says one South Dakota politician. "Farmers don't mind schoolteachers. A schoolteacher doesn't take their money. It's the people who take their money they mind, and there's only three sorts of those folks: the tax collector, the banker, and the lawyer." Harold Lovre, as it happened, was a lawyer. He was also a Republican, which put him in the same party as Ezra Taft Benson, who after four years as Secretary of Agriculture in the Eisenhower administration had earned a special enmity among farmers, and McGovern never let them forget it. In speech after speech McGovern assailed the conservative farm policies of

Republicans and made it seem to some people as if Lovre was not so much a Congressman as one of Benson's chief henchmen in the USDA. In fact, Lovre, who held a seat on the House Agriculture Committee, had little use for Benson or his policies. But the identification stuck. "McGovern," says Robert Nelson, then a publicist for the South Dakota Farmers Union and later McGovern's administrative assistant, "took Ezra Taft Benson and hung him right around Harold Lovre's neck."

As the campaign swung into fall, the "schoolteacher" Lovre had so contemptuously dismissed a few weeks before could no longer be ignored. The most damaging evidence was a poll early in September showing Lovre and McGovern running neck and neck. In something of a panic, Lovre and his supporters gathered to plan a counterattack. The plan that emerged was devastatingly simple: in a state fiercely anti-Communist, they would paint McGovern red.

The offensive broke with a series of full-page advertisements in every daily newspaper in the state, attacking McGovern's China policy as a "sellout" to the Communists. The charges were documented with quotations—invariably out of context—from McGovern pronouncements and speeches. In boldface type the headline challenged: "Do You Want McGovern for *Your* Representative?" The sponsors of the ad—a group of businessmen calling themselves the "South Dakota Volunteer Bipartisan Committee Opposed to the Admission of Red China to the United Nations"— obviously did not. "We do not believe South Dakotans of either party will want to vote to recognize and reward the godless Communist leaders of Red China by allowing them to shoot their way into the United Nations," one of the committee's mailings warned darkly. "Read . . . the words of Mr. McGovern . . . and come to your own conclusions. Our committee is only interested in making certain that we preserve world peace and protect our Christian civilization against the godless menace of aggressive, militaristic communism."

Other ads dredged up McGovern's support of Henry Wallace, while still others claimed that McGovern was a card-carrying member of the American Peace Crusade, which the U.S. Attorney

General had listed as a "subversive organization." From Michigan came a public testimonial from Lionel Stacey, one of McGovern's former students, taking up where the ads left off:

> Why did you make Communist propaganda compulsory reading? Why did you always criticize and condemn our government for removing Alger Hiss and all other Communists from the government payroll? Why did you never, never say nothing [sic] but slander for the Republicans and praise the Democrats to high heaven, fairly brainwashing your class in the perfection of socialism and the Democratic party without mentioning how closely socialism and communism are related? A man who will betray his trust in the classroom just might betray his country.

Stacey's letter, which the Republicans ran off in the hundreds, was promptly refuted by the Dakota Wesleyan administration, but by then of course most of the damage had been done.

In the rough and tumble of country politics such assaults were expectable. What McGovern did not expect was an assault from a friend, especially so dear and close a friend as Bob Pearson. Pearson's attack came in an open and supposedly friendly letter sent to all the newspapers in the state. "As your former high school history teacher and debate coach and as a friend since those days, I have been intensely interested in your analysis of the issues of this political campaign," the "Dear George" letter began. "Recently I have become frightened. You . . . have frightened me." Pearson was alarmed by McGovern's "appeasement" of Communist China and support of Henry Wallace and his proposals for nuclear disarmament and an end to the draft. "The fear haunts me," wrote Pearson, "that the same 'liberals' who fell for the Communist strategy in 1948 and 1951 are playing into the hands of these conspirators again."

Pearson's letter wounded McGovern deeply, "more deeply," his wife says, "than anything that has ever happened to him in politics." Hurt, angry, more stunned than anything else, he sat down to write a reply to Pearson that began: "Now I know how it feels to be stabbed in the back." It had been a stab in the back. But Pearson had done it only under extreme pressure. For months

Pearson searched for a way to leave Mitchell and return to his family home in Webster, in the northwestern corner of the state, where both his parents lay seriously ill. A postmastership seemed the ideal solution, and Lovre, who knew of Pearson's anxiety to go home, offered to secure it for him, on one condition. The price was a statement about McGovern's past, specifically, how red it was. At first Lovre demanded that Pearson make his testimonial on television, but Pearson balked at that. A letter or nothing, he said, and Lovre agreed. According to Pearson, he resisted Lovre's demands to strengthen the language of the letter. Pearson's letter was strong enough, especially for McGovern, who after he won the election saw to it that the postmaster appointment that Pearson so desperately wanted was denied him for almost two years. Eventually, McGovern relented and allowed Pearson to have the job. Today a far more liberal Pearson and a far less bitter McGovern are once again, in McGovern's own words, "close and trusted" friends.

The smears produced their desired effect. The next poll taken after the publication of the "China" ads showed McGovern slipping badly. Lovre's share of the voter sample remained unchanged. That was cold comfort in the McGovern household. For a time Eleanor stopped reading newspapers altogether, afraid of what she would see next. When friends tried to console her, she could not keep from bursting into tears. Finally, she began avoiding friends. George took it far less emotionally but no less seriously. To a friend who urged him not to take it personally, he snapped: "How would you like to wake up in the morning to find out that someone had just called you a Communist?" For several weeks he was on the defensive, trying to explain away his past or, more accurately, what was being represented as his past. Finally, late one afternoon after a full day's campaigning, he was in a bar shaking hands when he spotted a copy of the *Sioux Falls Argus-Leader* open to one of the full-page ads. "Hello," he said to an old man. "I'm George McGovern and I'm running for the Congress." "I know," said the man, gesturing at the newspaper, "I've just been reading about you." "What do think about that ad?" McGovern ventured cautiously. "Oh," said the old man with a grin, "I just figured you were a big shot or something."

From that moment on McGovern did not seriously worry about the ads again. He went back on the offensive, slugging away at Lovre, his record, and his tactics. In a closing address McGovern proclaimed:

> I am running in this campaign against a "do-nothing" Congressman who is now completing an eight-year Washington excursion at the taxpayers' expense. I have always despised communism and every other ruthless tyranny over the mind and spirit of man. Mr. Lovre knows this. He also knows that I was quick to volunteer my services as a combat soldier in World War II while he was free to advance his fortunes at home. It is perhaps a combination of his feeling of inadequacy on this point plus his poor congressional record that has led Lovre to a desperation type of smear campaigning. . . . If I were to summarize the basic conflict between Lovre and myself, I would say he is primarily concerned with representing the interests of big business, whereas my interest in Congress rests on my determination to fight for the people's best interests. A prosperous, wholesome America and a peaceful world in which to rear my family are my goals in political activity.

On Election Day it was far from certain that McGovern had recovered from the Lovre campaign. It was true that in the final days of October and early November 1956 things seemed to have begun to turn around. The question was: Had they turned around enough? That night the McGoverns dined at the Nichols' with a few friends as they waited out the results. Through dinner, everyone kept up a pleasant banter, chatting about everything except the obvious, as if determined to keep their minds off the impending unpleasantness for as long as possible. Finally, it could no longer be avoided. They piled into the car and drove over to campaign headquarters, where something of a surprise was awaiting them. By 12,000 votes South Dakota had just elected its first Democratic Congressman in twenty years. "Everyone was simply stunned, shocked really," recalls Nichol. "But not George. He wasn't surprised at all. He acted like he knew it was going to happen all along." There was shock also in South Dakota. One weekly newspaper, bitterly Republican to the end, recorded the result as painlessly as possible. "Representative Lovre," it reported, "was defeated by his opponent."

The McGoverns celebrated Christmas early that year, figuring that when the real anniversary of Christ's birth came, they'd be stuck in a small apartment in an unknown city and in no mood to celebrate. They were wrong. Even in December Washington was not a cold city, not when the people living next door to their new house in Chevy Chase were so ebullient a couple as Muriel and Hubert Humphrey. So for once the McGoverns hanged frugality and celebrated.

There were seven of them now—another girl, Mary, had been born in 1955—and the Humphreys made them feel right at home. From Muriel, Eleanor took instructions in the art and drudgery of being a congressional wife. Hubert, then in his second term as Minnesota's junior Senator, schooled George in the vagaries of getting around Capitol Hill. It was a close relationship from the start. The two women got on "like sisters" and the men, who often rode to work together, were only slightly less intimate. Arthur Link, who spent a summer with the McGoverns, likened their relationship to that of a father and a son. They spent hours talking about the issues, over coffee in the Humphreys' kitchen or, once the weather warmed, stretched out in lounge chairs in the backyard. Humphrey naturally did most of the talking, and he had a most receptive listener in the young Congressman.

Not until Humphrey became Vice President and the war began to escalate did they drift apart. With Humphrey determinedly on one side of the issue and McGovern just as determinedly on the other, there was increasingly less to talk about. "Things," says McGovern, "began to get a little strained." A friend of McGovern's recounts that the friendship nearly broke shortly after Humphrey assumed the vice presidency. "George and Eleanor had Hubert and Muriel in for coffee one afternoon, and George began talking about Vietnam, warning Humphrey not to get too close to Johnson and his war policy or they would start calling it 'Hubert's War.' Well, Humphrey was incensed. He was angry that McGovern would question his loyalty to the President." And Humphrey was nothing, if not loyal. "I admired him for that," says McGovern. "You had to. He was a committed believer, a straight-out advocate of our involvement. He never said anything in private that he didn't say in public. It would have been easy for him to talk behind the President's back, but he never did. Not once." In the end, of course, Humphrey suffered for his loyalty. His friendship with McGovern, whom he persuaded Johnson to see, cost him dearly at the White House. "Humphrey tried to see that my dissent and similar dissenting views were presented to the President," says McGovern. "He never told me so, but other people have told me that that hurt him with Johnson. That was the kind of man Johnson was. It had to hurt him."

In the meantime, McGovern was carving out his own congressional career. He tried for a seat on the House Agriculture Committee, failed, and finally settled for a slot on Education and Labor. In his very first roll-call vote in the House, he was one of sixty-one Congressmen who resisted heavy bipartisan pressure and voted no to the "Eisenhower Doctrine," which McGovern today describes as "a sort of Gulf of Tonkin resolution for the Middle East." McGovern was also on the small end of a lopsided vote in the House in favor of the so-called Jencks bill, a proposal that would have reversed a Supreme Court decision protecting the rights of the accused to examine evidence from government files used against them. On the positive side, McGovern authored a successful bill providing federal grants to educate teachers of the mentally retarded. Of more pertinence to his own constituency was his sponsorship of an amendment calling for 90 percent parity for farmers. The amendment, which McGovern brought to the floor within weeks of taking his oath of office, failed by a bare four-vote margin. McGovern was still, says one of his friends, "very much the country boy, rough and unsophisticated. You could almost see the hayseeds in his hair." He was also full of bumptious exuberance. Harl Andersen remembers being roused from sleep late one night by a familiar voice announcing that he was at that moment in a Sioux Falls hotel and wondered whether the Associated Press would like his "impressions and reflections on being a first-term Congressman." Maybe it would, Andersen allowed, only in the morning.

There was nothing unsophisticated about the way McGovern

ran his House office. From day one, the emphasis was on what is politely called "constituency service." McGovern laid down an order that every letter from South Dakota, no matter from whom it came, was to be answered within twenty-four hours, and with few exceptions they were. McGovern got off his own first letter to constituents within a week after taking office. McGovern's dictum was more than courtesy; in South Dakota it was smart politics. Within months McGovern established a reputation in his home state "as the man you write to when you want something done," as Owen Donley, who oversaw the letter-answering operation puts it. McGovern's office was very big on dispatching congratulatory messages, for whatever occasion, from giving birth to twins to raising a prize heifer in 4H. With answers to request mail, McGovern's office churned out as many as 150 letters a day. Once again there was a political point. "In our state," Donley explains, "issues take a second place to what you can do for me, how well you can do it, and how quickly. A guy may not like the way you voted, but when you write his kid saying you were damn glad that she was the high school valedictorian, he'll be your friend for life."

McGovern had to have friends if he hoped to become something other than a one-term Congressman, and there were many who frankly doubted he would make it. The cause of their concern was his announced opponent in the 1958 election: incumbent Governor and Medal of Honor winner Joe Foss. When McGovern went home to campaign for reelection at the conclusion of the 85th Congress, a number of his friends on the Hill stopped by to say good-by. "They were paying their last respects," says McGovern. "They didn't think I would be coming back here again." Neither did many people. As a candidate, Foss seemed to have everything: ruggedly handsome good looks, a legendary record as a Marine flying ace (twenty-six kills over Guadalcanal), unlimited affability and charm, and a reputation as a skilled hunter and outdoorsman—no mean consideration in a state where a man's success shooting pheasants can count as much as the way he votes. Coming into 1958, Foss had served two terms as Governor, the maximum then allowed under South Dakota law. With nowhere to go inside the state, the congressional seat seemed a natural, or so at least Karl Mundt advised him. Mundt had a special interest in seeing Foss elected. His political instincts, keen as ever, sensed that McGovern had more in mind than a seat in the House. With his own reelection coming up in two years, Mundt wanted to dispose of McGovern there and then. Foss seemed the perfect weapon.

Or rather the almost perfect weapon. Because for all he had going for him, Foss still had his flaws. He was not, in the first place, a man of overpowering intellect, a fact which tended to show up at the worst possible moments. (Said one observer after a session with Foss: "He's either the dumbest smart man I ever met, or the smartest dumb man.") Nor had he been all that popular as Governor, especially after he upped property taxes late in his second term. Foss's gifts were those of a successful PR man (which he later became, as president of the American Football League), not a competent administrator. In attempting to make the switch from Pierre to Washington, Foss was also bucking a Dakota tradition that never the twain shall meet. What weighed most heavily against Foss, though, was something entirely beyond his control: the farm policies of the Eisenhower administration. If Benson had been unpopular in 1956, he was a positive pariah by 1958, as McGovern never failed to remind his farm audiences.

McGovern ran essentially the same campaign he had run so successfully two years before. Remarkably, the Republicans had apparently not learned from their mistakes, because they too ran a replay of the 1956 election. While McGovern worked the back streets and small towns, Foss stuck to the main roads and the cities. The old smears were trotted out, and the familiar faces of the professional Communist denouncers began to reappear on the hustings. There was even another letter from a former student, charging McGovern with aiding the spread of the Red tide. Here and there a few new twists showed up. Glenn Martz, the editor of a Washington-based weekly farm newsletter called *The Lowdown*, accused McGovern of belonging to Communist-front organizations. McGovern responded by producing a cable from the Chairman of the House Un-American Activities Committee testifying to his patriotism and loyalty. For good measure, he also named Martz in a $250,000 libel suit, which was dropped two years later when Martz printed a public apology.

Compared with the 1956 campaign, the 1958 congressional race was remarkably clean by Dakota standards. The candidates spent most of their time pounding away at each other's records. Foss and McGovern met several times in public debate during the campaign, and on each occasion Foss came off distinctly the worse for wear. Before a large crowd at Brookings, Foss stumbled so badly, that McGovern eased up, lest the outgoing Governor receive a sympathy vote. With the issues cut out from under him and his own record nothing to stand on, Foss traded heavily on his valor as a war hero, an unfortunate tactic, since McGovern too could—and did—claim almost the same distinction. "By the time we were finished," says one McGovern aide, only half-kiddingly, "there were a lot of people in the state who thought the Distinguished Flying Cross was a sight better than the Congressional Medal of Honor."

Poor Joe couldn't seem to do anything right. On an election eve telecast from the Governor's mansion, standing in front of a big fire and surrounded by his family, with the family dog at his feet, he earnestly began reading from the teleprompter. Which only prompted his young son to read from the teleprompter too, a few lines behind his father. Flustered and stumbling, Foss tried to wing it. "This is our old family dog," he said gamely, and reached out to pat the animal. But the dog wouldn't follow the script. The cur reached up to take a nip at Foss's hand. Foss should have quit right there, but the old Marine persistence wouldn't let him. "Well, honey," he said, turning to his wife, "what do you think?" She stared back at him blankly for a second and finally replied: "Think about what, Joe?" "The election, honey," Foss answered in desperation, "the election."

All of Mundt's horses and all of Mundt's men couldn't put Foss together again. Ezra Taft Benson and "the Republican recession" of 1958, as McGovern and the other Democrats called it, were simply too much to battle. On the other side of the coin, it was hard to fault McGovern's record, which was determinedly pro-agriculture, especially the family farm. Time and again McGovern hit at the plight of the small farmer, how big business and big agriculture were driving him off the land, how he had to be protected by high price supports and federal legislation, how America's abundance should be transformed "into an arsenal in the battle against communism."

Speaking before high school audiences, McGovern would emphasize the lack of opportunity in the state. Bit by bit, year by year, South Dakota was dying, and the people knew it. The young, the bright, the innovative—in short, the very lifeblood of the state—were slowly trickling away, going to places like Chicago and Minneapolis and Omaha and Des Moines, where, as the students said, there was opportunity. South Dakota's population nudged over 690,000 in 1930; it has never been that high since. Between 1960 and 1970 South Dakota's population declined by 20,000 (making it one of two states in the nation to lose citizens). When the birth and death rates are figured in, the actual loss is closer to 100,000, or almost 10,000 per year. Many of those who remained behind deserted the farms for the cities, like Sioux Falls and Rapid City, whose population has mushroomed since World War II. All these figures were stored in George McGovern's memory. He didn't forget them, and on Election Day neither did the voters. McGovern swamped the supposedly unbeatable Foss by 15,000 votes.

Back in Washington, McGovern's interests turned to the then bubbling issue of labor reform. One Teamster president, a balding, tight-lipped figure by the name of Dave Beck, would soon go to jail, and another, a two-fisted stump of a man named Jimmy Hoffa, was keeping the eyes of the nation riveted to their televisions as he did daily verbal combat with his equally determined opponent, the chief counsel for the Senate Rackets Committee, Robert Francis Kennedy. Kennedy and McGovern came to know each other during the legislative wrangling over the (John) Kennedy-Ives labor reform bill, of which McGovern was a leading sponsor in the House. The bill, which set standards for union officers and required public disclosure of union financial activities, drew the fire of much of organized labor, and Bob Kennedy worked closely with McGovern and other House sponsors plotting strategy to ram it through. In the end the planning failed, and the bill missed passage by a narrow margin.

But the friendship stuck. At first McGovern had been put off by the younger Kennedy's abrasive brusqueness; in temperament and style he was far closer to brother Jack. There was something about Bobby that made McGovern vaguely distrustful; not so much his "ruthlessness" perhaps as the passion with which he pursued life and everything about it. As the two came to know one another, however, McGovern's suspicion disappeared. Despite the apparent differences between the two men, there was much that linked them, not the least of which was an abiding ambition. In Bobby's case, the ambition was nothing less than seeing his brother elected President of the United States. For McGovern, the ambition was more personal and for the moment not quite so lofty— simply a seat in the U.S. Senate.

McGovern's motives were, as usual, far more complicated than they seemed. Certainly, the prestige of membership in the world's most exclusive club must have meant something for a man who grew up not being able to afford membership in *any* club. But there was more to it than position or acclaim or pictures in the paper, though they all played their role. McGovern wanted "to do more, to speak from a larger platform." In the House McGovern was but one of 400 members; what he said or did rarely made a difference anywhere but in Sioux Falls. In the Senate, though, McGovern would have his platform. If he spoke, people would begin to listen. All this, of course, required an extraordinary degree of self-confidence, almost an arrogance of a fine, intellectual kind, and McGovern lacked for neither. "I used to think it was sheer ambition that pushed him along," says one of his closest friends. "But it isn't that. And it certainly isn't money. What it is, I think, is George's conviction that he has a message, and that it is worth hearing. It takes a certain amount of balls to think that, and George has always had them."

Convinced as he was, McGovern might not have been pushed into giving up an apparently safe congressional seat and going after the bigger prize. What finally tipped the balance (in more ways than one, as it developed) was the identity of McGovern's prospective opponent: the senior Senator from South Dakota, Karl Mundt. Mundt's presence made the 1960 contest for the Senate more than an ordinary election campaign. It was for partisans of both sides an ideological crusade, an epochal confrontation of left and right, or as it was so often cast in the months that followed, good and evil. No one saw it more starkly in those terms than George McGovern. Since his days as a graduate student, when he turned out leaflets opposing the Mundt-Nixon Communist registration bill, he had been following Mundt's career with increasing loathing. Mundt, as he saw it, "represented the worst kind of holdover from the McCarthy days." And so he had prepared, girding himself for the battle that he hoped would be inevitable. Like a prosecuting attorney amassing evidence for a court case, he had for years kept track of Mundt's every public utterance. The clippings and papers he collected in that effort filled more than a dozen scrapbooks. As executive secretary of the state Democratic party, McGovern took it upon himself to match Mundt press release for press release. There were times when he seemed to go out of his way to court Mundt's ire. Shortly after McGovern took over the party job, Mundt waspishly expressed his sympathy and admiration for "the college professor who gave up his job to organize what's left of the Democrats." McGovern humorlessly retorted: "Before Mr. Mundt lavishes any more praise on me, I think he should know that one of the reasons I left the classroom was to play a larger role in combating the sensationalism which he has offered in place of statesmanship. For fifteen years Mundt, like his associate Joe McCarthy, has utilized one political weapon. That is his clever technique of exploiting the people's justified fear of totalitarianism by sensational attacks upon the loyalty of his Democratic opponents. Those who know the meaning of Americanism have had enough of 'McCarthyism.' There is reason to hope that South Dakota voters are growing tired of its counterpart, 'Mundtism.' " Mundt was too cool— and too savvy—to continue the debate by press release with the young party organizer. McGovern, however, couldn't put it down so easily. In the deepest sense Mundt offended McGovern's moral sensibilities. He became not merely an opponent but a blot to be expunged. "I don't know how he felt about me," says McGovern, "but I knew I hated his guts."

It is one of McGovern's greatest strengths—and some would say, among his most glaring weaknesses—that on certain issues he does see politics in moral, almost apocalyptic terms. Later Vietnam would be that way for him. It would summon up a sort of ministerial outrage, which in turn would produce denunciations of a fervor and intensity worthy of his father's pulpit. The righteous style has by and large gone out of contemporary American politics. In a society obsessed with coolness and all its implications, both hip and McLuhanesque, such an approach seems oddly out of place. Perhaps more to the point, it simply doesn't work. That reality was no less true in 1960. But one of the marks of the passionate state of mind is that it does not always perceive reality, political or otherwise. And George McGovern's mind the fateful summer of 1960 was passionate indeed.

McGovern did things and said things that in a calmer context he would never have considered. "It was my worst campaign," he admits today. "I hated him so much I lost my sense of balance. I was too negative. I made some careless charges. When the media in the state turned against me, the television and radio stations and almost all the newspapers, I got kind of rattled. I got on the defensive. I started explaining and answering things I should have ignored. It was hard to get a hook in Mundt."

One of the hooks McGovern tried and failed to get into Mundt was his own voting record. McGovern gathered a collection of Mundt's most outrageously mossbacked votes, printed them in a pamphlet called "The Black Record of Karl Mundt," for statewide distribution. The propaganda promptly backfired. "Everything in the pamphlet was true," McGovern explains. "These were nothing but his own votes. But people in South Dakota don't take to that kind of approach. It seemed as if I were smearing him." McGovern committed a far worse error late in the campaign, when he charged that Mundt, on the basis of prior knowledge, had built a motel on land adjacent to a projected interstate highway. McGovern had been put on to the story by a prominent lawyer and long-time Democratic pol, which should have been reason enough to doubt its authenticity. McGovern, however, accepted the charges at face value and blasted Mundt for the deal. Much of McGovern's allegation was true; unfortunately, not all of it. "I was terribly naïve," McGovern confesses. "I assumed that because a lawyer gave the story to me, he would have checked out the facts first." The reaction in the state was as instantaneous as it was unfavorable. The *Sioux Falls Argus-Leader*, the largest newspaper in the state and a rabidly Republican sheet, accused McGovern of conducting "the filthiest campaign in South Dakota history." "McGovern should apologize," the paper demanded in a front-page editorial. "The charge is a dirty smear, one of the worst in South Dakota history—an unconscionable attempt to blemish the record of a man who did only what any other citizen could have done and what many others did do. George McGovern and Jim Magness [the state Democratic chairman] owe Mundt an immediate apology. If it isn't made at once, they have forfeited all right to the respect of the good people of South Dakota."

Mundt played the incident beautifully, casting himself in the role of the understanding senior statesman who wouldn't stoop to such shenanigans. He and Mary, he said smoothly, thought George McGovern was a fine young man, the very essence of a Christian gentleman, and wasn't it too bad that he had become the stooge of the Kennedys and was letting Jimmy Hoffa call all the shots in his campaign. In mentioning the Kennedys and Jimmy Hoffa, Mundt in one breath managed to touch on the two most emotional issues in the entire campaign. In South Dakota, the most heavily agricultural state in the nation, there was little love lost for organized labor, and none at all for Hoffa. The Republicans did their best to link McGovern with both.

One of the more blatant ploys was dreamed up at a meeting of Republican party strategists, one of whom became so sickened by the cynicism of the affair that he tipped McGovern about what had gone on. The subject of the meeting, according to McGovern's informant, was what figure to use as the total for contributions McGovern had supposedly received from the AFL-CIO offices in Washington. The moderates had in mind something on the order of a quarter of a million dollars; the bolder members of the group wanted to hold out for something truly significant, say, half a million or even more. In the end, a lopsided compromise was reached. McGovern, they agreed, would be charged with receiving $454,000, the odd figure apparently having been chosen to give the accusation a ring of authenticity. In fact, McGovern's contributions from labor amounted to slightly more than $8,000.

Far more serious was the issue of the Kennedys and their Catholicism. South Dakota, like a number of states in the Midwest, harbored a particularly virulent strain of anti-Catholic prejudice, of which the notion of John Kennedy as President brought out the very worst. Matters weren't helped any by two other names on the ticket: Ray Fitzgerald for Congress and George McGovern for the Senate. There was even some suspicion that the good Methodist McGovern might secretly be a papist. "Do you think we'll be able to stand those three Irishmen in Washington?" was a none too funny joke heard throughout the campaign. Most of the anti-Catholic propaganda, though, was far more vicious. Crude leaflets appeared in Sioux Falls and elsewhere warning of the "Catholic plot" to take over the White House. All the old fears were dredged up: the jailing of Masons, the appearance of the anti-Christ, even the secret tunnels to the Vatican. As Election Day neared, more and more leaflets poured into the state, most of them bearing out-of-state postmarks. At least one Protestant clergyman informed his congregation that those who were planning on voting for "the Catholic ticket" would no longer be welcome.

When McGovern announced his candidacy for the Senate, months before the Democratic convention in Los Angeles, he personally felt—and hoped—that the presidential nomination would go to the more liberal candidate, his old friend Hubert Humphrey. Not all of South Dakota's Democrats shared McGovern's enthusiasm for Humphrey; they were frankly willing to settle for anyone but Kennedy. A number of Democrats, including Governor Ralph Herseth (who later blamed his defeat on "the Kennedy issue"), were so pained by sharing the ticket with Kennedy that when he came into the state to campaign late in September 1960 they pointedly refused to share the platform with him. McGovern was one of the few who did, accompanying Ken-

nedy ("my treasured friend . . . a leader who calls us to greatness") to the Corn Palace in his native Mitchell for a major speech
on farm policy. As he left, Kennedy turned to his brother and
remarked: "Bobby, I think we just cost that man a seat in the
Senate."

Kennedy's was a judgment shared by many people in the state.
In June a poll showed McGovern running ahead of Mundt. The
next poll, taken in July after Kennedy was nominated, showed a
shift of almost 20 percent. McGovern himself thought Kennedy
was the difference, though he never said so publicly, either then or
later, when a variety of Democratic also-rans, including former
governors Orville Freeman of Minnesota and Herschel Loveless in
Iowa, were blaming their losses on religious prejudice. The fact
was that despite the miscues and mistakes, McGovern was giving
Mundt the scare of his political life. People in the state still recall
the time when the Stock Growers Convention was readying a vote
on a resolution condemning McGovern's farm record and the
convention chairman asked, as a pro forma gesture, whether there
was anyone in the room who wanted to voice their opposition. "I
do," called a voice from the back of the hall, and McGovern
strode forward to the gasp of those present. He spoke for five minutes, then the microphone was literally yanked out of his hand and
he was shoved from the stage.

Whatever else he lacked, the Congressman was not wanting for
guts, and guts it took to take on Karl Mundt, the founder of the
National Forensic Society, in three public debates. The first time
they clashed was in the quiet of a television studio in Sioux Falls,
and by general reckoning McGovern emerged as the clear winner.
"I just slaughtered him," McGovern boasted.

Mundt, however, was not to be so easily handled again. When
McGovern showed up in Huron for the second debate, however,
he discovered that Mundt had quietly rounded up the most fanatic
of his supporters and bussed them in to pack the hall. "I was just
too gullible to think that they would let this kind of thing go on,"
says McGovern. "I looked down from the stage on the most hate-
filled audience I have ever seen in my life. They were the most
rabid, mean-spirited people. Their faces were actually contorted

in hate. They cheered everything Mundt said and booed and hissed everything I said." A third debate at Sioux Falls was a virtual replay of the second. "The tension in that room was so thick you could crack it," says Robert Nelson, who was in the audience. "It wasn't funny at all. It made me scared. I thought there was going to be violence." Evidently, the candidates felt the same way too, because the remaining debates were canceled.

It was said that Karl Mundt could outorganize and outpolitic anybody. During the election campaign of 1960, he certainly made a case for it. He whipped his organization to fever pitch, then toured the state to work the magic he did so well. "Cagey old Karl," as they called him, came on like a country boy, aw shucks and gee whiz. He even kept a special suit, permanently baggy and rumpled, which he donned only for campaigning and shed just as quickly each Election Day. With his battered felt hat pulled down around his ears, he looked like Willie Loman, out there on a smile and a shoeshine, only Mundt's sample case contained just one item: the "international Communist conspiracy." Wherever Mundt went the words were never far from his lips. He literally forged a career with them, and an impressive career it was: five terms in the House and four terms in the Senate, more than any man in South Dakota's history. Were it not for the stroke that left him paralyzed and all but speechless in 1969, Mundt no doubt could have gone on being reelected indefinitely. Even flat on his back, his power was such that he could prevent his own party from naming his successor and thus, in the minds of many, guarantee that when he did step down his seat would fall to the hated Democrats.

In 1960, however, the old master was in trouble, in need of a little help from his friends, and they were only too willing to provide it. Their masterstroke was a scheme devised by John A. Kennedy, the publisher of the *Argus-Leader*, who concluded, rightly as it turned out, that nothing would aid Mundt more than an endorsement from the big man himself, J. Edgar Hoover. Hoover was more than amenable. His only qualification was that other legislators be added to the endorsement—two Democrats and one more Republican—so that it would have the appearance of scrupulous nonpartisanship. Kennedy agreed, and on October 4 the *Argus-Leader* displayed Hoover's letter of endorsement in a page-one black-bordered box. Wrote Hoover:

> In my own humble opinion, these fearless men, knowing of the scorn and abuse that would be heaped on them by the Communists, pseudo-liberals, and others of like ilk, have constantly risen above personal consideration to strike out whenever possible against the treacherous enemy. The Communists, both here and abroad, have long felt the heel of Senator Karl Mundt.

Against such praise there was little McGovern—or even the Kennedys—could do. Bobby made one last effort to pull it out of the fire by returning to South Dakota for a Democratic rally in Watertown the Friday before the election, but by then McGovern had concluded that it was hopeless. On Election Day McGovern voted in Mitchell, then went home to write out his statement of concession. The final returns showed Kennedy losing to Nixon by some 50,000 votes. (In some counties, notably Minnehaha, where Sioux Falls is located, Kennedy ran behind Democratic candidates for constable.) McGovern ran some 35,000 votes ahead of him, coming within 15,000 votes of unseating Mundt. "Well," McGovern cheered his disconsolate supporters, "at least we won a moral victory."

Moral victories, however, do not pay the rent. McGovern was now out of a job, with no immediate prospects for another. A few days later he and Eleanor were dining with friends, cheerfully trying to make the best of the situation, when the telephone rang. "It's President Kennedy calling from Palm Beach," his host announced, committing a forgivable mental slip. While McGovern talked on the phone, the rest of the eavesdropping dinner party strained to listen. "No, Jack, it wasn't your fault I lost. I did that all by myself," they heard him say at one point. Then: "Gee, that's fine. I'll do that. Yes, we'll see you then. Good-by." Well, George, they demanded when he replaced the receiver, what did he say? What did he say? McGovern grinned broadly. "He said not to make any plans until he talked to me again."

6

War
Against Want

KENNEDY DID NOT want to talk about the price of wheat
or the weather in Palm Beach. McGovern was in line for some
kind of job; that much he knew. What he did not know was that
only three days after the election Kennedy had sat with Arthur
Schlesinger, sipping Bloody Marys in the living room of his Hyan-
nis Port home, and had named George McGovern as one of the
four men he wanted in his administration in important positions.
Halfway across the continent in Mitchell, McGovern could only
speculate. There his friends, inevitably, kibitzed with him. They
guessed that Kennedy might name him Secretary of Agriculture.
McGovern took it all as flattery at first; until the moment Kennedy called, he had not considered any job within the administration, much less a Cabinet appointment. He had not, in truth,
expected Kennedy to win. Now, suddenly, his own friends were
speculating on his overseeing one of the largest departments in

99

the government. The notion was a heady one. Gradually, as McGovern considered it, he came to the conclusion of his friends: Why not?

Once convinced, McGovern moved swiftly. He called Kennedy and told him he was interested in the Agriculture job. The President-elect was noncommittal: "Let's wait a while, George, and we'll talk." While he waited, McGovern started to enlist firm lobbyists for his cause. He called Arthur Schlesinger, whom he had never met before but who he knew had the President's ear, and confided his desire. "I thought it was a fine idea," says Schlesinger. "McGovern seemed 'tough,' and certainly didn't lack for ambition." Schlesinger agreed to do what he could. In the meantime, the National Milk Producers Federation started pushing his candidacy, as did various leaders in the Farmers Union as well as some Congressmen. It was Robert Kennedy, though, who was McGovern's real champion. With characteristic loyalty, he was determined to pay back the man who had gone down with the ship for the sake of his brother. Bobby pushed, and pushed hard, and his brother began to listen. According to Schlesinger, if Kennedy had had his druthers, McGovern would have been Secretary of Agriculture.

But it was not so easy a matter as the President of the United States simply choosing the man he wanted. Not when the President was a politician—and John Kennedy was a superb politician. To name McGovern, Kennedy had to follow certain rituals, and none was more important than having the nomination informally cleared with the senior members of the House Agriculture Committee, an institution as powerful as it was conservative. From the committee came the word that it would accept McGovern, but only with the most extreme reluctance. There were prestige factors to consider as well. Whatever else could be said in his favor, McGovern was still nothing more than a former Congressman from a small Republican state. Nor had his experience in agriculture been all that great. Even so, had there been no other strong contenders in the field, Kennedy might still have had McGovern. But there were, among them governors Herschel Loveless of Iowa and Robert Docking of Kansas. And there was another man: Orville Freeman, the former Governor of Minnesota. In the end, the decision was made on politics. "We owed Orville something," as Myer Feldman, who served as a special assistant to Kennedy, puts it, "and we didn't owe anything to George."

As Kennedy weeded through the nominees with increasing despair, McGovern began having second thoughts. He was still a man with political ambitions. In two years, he knew, Francis Case would be coming up for reelection in the Senate, and there would be another opportunity to take a shot at Mundt six years hence. He also knew that being Secretary of Agriculture was a post from which few politicians ever recovered. It was truly a thankless task, second only in opprobrium to being the director of the Internal Revenue Service. With the vast bureaucracy, the dependence on Congress, the claims and counterclaims from the various farm lobbies, it was virtually impossible not to offend some significant body of opinion. The internal opposition from South Dakota farmers— the group on which he depended most—could almost be guaranteed. McGovern could avoid most of the political pitfalls if a lesser job came his way. Kennedy had asked him to come by his Georgetown home on the morning of December 16 to learn his fate. The night before, as he called Eleanor in Mitchell, McGovern was still undecided. At that point, he didn't know what would happen; events were out of his hands. The old sense of fatalism was creeping in. Tomorrow's was one more mission he would have to ride out and see.

The next day McGovern sat in the drawing room of the Kennedy house, waiting and wondering. Harvard law professor Abe Chayes, who was waiting for his appointment as legal adviser to the State Department, sat with him. Finally, McGovern was ushered in to see the President-elect. When he emerged some minutes later there was a big smile on his face. "Well, you must have gotten some big post," exclaimed Chayes. "Yes," beamed McGovern. "He didn't name me Secretary of Agriculture."

The post Kennedy had given McGovern was the directorship of the Food for Peace program, a job which until that moment had not existed. "Food for Peace" was the name the New Frontier sloganeers had chosen for the Agricultural Trade Development and Assistance Act, or as it was more commonly known around the world, Public Law 480. Passed in the second year of the Eisenhower administration, PL 480 had a twofold purpose: the humanitarian mission of providing food to the needy of the world, and the more practical consideration of helping the United States get rid of its vast store of surplus commodities, which had been mounting steadily since the end of the Korean War and was then costing the federal government more than a million dollars in storage costs each day.

The law worked three different ways. Under Title I the United States sold food to developing nations under a scheme similar to the Marshall Plan. If the host government lacked dollars or gold, it paid for the food in its own currency at the export market value of the product. The host government then sold the food to its wholesalers and retailers. The United States, meanwhile, granted or loaned back 80 percent of the purchase price for economic development, "mutual defense" (which in later years meant selling M-16 rifles to the dictatorship in Thailand), and other purposes, such as the Indian government's successful malaria eradication campaign. The remaining 20 percent of the purchase price was devoted to such things as Fulbright fellowships, the United States Information Service, the translation of scientific journals, and the maintenance of American embassies. As of 1964, when McGovern summarized the accomplishments of Food for Peace in a slim volume entitled *War Against Want*, more than one-third of the American aid program consisted of Food for Peace—70 percent of it under Title I foreign currency sales. Since that time, both percentages have declined somewhat.

Under Title II the United States could make outright grants of food in cases of emergency or disaster. Under the same provision food could be used for economic development projects, payment of wages, and school lunch programs. As PL 480 expanded, this provision became increasingly popular—at one point, 700,000 people were working for food wages.

Title III of PL 480 authorized the distribution of foodstuffs by private volunteer agencies, such as CARE, and by a score of church-connected agencies, such as Catholic Relief Services, Lutheran World Relief, and the Joint Jewish Distribution Committee. By far the largest of the PL 480 programs, Title III still feeds some 80 million people in 112 countries. In 1959, after PL 480 had been in operation for five years, a fourth title was added to the act permitting the extension of long-term credit at low interest rates on dollar sales of food and fiber. The theory behind the title, which was not put into operation until 1961, was that some countries would be able to pay dollars for food in favorable credit terms that could be extended.

During the Eisenhower years PL 480 was given a distinctly secondary priority. The program was coordinated by Dr. Don Paarlberg, an able academician who served both as the Department of Agriculture's chief economist and as a member of the President's Council of Economic Advisers. Paarlberg's problem was lack of support from his own administration, which regarded the law as little more than a convenient wastebin for surplus commodities. Some of the host countries looked on the law as a covert dumping program (which indeed it was), while others, as Schlesinger points out in *A Thousand Days*, "acted as if they were doing the United States a favor by relieving the American economy of the embarrassment of surpluses." Ironically, PL 480 did not do well even at its most cynical purpose. Between 1954, when the law was passed, and 1961, when Eisenhower went out of office, the annual average rate of food exports was $891 million, not enough to prevent grain elevators all over the Midwest from filling up with more and more surplus commodities.

The arrangement seemed to satisfy no one—neither the farmers, whose price supports kept dwindling, nor the host countries, which wanted more food and without strings, nor the American taxpayer, who stood appalled as the cost of the already burdensome farm program tripled, thanks in part to huge storage costs for unwanted food. By the late 1950s liberal Democrats in Congress began demanding a major overhaul of the program. In the House no one was more vocal than McGovern, who campaigned for "more effective use of our God-given abundance in a hungry world," invariably coupling his suggestion with a reminder that "hunger and communism go hand in hand."

By the 1960 presidential campaign the Food for Peace call had become the most popular part of the Kennedy farm program. The appeal was demonstrated during a swing through South Dakota.

At Sioux Falls Kennedy spoke to 50,000 farmers gathered in a chilling drizzle for the National Plowing Contest. "Kennedy spoke of farm price supports and supply management with his usual eloquence and urgency," recounts McGovern in *War Against Want*. "[But] I felt that he was not at ease with the prepared manuscript, and the crowd reacted indifferently. Two hours later he walked onto the stage of the Corn Palace at Mitchell, South Dakota, my hometown, where a jam-packed crowd had been waiting for two hours. This time, without a note, he spoke in terms that deeply moved his listeners. 'I don't regard the agricultural surplus as a problem,' he said. 'I regard it as an opportunity . . . not only for our own people but for people all around the world.' "

In October Kennedy appointed a task force to develop new ways of using American agricultural, abundance abroad. In its final report the committee condemned "the conception, the philosophy, and the nomenclature of 'surplus disposal.' " Instead, it called for a change in approach.

What was holding PL 480 back, Kennedy and his advisers concluded, was that bane of most good ideas: the federal bureaucracy. The bureaucratic machinations of one agency would have been enough to emasculate the most promising program, but in PL 480's case, there was not one but nine at work, representing the number of different departments and agencies with some sort of claim on the law. They staked that claim by membership on PL 480's "coordinating committee." Agriculture naturally dominated, but State was there too, and so were Commerce and Defense, to name but the principal actors. Each week, representatives of all nine agencies would meet at the USDA to review the triumphs and failures of the past week and plan for the next. The atmosphere, says one critic, was "like a union: comfortable, smug, a real closed shop. And they didn't want any apprentices." The new administration could have chosen to eliminate the monster once and for all by creating a new agency with sole responsibility for Food for Peace. But that would have required legislation, and Food for Peace was one area where Kennedy wanted to move fast, because the faster he moved, the more dramatic the results, and of course the greater the credit for the fledgling administration. So as he did with similar problems, he "bypassed the pool of stagnant water," as one administration official put it, "instead of cleaning it up." Later this approach would prove of dubious value, not only with Food for Peace but with the other agencies. But for the moment it seemed the quickest, most effective answer.

The "special office" that Kennedy proposed lacked offices, staff, and budget—in government or elsewhere, the makings of clout. "It was kind of a poor relation," says Myer Feldman. McGovern saw this sooner than anyone. To lend the office more prestige, he asked for and got the rank of "special assistant to the President." Bob Kennedy aided by having his job description switched from "program coordinator" to "program director," figuring that a "coordinator" wouldn't mean anything to South Dakotans. Kennedy also persuaded his brother to raise McGovern's protocol rank, which normally would have been equal to that of an Assistant Secretary, up one notch to Under Secretary, a move that, as McGovern notes, "helped take the sting out of not getting the Cabinet job." * Kennedy himself demonstrated the importance he attached to the program by making its creation the subject of his second Executive Order (the first order mandated the distribution of surplus commodities to needy Americans). In the order, dated just three days after he took office, Kennedy instructed McGovern to exercise "affirmative leadership and continuous supervision over the various activities" of the food distribution programs.

Kennedy's fine words did not provide McGovern with offices or staff. McGovern solved the latter problem by "borrowing" half a dozen consultants and secretaries from other departments. His special assistant, Nelson Post, a big, bluff former lobbyist for the dairy industry, was paid out of Agriculture funds. James Symington, the son of the Senator and later a Congressman himself, came on as deputy and was charged to the State Department. From the House McGovern brought over his personal secretary, Pat Donovan, a deeply religious Irish Catholic whose competence

---

* While exploring job possibilities with McGovern early in December, Kennedy had asked McGovern whether he would be interested in an under secretaryship or an ambassadorial post. McGovern replied that if he didn't get a Cabinet job, he would prefer to be director of Food for Peace. When that was the job he was named to, Kennedy assured McGovern that it was "virtual Cabinet-level."

was matched only by her devotion to her employer. ("Two of Pat's brothers and one of her sisters chose to follow Holy Mother the Church," says one co-worker. "Pat chose to follow Mc-Govern.") Both State and Agriculture invited McGovern to share their quarters, but McGovern politely demurred. The closer he was to the President, he calculated, the better off he would be. He turned his attention to the Victorian confines of the Old Executive Office Building. In one corner of the second floor, behind a door marked EO 10940, he found a suite of rooms whose sumptuousness at least partially made up for his penury. Without bothering to inquire further, he exercised what could be best called "squatter's rights." Unknown to McGovern, the newly elected Vice President of the United States had also been attracted by the Texas-sized grandeur of the offices. "For a time," says Post, "it looked like we all might be moved out into the street." The crisis passed when, unannounced, Lyndon Johnson appeared at the door one day, strode through the offices to inspect them, and strode right out again, apparently having made up his mind that the real estate wasn't worth the fuss.

Washington in the winter of 1961 was a special place, a city coming alive against after the decade-long sleep of the 1950s. There was a sense of newness, of purpose; a sense, more than anything else perhaps, of the sheer possibility of things. The spirit did not fail to penetrate the offices of Food for Peace. "He was filled with an infectious enthusiasm," says James Symington of McGovern. "He conveyed a sense of the urgency of what we were doing. It was an exciting time for us. We all felt we were taking fortune at the flood." The waters rose more swiftly than anyone could imagine. Within a week on the job McGovern was listening to a proposal from the ordinarily mossbacked Bob Poage, the Texan chairman of the House Agriculture Committee, that the United States immediately dispatch three shiploads of wheat to Communist China, then in the midst of a severe famine. If the Communists refused, Poage figured, the wheat could always be diverted to Hong Kong to aid Chinese refugees. Mc-Govern bought the idea on the spot.

Kennedy, however, was less than enthusiastic. The Red Cross, he informed McGovern, had already broached such an idea to the Chinese at Geneva and had been angrily rebuffed. Moreover, he doubted that domestic opinion would tolerate an overture to China less than a month after a Democratic President had taken office. McGovern was only slightly deterred. He had other plans afoot, several of which he had outlined in a memo to the new President. His idea, basically, was to dramatize the Food for Peace concept, as well as help sell it to suspicious host governments, by dispatching Food for Peace missions to Africa, Asia, and Latin America. The next McGovern heard of his suggestion was Kennedy's announcement of a Latin America mission in his first State of the Union message.

McGovern's trip to South America was the first official mission dispatched by the Kennedy administration. On this his first excursion for the government, McGovern confined his itinerary to two stops: Brazil, the most populous country in South America, and Argentina, the continent's largest food producer. While McGovern toured these two nations, Symington would cover most of the others, including Bolivia, Colombia, Chile, Ecuador, Paraguay, Peru, Uruguay, and Venezuela. Accompanying McGovern would be Arthur Schlesinger, who, as Kennedy told McGovern, would be going along "to look into some things for me." The things, as it turned out, were Castro and what other Latin American leaders thought the United States should do about him.

They departed from New York on the evening of February 12. McGovern and Schlesinger knew each other only vaguely, their chief contacts having come during McGovern's unsuccessful bid to be Secretary of Agriculture. But the fellow historians quickly established a bond. "Like everyone else (it seemed) in the Kennedy administration," Schlesinger wrote, "he was five years younger than I—a fact which continued to disconcert one who had long been accustomed to regarding himself as the youngest man in the room. . . . His modest and diffident manner concealed deep liberal convictions, a sharp intelligence, an excellent sense of humor, a considerable measure of administrative drive, and unusual physical courage." By the time they arrived in Buenos Aires, the first stop on their tour, Schlesinger had wheedled from McGovern the story of his wartime exploits, and the two were well on their way to becoming fast friends.

Their mood chilled after their meeting with President Arturo Frondizi. Frondizi was suspicious, if not outright hostile, to the Food for Peace idea, or, for that matter, any notion of "social investment." He was a big capital and heavy industry man; once those were established, he argued, all the rest would follow. McGovern found Frondizi's skepticism shared by many other government officials, as well as leading private businessmen. The previous administration of PL 480, with its emphasis on "dumping" surpluses, had moved many of them to regard Food for Peace as a Yankee euphemism for an American takeover of traditional Argentine beef markets. At each stop McGovern went out of his way to assure the Argentinians that the United States intended only to complement their markets, not absorb them.

Brazil was a wholly different story. Where Argentina could boast at least nominal abundance, fully one-third of Brazil's 93 million people teetered on the brink of starvation. McGovern had seen poverty before, but never anything quite like the scene that awaited him. From Brasilia, where they conferred briefly with the brilliant but erratic President Janio Quadros ("a leaner Jerry Colonna," Schlesinger commented), they flew to Recife in Brazil's ravaged northeast, a nine-hour overland tour of some of the most depressing scenes on earth. "I had never seen such an area of despair," Schlesinger later reported, "one bleak stagnant village after another, dark mud huts, children with spindly legs and swollen bellies, practically no old people." At one stop Schlesinger and McGovern entered a hut to see a baby lying in its mother's arms, dying of measles. The rest of the family—six people in all —were huddled on the dirt floor eating beans and farina. As the Americans approached, a naked baby, no more than eighteen months old and covered with hideous scabs and pockmarks, rushed toward them, arms out, begging to be picked up. The Americans backed off, repulsed by the disease. Later they were told that those who are lucky enough to survive the first year of life can look forward to an average life span of twenty-nine years.

McGovern and Schlesinger separated in Brazil, with Schlesinger continuing on to Peru with Symington and McGovern heading back to the United States. On the way home McGovern reflected on what he had seen during the last few days. The implications were ominous, not only for his own program but for U.S. policy as a whole. Already in the northeast what McGovern called "a counterpart Castro" had appeared. His name was Francisco Juliao and his message was simple: the land belongs to those who work it. In the following months McGovern would continually harken back to the image of "the flaming peasant leader, urging his wretched followers to seize the land and destroy the suppressors," as a means to sell Food for Peace. His thesis, in the typical Kennedy style, was a tough, pragmatic one. Food could beat communism, or as he melodramatically put it once: "In the Cold War our grain elevators are more powerful than the mightiest nuclear-tipped missile."

The cold-warring lay ahead. For the moment, the very real problem of what to do about South America in general, and Brazil in particular, had to be solved. "When George came back from that trip," says Nelson Post, "he was more impatient with people. You just knew that, somehow or other, without violating the law, things would have to move." Within weeks after McGovern's return the initial shipments of what would eventually amount to 60 million pounds of powdered milk for a child feeding program and 30,000 tons of other commodities were on their way to Northeast Brazil. The milk shipment was one of the largest in PL 480's history, enough to feed 2 million people daily for a year.

Sometimes McGovern's enthusiasm ran ahead of his authorization. He was so moved during a Washington meeting with Peruvian Prime Minister Pedro Beltran that he committed the United States to providing a pilot school lunch program for 30,000 Peruvian schoolchildren. On May 11, the day before Beltran was to sign the formal agreement in McGovern's office, the Bureau of the Budget informed Post that McGovern had no authority to make the agreement. "Well, he's gonna," said Post, "and if you want somebody else to sign the agreement too, you better get him over here by tomorrow morning." The bluff worked. As a result of the school lunch program, dubbed "Operation Niños" (Operation Children) by Food for Peace, school attendance in Peru shot up by 40 percent. Eventually a million Peruvian schoolchildren were eating U.S. foodstuffs for lunch. And there were equally dramatic results elsewhere. Before McGovern took over

the program, U.S.-donated food had been used as a partial payment of wages in only two countries. By the end of his first year
in office nine more countries had been added to the list, and
negotiations were under way with twenty-five others. In 1960,
the last year of the Eisenhower administration, 54 million people
were being fed with food provided by the United States and
distributed through private voluntary agencies like CARE. By
the end of 1961 the figure had increased by 10 million. In all,
Food for Peace distributed some 60 billion pounds of surplus commodities during 1961, far more than in any other year of PL 480's
existence. One of the most important changes wrought was the
psychological one. The word "surplus" was officially banned.
From then on, extra food was to be termed "abundance."

There was a certain amount of public relations in the way
Food for Peace went about things; in fact, a great deal of it. Short
of staff and money and surrounded by covetous superagencies
with plenty of both at their command, Food for Peace fought
back with one of the few weapons it had: the press release.
"When the strongest word in your Executive Order is 'coordinate,'" says Post, who directed most of the campaign, "you
don't have much choice." More cynical observers explained the
blizzard of press releases from the Food for Peace office as the
opening shots of McGovern's campaign for the Senate in 1962.
Whatever the precise explanation, there was no denying the importance of public relations. A film was ordered to document
Food for Peace's activities around the world, and when it was
finished prints were made available to all the major TV networks,
as well as to civic groups across the United States. Photographic
teams brought back Food for Peace pictures from India, Brazil,
Indonesia, Colombia, Iran, Tunisia, Korea, Afghanistan, the
Congo, and Peru. Food for Peace also distributed 50,000 copies
of an eight-page brochure detailing its progress to what were
described as "educational groups, organizations, and interested
individuals." A "Freedom from Hunger" publicity campaign was
launched, complete with a "Freedom from Hunger" newsletter.
There was even a contest to design a Food for Peace emblem,
which drew half a million entries.

Meanwhile, Symington traveled across the country, bringing

the Food for Peace gospel to the creamed chicken and peas circuit. "How can you be against something like that?" said one frustrated critic. "They present it like it was the flag, motherhood, and apple pie all rolled into one."

In February 1962 McGovern set off on a five-week round-the-world trip to inspect Food for Peace projects in Hong Kong, India, and Tunisia. The second stop was by far the most important. India was the biggest recipient of Food for Peace shipments. By the end of the Kennedy administration 29 million tons of wheat had been either delivered or committed. Combined with the 1.6 million tons of rice shipped by Food for Peace, it was enough to provide one hundred forty pounds of food to every person in the country. In addition, Food for Peace provided 2 million bales of cotton—or seven yards of cloth for every Indian man, woman, and child. In 1960 the United States committed itself to sending India $1.4 billion worth of wheat, rice, corn, cotton, and soybeans—or roughly one shipload of wheat every day for the next four years. Much of the money from that vast transaction, as well as from four previous sales, was loaned back to the Indian government to finance a variety of development projects. Other money was returned as an outright grant, including funds to underwrite the country's campaign against malaria, which, up to the time of Indian independence in 1950, struck 100 million Indians annually, killing 2 million. After a decade of U.S. assistance, however, the disease, once India's number-one health problem, had been virtually eradicated.

One of McGovern's earliest acts as Food for Peace director had been to write the Indian government in April 1961 indicating U.S. willingness to participate in a sharply expanded school lunch program. Now, less than a year later, he was on hand to personally augment a major portion of it. In Punjab he inaugurated one large program, and in Madras he witnessed "cornmeal from Iowa and Illinois, wheat flour from the Dakotas and Kansas, milk powder from Wisconsin and Minnesota, rice from Arkansas and Louisiana, eaten by happy, vigorous, growing children." In Madras, as elsewhere, the school lunch program was the most popular of all Food for Peace's projects. By 1964, thanks largely to McGovern's goading, the program was reaching one of every five Indian chil-

dren. Not coincidentally, school attendance also increased, dou-
bling during the same period.

On the way back to the United States, McGovern and his
party stopped off in Rome for an audience with Pope John XXIII.
The Pope had a special interest in the problems of world hunger.
The preceding July, in *Mater et Magistra*, he had warned: "To
destroy or squander goods that other people need in order to live
is to offend against justice and humanity. The rich lands must aid
the poor." Now in the audience room Pope John, his eyes twin-
kling, his arms waving merrily in greeting, moved forward to meet
the Americans. When he came to McGovern, the South Dakotan
explained that he was director of the United States Food for
Peace program. "Ah," said the Pope, his smile brightening. "When
you meet your Maker and he asks, 'Have you fed the hungry,
given drink to the thirsty, and cared for the lonely?' you can answer, 'Yes.' "

It had been little more than a year since McGovern had taken on
the Food for Peace directorship. There was a record of startling
achievement to look back on. Aside from the most obvious benefit
of feeding a portion of the world's hungry, the program had
played an important developmental role, not to mention its ideological function. Later Schlesinger would judge it "the greatest
unseen weapon of Kennedy's third-world policy." Hubert Humphrey, reflecting on the good it had done at home as well—reduc-
ing storage charges, boosting farm income, and offering a partial
subsidy to the ailing U.S. maritime industry—termed it, with usual
hyperbole, "a twentieth-century form of alchemy." But the record
had not been compiled without pain and disappointment. Late in
June 1961 McGovern had come down with hepatitis, from an
infected needle used in the White House dispensary to give him
his shots for his South American trip. The disease put him out of
action for a full sixty days. At first he tried to administer the program from his bed in Georgetown University Hospital, firing off
memos, conferring by telephone, and meeting with Pat Donovan
and Nelson Post every morning and night. McGovern relied on
cortisone to keep him alert and active. Instead it made him
dreamy, and sometimes it worked only too well. Once, while

under the influence of the hormone, McGovern composed an uncommonly tough memo to Kennedy, stressing the importance of
Food for Peace and demanding that the administration give the
program its fullest backing. The thrust of what McGovern wrote
was fine; it was the language in which he couched it that was out
of place. "It was not," says Pat Donovan, "the kind of note you'd
send to the President of the United States." Fortunately, the staff
caught it and revised it before it was sent to the Oval Office.

Far more serious than the sickness were the rows with the
other government agencies, particularly the Department of Agriculture and its Secretary, Orville Freeman. On the surface the dis-
putes centered on what and how much was to be sent overseas.
"George was always more interested in the giveaways than the
sales," says one man who was party to the dispute. "Orville liked
sales, but more than anything else he liked getting rid of all that
stuff he had on his hands. Sometimes the two didn't match." On a
deeper level Freeman resented the way McGovern ran the program, with its high emphasis on publicity, to the exclusion, it
sometimes seemed, of the Department of Agriculture. Once one
of Freeman's aides accused Post of "running the program by mimeograph." The conflict between the two men, each a politician
with the usual quotient of vanity and ambition inherent in that
profession, was probably inevitable. "Freeman," says McGovern,
"seemed to resent the fact that he was stuck administering price
supports while I was overseeing a glamorous, humanitarian effort
like the Food for Peace job."

In the beginning McGovern tended to give way to pressures
from Freeman and the representatives from other agencies. According to Myer Feldman, who served as McGovern's liaison with
the White House, McGovern became more aggressive in defending his prerogatives "once the President made it clear he would
support him. Then he began to make himself heard." But not as
much as his staff would have liked. Post was continuously pushing
McGovern to take a tougher stand with Freeman, even if it meant
taking his case to the White House. McGovern, however, was
reluctant. "At certain critical times," says Symington, "he would
recede in order not to present the President with problems that
were not solvable anyhow in the long run. George was not the

kind of guy who ran to teacher. You can only spend that credit once, and he didn't want to do anything just for show. He wasn't interested in power just for power's sake."

Once, however, McGovern did stand up, and quite firmly. The occasion was during the summer of 1961, when a proposal to absorb Food for Peace and the Peace Corps into the State Department's Agency for International Development (AID) was pending before Congress. In an administrative sense, the plan had a certain tidy logic to it. Practically, it would have gutted both programs. McGovern decided to make his protest in person. On his way to the Oval Office he bumped into Freeman, who would have liked Food for Peace for himself. They exchanged the briefest pleasantries; then McGovern went inside to make his plea to the President. In fifteen minutes he was finished. He walked back across the street and through the doors of his own office. "Well," he said, grinning at his worried staff, "we're staying."

But the pressure did not relent. The maritime unions insisted that the huge stores of food going overseas should be transported in U.S. ships. Food for Peace and the Kennedy administration were opposed on the grounds that U.S. flag shipping rates were invariably higher, and that in any case there were not enough American ships to bear such a load. Eventually a compromise was worked out, whereby at least 50 percent of Food for Peace shipments would be carried in U.S. bottoms. Then the fiercely anti-Communist unions balked at loading shipments of wheat bound for the Soviet Union. In time this dispute too was worked out, though the final tonnage of grain reaching Soviet shores was far less than either Kennedy or McGovern had hoped. McGovern never did convince the administration to sell wheat to China and provoked private criticism from members of his own staff for continuing to push for the deal. "What he was proposing was politically impractical," one disillusioned former aide commented later. "There was in him an element of childish trust in events or people. He was of the school that the wish is the father of thought, and sometimes we were left hostages to fortune in the belief that goodness will win out."

The essential problem was the nature of the office McGovern administered. Food for Peace's credibility rested entirely on the

personal prestige of the President of the United States. In the beginning Kennedy lent the office the power it needed. Kennedy
personally instructed his staff to give McGovern "all the help we
can." But as the months wore on, the once pressing issue of agricultural surpluses seemed increasingly remote. There were other
thing to occupy Kennedy's attention: Laos, Vietnam, Cuba, the
beginnings of the civil rights revolution. Never enamored of agriculture ("I don't want to hear about agriculture from anyone but
Ken Galbraith," Kennedy joked at the beginning of his term,
"and I don't want to hear about it from him"), Kennedy, according to Feldman, became "increasingly bored by it." "There wasn't
really much we could do about it," says Feldman. "It just wasn't
at the top of our agenda." Symington first sensed the shift in
mood toward the end of the summer of 1961, when his customary
announcement "This is the White House calling" was answered
by a curt "*Who* at the White House?" The erosion was gradual:
a hint dropped here, a message left unanswered there. Symington
likened the deterioration to "an almost biological process," in
which the antibodies slowly rejected Food for Peace, the foreign
transplant. "In time," Symington says, "it became difficult to get
appointments not only with the President but with the assistants
to the President. . . . By January of 1962 I could see our house
of cards collapsing. The seas of bureaucracy were closing over
us."

In fact, Food for Peace had completed the major part of its
mission. Hundreds of millions, of course, remained to be fed, but
a pattern of assistance had been established. The most dramatic
days were behind them. As Post puts it: "After a while there just
weren't any more northeast Brazils." There were also doubts about
how large a role food should play as an instrument of development. A number of people, both within the administration and in
the underdeveloped countries themselves, argued that rather than
providing food the United States ought to be granting technical
assistance so that countries could raise their own food. Meanwhile,
the United Nations was pressing for a multilateral solution to the
problems of world hunger. If successful it would lead to a larger
UN role—and a correspondingly smaller role for Food for Peace.

Thus it was not surprising that the winter of 1962 found

George McGovern increasingly frustrated, even bored. In his own mind he had fulfilled what Kennedy had asked him to do. He did not relish the prospect of staying on simply to administer another government agency. For one thing, he was not cut out for it. Post kidded him that "as an administrator, you're a helluva fine history professor." McGovern didn't need to be reminded. Administration had never been his long suit, and he admitted it. The second thing was McGovern's own temperament. He didn't like overstaying any job. When he played it out, he moved on. This too was no secret to him. "I tend to get restless and easily bored," he says today. "I try things for a while and then I move on to something else if it doesn't seem to be getting any results." In 1962 Food for Peace was getting results, but not the results McGovern wanted. So now he was leaving. But not to find an escape; politics was hardly that.

There had never been any doubt in McGovern's mind that he would try for the Senate again.* When he accepted the Food for Peace job, it was with the understanding that when the right political opportunity presented itself he would go for it. In 1962 there was opportunity, though there was considerable doubt in many Democrats' minds whether it was the right one—for Mc-Govern or anyone else. In November Francis Case, the junior Senator from South Dakota, was up for reelection to a third term. South Dakota had not often granted third terms to its Senators; besides Karl Mundt, there was one other in the state's history, and that was the legendary Peter Norbeck. But early in 1962 there was every expectation that Case would be the latest to break with tradition. Unlike Mundt, Case aroused no great passions on either side. A deeply conservative, decent man, Case mainly evoked respect. On the agricultural issues he had done nothing to outrage the farmers; it was now the Democrats' turn to take the heat. He

* The election was already in McGovern's thoughts in June of 1961, during his hospital bout with hepatitis. From his sick bed McGovern composed a memo reminding himself to "make a pact with self on 1962 campaign—the highest and most educ[ational], inspiring, friendly, and Xtian I can make it with complete Xtian resign, in a happy warrior spirit as to the outcome. No tears or joy—win or loose [sic] and no concern over outcome—except high-mindedness and inspire as many S. Dakotans as possible."

was popular in his own party, and "a good old boy" as far as the state's major economic interests were concerned. The most that could be counted against him was his advancing age and deteriorating health. On balance, he would be a hard man to beat.

But McGovern had made up his mind. In January he lunched with Myer Feldman and told him his plans. Feldman was enthusiastic and promised McGovern that he would relay word to Kennedy. On hearing the news, Kennedy had instructed his aide to "do everything we can for him." Eventually the administration got McGovern what Feldman calls "a small sum of money." They also recommended that McGovern enlist the services of political documentary film maker Charles Guggenheim, a suggestion that McGovern adopted and one that would later serve him in good stead.

To almost everyone outside the White House, McGovern was being very circumspect about his plans. There were still details to attend to in Food for Peace. Nor did he want to make it appear that he was in an unseemly haste to get back to South Dakota. And there was an even more practical reason. Until the campaign season got under way, he needed a job and the $22,500-a-year income that the directorship of Food for Peace provided. McGovern's hope was that while he stayed in Washington a weak, stand-in candidate would hold the field against other potential rivals. Then, in July, McGovern would make a triumphal return to the South Dakota Democratic convention, and the stand-in would unanimously step aside, clearing the way for the party's strongest candidate.

Both Peder Ecker and Bill Dougherty knew what McGovern had in mind, and neither one particularly liked it. On a Tuesday evening late in March the two men sat in Kirk's Café in downtown Sioux Falls talking, as usual, about the deplorable state of the Democratic party. They were especially upset about the Senate race, and the fact that this late in the political season a Democrat had yet to declare for it, and if McGovern had his way no Democrat would for four more months. They talked and they drank, and talked some more. Finally, they hit on a plan. Why not run a candidate of sufficient strength to scare McGovern into the race? They had just the man: John Lindley, a corpulent (five-feet six,

260 pounds) country lawyer from Chamberlain who had served as Lieutenant Governor under Ralph Herseth and who had himself come within an eyelash of being elected Governor in 1964. The polls showed that Lindley didn't have a chance against Case. All the same, Dougherty and Ecker figured, he possessed enough stature to throw a real fright into the man who might beat him, George McGovern. A telephone call went out to the state party chairman, Jim Magness, who readily approved of the plot. Another call found Lindley all too willing to serve and a little surprised that someone would have asked him. Chuckling over their prank, Dougherty and Ecker sat down to add the *pièce de résistance*. "A wildly cheering, foot-stomping group of Democrats," their press release began, "today named former Lieutenant Governor John Lindley of Chamberlain as their candidate for the United States Senate."

McGovern was back in the state by Saturday. Once again Dougherty and Ecker trooped down to Kirk's Café, but this time with the director of Food for Peace in tow. McGovern came right to the point. All right, he acknowledged, their ploy had worked. He would announce for the Senate immediately. But Dougherty was not about to let him off the hook so easily. "What trick?" he asked, feigning perplexity, while Ecker kicked him under the table. "We already have our candidate for the Senate." The charade lasted only a few seconds more, then all of them collapsed in laughter. But there were serious problems to be solved. Lindley now had to be talked out of the race he had been talked into only a few days before. McGovern volunteered for that chore. More important, the filing deadline for the Democratic primary was only three days away, and for McGovern to qualify as a candidate he needed 10,000 signatures on his petitions. Could they do it? McGovern asked earnestly. For him, said Dougherty and Ecker with a smile, they could.

7

Return
of the Native

McGOVERN'S RETURN to South Dakota politics was greeted
as something less than the Second Coming. The *Sioux Falls
Argus-Leader,* reflecting a not uncommon view, grudgingly conceded that as Food for Peace director McGovern had "made
some sense out of the usual Washington scramble." But since he
was doing so well, the newspaper wondered, why didn't he stay
there? Could it be, asked most other newspapers in the State, that
the Kennedys were hatching a plot to "take over" South Dakota?
As the *Argus-Leader* put it: "The President has decided that
South Dakota is a state with a Republican Senator who could be
beat. The big Democrats presumably figured that John Frank
Lindley could never beat Senator Case. McGovern's now in the
race. Everyone knows lots of nice Democrats, some of the
nicest people are Democrats. But McGovern being allowed to

come back to South Dakota so that Kennedy or Kennedys can control South Dakota is different. Isn't it?"

Resentment of "the suave, handsome, and urbane Kennedy man" coming back to fleece the yokels, as the Brookings *Register* characterized McGovern, reached hysterical proportions after McGovern attended a fund-raising cocktail party in New York, arranged by Schlesinger and Humphrey, at the townhouse of former Governor Averell Harriman. At the South Dakota Republican convention the keynote speaker bellowed that "arrogant left wing Democrats" were moving into the state "to buy themselves a seat in the United States Senate." In the keynoter's breathless words: "The Kennedy lust for power bared its stark brazenness in a nighttime coup held high in the skyscrapers of New York City with Democratic nominee George McGovern the center of interest. Brain trusters Hubert Humphrey and Arthur Schlesinger had assembled a select group of their fellow thinkers and demonstrated how brutally practical as political bosses they could be by suggesting that the liberal Democrats of New York City could buy a Senate seat in South Dakota cheaper than they could in populous New York." *

McGovern ignored the taunts and went on for the next several months with the business of being Food for Peace director. He did find time to come back to South Dakota now and again for what were somewhat elastically billed as "nonpolitical" appearances. In fact, there was much to attend to in Washington in preparation for the transition of power. His successor was to be Richard W. Reuter, then head of CARE. As an administrator, Reuter was probably more able than McGovern. Certainly, he shared his compassion and concern for the the world's poor. What Reuter lacked was McGovern's political sense and, more crucially, his standing with Kennedy. Only after McGovern's departure did it become obvious how Kennedy had tailor-made the job for him. By the end of 1962, according to one holdover

---

* The supposedly extravagant cocktail party raised a grand total of $980 for McGovern's campaign. McGovern was more indebted to Schlesinger for a speech the presidential assistant ghosted for his campaign. "The speech is terrific," McGovern exulted in a note of thanks. "You sound more like a South Dakotan than South Dakotans do."

from the staff, "there was no effective impulse left in that office." Food for Peace was all but forgotten, tucked away, as McGovern himself put it, "in some back room in the State Department."

Meanwhile, an event occurred in South Dakota that changed the complexion of the Senate race entirely. Senator Case succumbed to a heart attack late in June. Case's death threw the Republicans into an uproar. As usual, the party was in control of the statehouse in Pierre. Under South Dakota law it would have been an easy matter for Governor Archie Gubbrud to name Case's successor. But Gubbrud, who had won office largely because Kennedy had headed the Democratic ticket in 1960, was leery of offending any of the competing Republican factions. Instead, he left the choice of Case's successor to a convention of the Republican central committee.

For the Republicans, it was the worst thing Gubbrud could have done. No less than seven of them jumped into the race, including two former Governors (Joe Foss among them), a Congressman, and the state's Attorney General. Joe Bottum, the state's Lieutenant Governor, also ran, but at the time few people took the candidacy of the party's "hatchet man" seriously. An informal poll of Democrats by *The Aberdeen American News* named Bottum the "easiest" candidate to beat, with either of the former Governors picked as the toughest. The convention met in mid-July, with no candidate holding a clear majority of the votes. Foss started strongly, faded less than midway through the balloting, then briefly picked up again. On the thirteenth ballot Foss finally withdrew. Gradually, it shaped up as a race between two men: former Governor Sigurd Andersen, the choice of the eastern half of the state, and of all people Joe Bottum, the pride of Rapid City. Finally, after ten hours and twenty ballots, Bottum captured the necessary majority. The Republicans tried to put the best possible face on the affair. "Joe got there the hard way," commented the Brookings *Register* in the understatement of the campaign, "via the democratic process of an open race in an open meeting. It took ten hours and twenty ballots to nominate him from a field of seven, with South Dakotans making the selection, not someone on Pennsylvania Avenue." But fine words couldn't cover the Republican debacle. The party had been split.

From a field of attractive, proven vote getters, it had nominated perhaps the one man who could not possibly beat McGovern.

In the meantime, McGovern was being nominated by acclamation. In his address to the Democratic state convention McGovern touched on all the familiar themes. On Food for Peace: "I have seen in all parts of the globe wheat and milk and corn from South Dakota clearing up the swamplands of hunger on which communism breeds. This nation has no stronger asset in our competition with Mr. Khrushchev than the American Farmer." On his relationship with the Kennedys: "Some Republican critics say that I should not be elected because I have had a close working relationship with President Kennedy. But is this a liability? Would it not be helpful for South Dakota to have at least one Senator who has some influence with the President of the United States?" On the farm program: "Every thinking farmer knows that in the absence of a federal farm program, we would be buried in surpluses and our farm economy would collapse as it did in the 1920s. And make no mistake about it; if feed grain prices collapse, livestock prices will collapse with them. In the long run, the greatest enemy of the livestock industry is cheap, surplus food." On his opponents: "The growth of South Dakota has been slowed by leadership that is timid and fearful of the demands of the twentieth century." And, finally, on his own politics: "I hope that you who believe as I do that we can build a world of peace and freedom will not mind if you are called dreamers, because the people who first opened homesteads on the Dakota frontier were called dreamers. And I hope you don't mind if you are called idealists, because the founders of this country were called idealists. And I hope you won't even mind if you are called dogooders, because one of the most eloquent passages in the Bible is the simple sentence: 'And he went about doing good.'"

Unfortunately, the campaign was not always so highly principled. The Republicans, for their part, were tireless in their efforts to paint McGovern's candidacy as "an expansion of the New Frontier." Suspiciously unsigned letters appeared in the editorial columns of staunchly Republican papers. One such letter in *The Aberdeen American News*, signed only "A Reader," charged that among other things Kennedy gave the go-ahead for free use of the U.S. mails to Russia for sending out tons of Russian propaganda. . . . That's what comes of having a millionaire, who has never had to earn a day's wages, in the White House. . . . The security of America is threatened as never before. It is a tragedy that the Democrats were ever put in control of American security. Nothing George McGovern can ever say will erase this mortal danger in which Kennedy has put us.

Another letter, this one in the Pierre *State News*, claimed that "the left wing extremists seem to be making an all-out concerted effort to place their George McGovern into office. . . . If they can do this, then, and only then, can their Keynesian or Fabian socialistic philosophy be promoted and the planner have full control to direct and control our lives." The anonymous hand also composed leaflets. One of them, a crudely printed 3 × 5 flyer, urged South Dakotans to "vote for McGovern to help to make a fascistic government our goal." Another asserted that McGovern was "trying to take away the people's freedom to live and work in a free enterprise system." In Madison a woman with a history of mental illness began distributing a picture of what she claimed was McGovern's illegitimate child.

But the Democrats were not wholly blameless. *The Edgemont Herald-Tribune*, one of the few newspapers in the state to support McGovern, asserted that "the radical right wingers [are] clearly in control of the state's Republicans." "If you believe in radicalism, minority hatred, denying the vote to the poor, and control by self-appointed Fascist dictators," advised the *Tribune*, vote for the Republicans. The Democrats, by contrast, offered "only high-type, intelligent Americans who believe in our country and what it has achieved and who wish to participate in preserving and enlarging upon the things that make it good to live in America. You won't find a Bircher among them, thank God."

Elsewhere, Bottum was accused of belonging to a variety of right wing extremist organizations,* everything from the Minute-

---

* Playing on the extreme right wing theme was one of the recommendations included in a confidential report prepared for McGovern by Joe Napolitan, a political public relations man whose most famous client

men on down. The lowest blow, however, was the implication that Bottum, his wife, or both of them, were alcoholics. Where the rumor first got started is hard to pin down. Eventually, though, it was pushed along by at least one person, then McGovern's aide. He had a cartoon printed up that depicted Bottum, dressed in a Boy Scout uniform (a reference to Bottum's "Silver Beaver" award from the Scouts), spraddled drunkenly over a barstool. The caption of the cartoon had Bottum asking the bartender: "What time's church?" It is dubious whether this tactic won McGovern any votes. It certainly wounded Bottum, who appeared on television, eyes brimming with tears, to deny that either he or his wife was a drunkard. By so saying, of course, Bottum only succeeded in spreading the story to those who hadn't heard it.

It was hard to stick pins in Bottum. By nature he was not a malevolent man. He was, according to the testimony of his friends

---

was John F. Kennedy. During May Napolitan journeyed to South Dakota to survey the political terrain and came away convinced that the two major issues in the campaign would be farm problems and communism. Napolitan also concluded that McGovern had done several things wrong during his 1960 campaign, from peaking too early to not shaking hands firmly enough. For 1962 Napolitan urged among other things that McGovern use television film clips; increase Eleanor's public exposure; avoid open labor support; stay out of local controversies; and "get a good hatchet man" ("should be a reputable person, whose views will carry some weight").

McGovern drafted some recommendations of his own in longhand on a yellow legal pad. Among them: "campaign in modest station wagon with loudspeaker—not fancy"; "never attack Case or his record except in the most high-minded and kindly way"; "counter labor domination and soft-on-communism image"; "organize 'letters to editor' of most genuine sort"; "study Larry O'Brien campaign guide"; "ask Jim Symington for entire month of October 7 to November 7 in S.D. with guitar before every school assembly, every street corner, and every other suitable group we can assemble." The final reference was to Symington's expertise as a political troubador. In 1960 he had traveled with McGovern, entertaining the small crowds they met along the way with such ditties as the following (sung to the tune "I Wear a Bandanna"):

> For years South Dakota has borne the whole brunt
> Of falling farm prices and Karl E. Mundt.
> So vote for McGovern and you will find
> A man of your choosing, a man of your kind.

and enemies alike, something of a humble soul, easygoing and gentle-mannered, not unlike the model of the Boy Scout oath itself. But Bottum had been cursed with the demeanor of a barroom brawler, and the party he belonged to seemed to regard him as such. In 1960 he was assigned the task of verbally belting the Democrats, while the other Republican candidates kept to the high ground, and thus gained the reputation of being a political hatchet man, a phrase McGovern used so often, that after a time, even the newspapers picked it up. Bottum and his organization strove mightily to convey precisely the opposite impression. He was portrayed as the quiet family man, who liked nothing better than to relax in the evening playing the organ. Bottum's most widely publicized trait was his affinity for baking cookies. One ad showed Bottum taking a fresh batch out of the oven. Bottum himself confessed, "whenever I feel tense, and can't get to sleep at night, there is nothing I like to do better than getting up to bake some cookies."

Throughout the summer and into the fall, the campaign teetered on farce. Then early in October McGovern felt faint after delivering a speech at the Corn Picking Contest in Sioux Falls. Cunningham and his other aides stretched the candidate out in the back of a Ford station wagon and in order not to provoke alarm in South Dakota drove ninety miles to St. Joseph's Hospital in Sioux City, Iowa. There the worst fears were confirmed. McGovern was suffering from a recurrence of hepatitis. The campaign staff was inoculated, and Cunningham put out a cover story that McGovern was suffering from "a mild kidney infection." Meanwhile, Eleanor filled in at all her husband's speaking dates. In a week McGovern was strong enough to come home, where he announced that he would "rest up a few days" before resuming the campaign.

The "few days" stretched into two weeks. Luckily, Eleanor proved herself an adept campaigner. "She did better before some audiences," said an aide, "than George would have." Ethel Kennedy flew in for a day's campaigning and pronounced the would-be Senator "our great pal," a designation that perhaps did him more harm than good. Later she was indefatigable in barnstorming round the state.

In the opinion of many, though, it was the Charles Guggenheim film, recommended by the Kennedys, that really came to McGovern's rescue. As a work of visual propaganda it was a masterpiece. Opening with a shot of McGovern driving home in a battered Chevrolet, it proceeded to depict McGovern as a man of courage (World War II battle footage), faith (stills of the old family church and McGovern's own parish at Diamond Lake), learning (Northwestern and Dakota Wesleyan), and patriotism (Food for Peace as the bulwark against communism). There were a number of scenes of McGovern walking through the fields and talking with farmers. But the capper was a shot of McGovern sitting in his easychair with a framed photograph of Mount Rushmore at his elbow. Strangely *A Dakota Story*, as the film was called, never mentioned Henry Wallace or McGovern's crusading on behalf of mainland China. Of course, Guggenheim's purpose was to persuade rather than educate, and that he did. During the last two weeks of the campaign the film was aired on statewide television, while prints were shown locally across the state. "In some ways," says one campaign worker, "that film really saved us."

McGovern was back on his feet ten days before the election, but only barely so. The station wagon, now permanently equipped with a mattress in the back, always had to be kept handy for his rare public appearances. He spent most of his effort that final week in a series of half-hour telethons, in which he answered questions phoned in from all over the state. On Election Day most observers were predicting Bottum the winner by a razor-thin margin. McGovern was just as confident that he would win, though he too suspected that the vote would be close. It was. With more than 250,000 votes cast, McGovern was the victor over Bottum by an even hundred votes, 121,581 to 121,481.

The morning after the election, Pat Donovan found McGovern sitting in the Lawler Café poring over lawbooks while he ate his breakfast. He had already spent several hours in the Mitchell Carnegie Library, he announced, researching South Dakota's election law. One thing he discovered was that the state hadn't had a recount in twenty-six years. He was sure, however, that history was about to repeat itself. "Psychology will be more

important than anything else," he said. "We've got to go into
this thing as winners. If we think we've won, we will win. If
we think we've lost, we will lose." McGovern assigned Cunningham to organize the recount drive. Cunningham figured that
Bottum would challenge only in those precincts where he was
the loser. Cunningham felt that was a good tactic for the
McGovern forces to adopt too, but in reverse, challenging only
where they had been the losers to Bottum. Next Cunningham
sought out expert legal advice. A cadre of young Democratic
lawyers was gathered to oversee the recount on a regional basis.
Meanwhile, Cunningham transferred the main points of the recount law onto film and conducted a slide show for McGovern
volunteers in ten locations around the state. To coordinate their
efforts a statewide phone hookup was installed inside campaign
headquarters.

The recount began on November 26 and in some counties
lasted more than a week. In each county a recount board, composed of the county judge and one member of each political
party, checked every ballot in 94 percent of the local precincts.
After that, one more hurdle remained: certification of the results
by the state canvass board.

Cunningham was worried. It was bad enough that the board
was dominated by Republicans; even worse, it was chaired by
Archie Gubbrud, the Republican Governor. Before he went into
the meeting with the board, Cunningham arranged the boxes of
certificates from each county alphabetically in the back of his
station wagon and posted a young volunteer by the car. If he
wanted something, Cunningham instructed the youth, he would
lean out the window of the board's offices and shout for it. But
the theatrics weren't necessary. The board voted unanimously to
settle the returns from the first two precincts in McGovern's
favor. At that point, Governor Gubbrud announced that he was
leaving for a dental appointment. Cunningham knew he had won.
The final tally increased McGovern's edge to 504 votes. When
Cunningham phoned the news back to Mitchell, McGovern was
almost incredulous. "Are you sure you have the certificate of
election?" he demanded. "Yes, George, I've got it," Cunningham
assured him. "Are you sure?" McGovern persisted. "Are you

sure?" A couple of hours later Cunningham drove into the yard of McGovern's home, and in Cunningham's words: "McGovern bounded out of the house. I've never seen such a big smile on anyone's face in my life."

McGovern took to the Senate more readily than most people imagined, and more than some people would have liked. Like any new lawmaker, especially one who had been elected by two-tenths of one percent, his first thoughts were of self-preservation. He volunteered for assignment to the Senate Agriculture and Interior committees, where his work would be most visible to South Dakotans, and was granted both his wishes. He was in those first months still a bit shy. "He seems to shrink from the rough and tumble of politics," a profile in *The Washington Star* quoted one of his colleagues as saying. "George will have influence in the Senate by winning gradually the confidence and respect of the other members. But it will take time."

There was nothing gradual or shy, however, about McGovern's choice of topics for his maiden Senate speech. In March 1963, when McGovern rose on the Senate floor to speak for the first time, the Cuban missile crisis of the preceding fall was still fresh in memory. The Kennedy administration was in a boisterous mood, flush with its biggest international success. Dean Rusk was being quoted approvingly as saying: "We were eyeball to eyeball, and the other side blinked." Not many people seemed to realize just how close the United States had come to nuclear war, and even fewer were looking beyond Cuba to the more grievous problems of the hemisphere. It was a time, in sum, to rally round the flag—and ask few questions.

Which is what made McGovern's speech so startling. Because it not only asked questions, it challenged the entire logic of U.S. Latin American policy:

> As a freshman Senator, I have been reluctant to add my voice to the current clamor over Cuba and Castro. But . . . I am constrained to speak out against what seems to me to be a dangerous Castro fixation that is not worthy of this great nation. . . . We have a smoldering blockbuster at our doorstep

to the south which potentially makes Mr. Castro seem like a mouse trying to bring down an elephant. Neither Fidel Castro nor Nikita Khrushchev nor international communism is at the base of this explosive situation. They are the exploiters and would-be beneficiaries of the tensions and illness which threaten the security of the hemisphere, but they are not the fundamental factors. They are effects rather than causes.

McGovern then ticked off the various social atrocities he had discovered during his tenure as Food for Peace director. He concluded:

We have had too many willing to shed the blood of our soldiers in an invasion of Cuba and not enough courageous and thoughtful men giving their attention to the real problems confronting the *Alianza*. We have had too many self-styled experts telling the President the inside dope from their private intelligence sources and not enough expert analysis of depressed commodity prices, rural credit problems, land reform, and population pressures. We have had too many post-mortems over the ill-conceived Bay of Pigs invasion, which might have damaged our standing in the hemisphere more if it had succeeded through American military intervention than it did as a miserable flop. . . . Why compound the error by probing the ruins of a mistaken venture and then calling for a repeat performance?

McGovern's words did not attract much press attention,* but they did catch the notice of a number of liberal academics and intellectuals, including Columbia University professor Seymour Melman, who was to advise McGovern on a number of national security matters; Cornell's George Kahin, who worked with him on Vietnam proposals; Sanford Gottlieb, executive director of SANE and a counselor to McGovern on strategic disarmament; and Marcus Raskin and Richard Barnet of the Wash-

* The single exception seems to have been the *Sioux Falls Argus-Leader*, which reported, without comment, that McGovern and Mundt were "poles apart" on the Cuban issue. Mundt at the time favored using the Guantanamo naval base as a government-in-exile for Cuban refugees.

ington-based Institute for Policy Studies. Melman particularly influenced McGovern's thinking on a number of matters, especially on the dubious wisdom of nuclear "overkill." Throughout 1963 a group of respected academicians headed by Melman had been attacking the Pentagon on just this point, arguing that a strategic capability of killing every living thing a hundred times over was not only wasteful from an economic standpoint but potentially provocative.

Early in August, partly because of Melman's influence, McGovern introduced an amendment to cut $5 billion from the projected military budget of $53.6 billion. On his way into the Senate chamber to deliver a major speech in support of the amendment, McGovern was stopped in the corridor by Hubert Humphrey, then the majority whip. "I've read that speech of yours, George, and it's a helluva great one," said Humphrey, "but are you sure you want to give it now? It might scare the opponents of the Test Ban Treaty." Gottlieb, who was at McGovern's side, recalls: "Humphrey showed no understanding of the political advantage of having someone further out than you are. But George did, and he told Humphrey that he was going to have to give that speech." A few minutes later McGovern sought the recognition of the President of the Senate to deliver an address that reflected the thrust of Melman's logic. The speech began:

> As a freshman in the House of Representatives in 1957, I was tempted to raise some questions about what seemed to me to be a staggering military appropriations bill. But I lapsed into silence when an older colleague took the floor to say, "If our military leaders are wrong and we listen to their advice, it will cost us some money. But if these experts are right, and we do not heed their requests, it may cost us our country." . . . I share the conviction that America ought to have a defense force second to none. But has the time not come to question the assumption that we are adding to defense and security by adding to the nuclear stockpile? . . . Today, the two superpowers, America and Russia, have piled up nuclear weapons with an explosive power of 60 billion tons of TNT—enough to put a twenty-ton bomb on the head of every human being on the

planet. . . . How many times is it necessary to kill a man or nation? When a nuclear exchange of a few minutes' duration means instant death and indescribable devastation to both sides, what consolation is there to the dazed survivors to know that there remains under the poisoned skies amidst the rubble some unused "overkill" capacity?

McGovern's eloquence did not save his proposal. Nor, a month later, was he able to rally more than one other vote on another of his amendments, a proposal to trim arms spending by $2.2 billion—10 percent of the Appropriations Committee's recommendation for military procurement, research, and development.

One of the arguments McGovern marshaled in his unsucessful brief against the defense budget was that extravagant arms spending was "distorting" the U.S. economy. By allocating such a high percentage of trained manpower, research, and technology to weapons production, McGovern pointed out, the United States was proceeding at a much slower rate than Japan and Western Europe in modernizing its civilian industrial plants. This, McGovern contended, "has added to our civilian production costs, decreased our efficiency, undercut our competitive position in international trade, and aggravated the balance-of-payments problem." McGovern urged that even as defense spending was being cut, there should be planning for a "conversion to a peace economy."

In August he sketched the bare outlines of his proposal: all companies with 25 percent or more of their employees in defense work would establish management committees to plan for the switch to civilian work, and an Economic Conversion Commission would be set up by the President with responsibility for blueprinting action by federal agencies to facilitate the conversion from a military to a civilian economy. McGovern's hypothetical commission would, within twelve months of its creation, "convene a National Conference on Economic Conversion and Growth to focus nationwide attention on the problems of conversion and economic growth and to encourage appropriate study and organization in all relevant parts of the nation's economy."

McGovern envisioned the savings from a smaller defense budget going into social needs: classrooms, laboratories, libraries, teachers, hospitals, nursing care, foreign aid, even the cleaning of streams and rivers.

After the ratification of the Nuclear Test Ban Treaty on September 24, 1963, there was some hope that defense spending might decrease. For a time it actually did, if only fractionally. McGovern felt that the chances for a meaningful sustained cut in arms spending would be enhanced if there were a plan, similar to the one he had alluded to during the summer, for channeling the new tax dollars into civilian needs. McGovern was not alone in his thinking. The cancellation of several defense contracts and the closing of a number of military installations late in 1963 and early in 1964 stimulated interest in the problems of economic conversion. Thus it was not entirely surprising that when McGovern formally introduced his national economic conversion bill late in October 1963, he was able to find thirty-three co-sponsors to stand up for it. A month later President Johnson signed an Executive Order establishing a small, ad hoc study group on the problem. But Johnson's order was form more than anything else. In reality the White House was "cool, if not hostile," to McGovern's scheme. However, the following spring hope flickered again when the Senate Commerce Committee scheduled hearings on the bill. Two days of testimony were heard, but the bill got nowhere. Vietnam—not economic conversion—now had the Senate's attention.

But McGovern did not give up easily. According to some members of his staff, economic conversion became one of his lesser obsessions. In substantially the same form he reintroduced his bill in 1969 and again in 1971, each time with similarly unproductive results. As he campaigned for the presidency through the spring and summer of 1971, he was still talking economic conversion, in words not unlike those he had used eight years before. The concept seemed so practical and so simple that it remained something of a puzzle to McGovern why it never managed to attract more support. Early in 1964 in a White House visit with Ted Sorensen, who was then in the final stages of leave-taking from the Johnson administration, McGovern asked Kennedy's chief counsel what JFK had thought of the idea. "He thought it was naïve," Sorensen answered bluntly. "He didn't think you realized the tremendous pressures there are in this country to keep defense spending high—the industries, the unions, the Pentagon, and all the other special interests." If Kennedy had attempted something like McGovern proposed, Sorensen continued, some of the nation's leading military men might have resigned, charging that the country's defenses were being sold out, just as Generals James Gavin and Maxwell Taylor had done during the Eisenhower administration. There could well have been, Sorensen reported Kennedy as saying, a major crisis of confidence in the administration. "These things," Sorensen concluded, "aren't as easy as they seem."

McGovern never thought that reversing the momentum of the military machine would be easy. But he disagreed with Sorensen that it was quite the impossible task it seemed. "He understood before all the others," says Sanford Gottlieb, "the thrust of American foreign policy, the growth of the military-industrial complex, and the dangers it represented." McGovern's record wasn't perfect (in 1967 he voted against an amendment by Wayne Morse of Oregon to cut the appropriations bill by 10 percent), but it was better, from a liberal viewpoint, than almost all his colleagues'. He voted for percentage reductions or ceilings on either procurement authorizations or defense appropriations in 1963, 1964, 1966, 1968, and 1970, and in 1969 and 1970 he voted against procurement authorizations altogether. Moreover, McGovern opposed some of the military's most glittering pieces of hardware, including the Air Force's medium-range mobile missile (1963), the advanced-man bomber (1964 and 1969), the Nike X ABM system (1966), Army missile procurement (1968), ABM construction and deployment (1968, 1969, and 1970), naval vessel construction (1968), and the C5-A transport plane (1969 and 1970). At the same time, McGovern opposed military assistance to other countries—in 1965, when he supported a series of reductions proposed by Morse and Frank Church of Idaho; in 1966, when after his own amendment proposing a $250 million reduction in the fiscal 1967 authorization failed, he voted against the authorization altogether; and in 1967, when he helped defeat an effort to restore authority to use the military assistance credit fund to finance the international sale of arms. In 1970 he supported an attempt to cut out military aid to the Lon Nol regime in Cambodia, and when that failed, voted against the foreign aid appropriation altogether.

McGovern was not always first on these issues or even in the forefront of those pushing them, but he was there nonetheless, and his presence counted more than some others. "Morse and Gruening were not guys who were breaking new ground," says Gottlieb. "They had a view and they were not about to be turned around. It was people like McGovern and Fulbright, reaching out, seeking new advice, who broke new ground. McGovern was really on the cutting edge."

McGovern could cut all he wanted to, as far as South Dakota was concerned—just so Ellsworth Air Force Base remained protected. In fact, McGovern's arguments about nuclear proliferation and economic conversion attracted little attention in his home state. What mattered was where McGovern stood on agriculture. And there his position was very firm indeed.

McGovern didn't have any problem getting assigned to the Agriculture Committee; he was the only member of the 1963 freshman class to volunteer for the job. The powerful committee, once a much sought-after assignment for ambitious young Senators, had in the last two decades been increasingly scorned by newcomers to the Senate. Agriculture was among the most conservative committees in the Senate. McGovern was one of the few liberals on the committee, and the only Democrat from the Plains States. The committee's membership was dominated by an unlikely oligarchy of Republican farmers and Democratic planters. But while ideology sent a chill into many new members, it was not the committee's main drawback. Agriculture, under Allen Ellender of Louisiana and later Herman Talmadge of Georgia, was one of the last bastions of tradition in the Senate, a place where a newcomer was to be seen and not heard. Upstarts hoping for a quick career could look elsewhere. Thus for McGovern to have gotten anywhere at all during his first term on the committee would have been remarkable. For him to go as far as he did was little short of astonishing.

One of McGovern's more notable victories was engineering the successful drive in 1964 to place controls on the importation of beef. The move seems anomalous to McGovern's reputation as a free trader and foe of tariff walls, until it is remembered that beef cattle is South Dakota's largest cash product. Only wheat rivals beef in importance to South Dakota's economy. Here too McGovern delivered. The issue was the Department of Agriculture's proposed compulsory wheat certificate program, which had run into tough opposition. McGovern sensed that the chief objection to the proposal was not the dollar level of certification but its compulsory nature. The farmers of his acquaintance didn't mind federal subsidy, but they did most emphatically mind being told that they had to take it. Why not, McGovern reasoned, keep the best features of the wheat certification plan but put it on a voluntary basis? Secretary of Agriculture Freeman, however, was not receptive. "Freeman," says one agricultural expert, "was of the mind that the farmers had made their bed, so let them lie in it." But McGovern succeeded in pushing the bill through Congress. He was also right in guessing that most farmers would go along with it. In the end, some 85 percent of them did.

The price of McGovern's victory was a further strain on his already poor relations with Freeman. The relationship was stretched to the breaking point in 1966 when as a hedge against inflation Freeman began releasing surpluses to keep farm prices down. McGovern took to the Senate floor to scold Freeman and point out that full parity had been a government goal for some time. A McGovern resolution, directing Freeman to "honor" and "observe" existing Senate directives to try to attain 100% won co-sponsorship from 42 other Senators and passed the Senate unanimously. When McGovern went back to South Dakota to campaign for reelection two years later, more than one farmer was quoted as saying: "We like him because he gives Freeman so much hell."

McGovern worked more quietly in bringing fellow Senators around to his own position. With the single exception of the war, and then only in later years, he was never so dogmatic as not to accept compromise. One area where McGovern compromised, and still succeeded in not only saving but substantially improving a program, was Food for Peace. In 1964 he had published *War Against Want*, a 148-page brief for Food for Peace. Rather than being cut back or eliminated, McGovern argued, Food for Peace ought to be expanded. At the conclusion of *War Against Want*, he proposed ten ways to do it, including tripling the number of "food for wages" projects, enlarging the school lunch program to cover every needy child in the world, and adopting an agricultural policy that would foster *increased*—not *decreased*—production. McGovern had the backing of various anthropologists and demographers who were freely predicting that large areas of the underdeveloped world faced famine within the next fifteen years. As it developed, their projections were grossly exaggerated, but at the time they seemed real enough. Thus armed, McGovern introduced a bill that would have raised the Food for Peace allocations by some 75 percent, or slightly more than a billion dollars. For political reasons, the Johnson administration introduced its own bill, which essentially duplicated the terms of McGovern's proposed legislation. After protracted wrangling, during which McGovern soothed Ellender and brought a number of skeptics around, Congress finally passed the Food for Peace bill, increasing the program's authorization by $700 million—or nearly all the money McGovern had requested—and upping the interest rate on concessional sales only .5 percent.

Food for Peace was the one aspect of agriculture in which McGovern had a special interest. As with everything else, when he was interested—or more precisely, "when he could relate policy to his own experience," as John Holum puts it—he was also enthused. The rest of agriculture seemed to bore him. He worked at it only because it was necessary. The fact that he did it quite well—*The Kiplinger Agricultural Letter* lauded him as being "as close to a statesman of agriculture as anyone on the scene"—was a tribute more to his application than to his enthusiasm. Ben Stong, a former legislative aide to McGovern with expertise in agriculture, states that McGovern "does not have a detailed grasp of the farm problem. He is not a close student of the gears and wheels and machinery that make a program work.

He has got a preoccupation with the broad strokes of turning policy in a particular direction. He needs people around him who know the details."

The economy is another field where McGovern has found it difficult to develop any interest or expertise. Generally his friends, not to mention his critics, cite economics as McGovern's weakest point, both politically and intellectually. Once again the reason seems boredom, an unwillingness or inability to cope with the technical details of a complex subject. During his years in the Congress only one economic issue, apart from his outspoken reaction to the Nixon wage freeze in 1971, has really taken his fancy. That was his own proposal in 1968 to impose an "excess profits" tax on defense industries, similar to the one in operation during World War II. While McGovern's idea perhaps made fine sense, it was somewhat extraneous to the pressing economic issue of the day, which was whether or not to pass a 10 percent surtax to finance the war. (McGovern voted against the proposal.) "He wouldn't have been interested in taxes at all," says one former aide, "if they didn't relate to the war. It was the war he was interested in, not the taxes."

McGovern has always been open to advice on economic issues, even though he has not always been sure what to make of it. *Time* magazine correspondent John Stacks, who briefly served as McGovern's press secretary in 1969, remembers the day when McGovern came bustling into the office after a lunch with NBC newsman Sander Vanocur, a McGovern confidant. "Sandy Vanocur says the economy is going to be a hot issue," exclaimed McGovern. "We're going to have to do something about the economy." "What?" an aide wondered. "Something," McGovern repeated.

In more recent months McGovern has worked hard to improve his grasp on economic affairs, but it has still been a struggle. After one meeting in New York during the summer of 1971 with a group of distinguished economic advisers, McGovern came away shaking his head. "It sounds like there is a big difference between the various economic theories," he said, "but when you reduce them to their lowest level, there isn't much difference at all."

McGovern is at his best when he can put an issue in human terms, like suffering, misery, and poverty. He is not an abstract theoretician, nor is he a master legislative technician, like William Proxmire or Philip Hart. Occasionally this has gotten him into trouble, and he has developed a reputation among some Senators for "not doing his homework." McGovern's interest, in the words of one of his aides, is "in the broad brush strokes of policy." "He likes to see things done," says one veteran journalist and observer of the Senate, "and he is not always patient about waiting to see them happen. In the Senate, though, if you want to see things done, you have to be patient." Richard Barnet cites economic conversion as one example. "He didn't have the follow-through except to make good speeches. The legislation was never adequate. I was never sure how serious he was about economic conversion, whether it was just an issue to him." No one makes this criticism of McGovern when it comes to the war. "That is one issue," says one critic, "where he has done his homework better than all of us."

The fact remains that though McGovern likes the Senate, is obviously stimulated by it, and even pays obeisance to its courtesies and protocols,* he has never, to quote Holum, "had a deep-down understanding of its rules and byways." McGovern, unlike Edmund Muskie of Maine, has never been a member of the Senate "club." He has purposely passed by those few opportunities which, says one of his staffers, "would have made our lives a little easier around here." At the beginning of the 1969 session of Congress, for example, he was offered a seat on the powerful Senate Rules Committee. But McGovern, noting sarcastically that the chairmanship of the Senate Restaurant Sub-

---

* He enjoys, for example, a working relationship with such unlikely figures as John Stennis of Mississippi and his old nemesis, Karl Mundt ("a professional all the way—there has never been any trouble between us since I got here"). Conversely, he holds a special loathing for people like Kansas Senator Robert Dole, who he feels goes beyond the bounds of partisanship and good taste. He became especially miffed at Norris Cotton when the New Hampshire Senator referred to him on the floor as "McGovern" without affixing the customary prefix "Senator" to his name.

committee would have gone with it, declined, saying: "What do
I want those housekeeping chores for?" A political student of
the Senate would have leaped at the chance. But McGovern
looks at the Senate, and his role in it, entirely differently. He
feels that he is there as a catalyst for change. Sometimes this
means simply speaking out on what he perceives as the great
issues, bringing them to the public's attention, while other men
work the mechanism of legislative change. At other times it means
introducing far-ranging, if technically imperfect laws for others
to act on. At still others it means molding amendments to shape
or strengthen the purpose of another man's bill. "He doesn't care
so much whether a bill has his name on it," says Holum, "as
whether it does what he wants it to do." Food for Peace is one
example; the school lunch program is another.

Sometimes McGovern's name and a bill that does what he
wants it to do come together. Out of fourteen bills which the
authoritative Congressional Quarterly deemed as "major pieces
of legislation" in 1970, McGovern sponsored two—the McGovern-Hatfield amendment and the Food Stamp Reform Act—one
of which passed. By contrast, no other presidential contender
sponsored even one. Eugene McCarthy, with whom McGovern
is frequently compared, sponsored not a single piece of significant
legislation during twenty-three years in Congress, according to
Congressional Quarterly's survey. As one of McGovern's friends
puts it: "McGovern is a Senator, but he really isn't in the Senate.
We'd be damned unfortunate if we had a hundred Senators who
were that way, but we'd also be damned unfortunate if we
didn't have at least one who did."

McGovern has flaws, but the fidelity of his liberalism is not one
of them. During his nine years in the Senate he has, with one
notable exception, scored consistently in the upper percentiles
in the Americans for Democratic Action's "scale" of liberalism.
The one exception was during the 90th Congress, which immediately preceded his bid for reelection in 1968. Then McGovern's liberal rating as measured by the Congressional Quarterly
skidded to below 40 percent, virtually the same score, it hap-

pened, as that of Karl Mundt. Generally, though, if McGovern is not briefed on a particular issue, he will simply ask one of his aides, "What are the liberals doing?"

McGovern has opposed the draft ("forced labor"), supported the environment, and been against the space program (voting to cut back appropriations for NASA every year he has been in the Senate). Despite the fact that he represents a state with no real cities, much less city problems, he has supported all the various urban renewal, housing, mass transit, and model cities programs. In education McGovern's record has been equally consistent. He voted for a bill authorizing a five-year $1.75 billion construction program for colleges and universities in 1963, for the Elementary and Secondary Education Act and the Higher Education Act in 1965, and for the Emergency Insured Student Loan Act in 1969. He voted against an amendment eliminating the work-study program in 1963, in favor of higher appropriations for the National Teachers Corps in 1966, 1967, and 1970, and against efforts to reduce the authorization for elementary and secondary schools in 1966 and 1967. When Nixon vetoed the $4.4 billion appropriation for the Office of Education in 1970, McGovern voted to override it. In health his record has been the same: support for medical schools and medical students, better care for the mentally retarded, and reduced penalties for possession of marijuana. ("[It is] hypocrisy [to] send a youngster to jail for marijuana while making rich men out of those who sell cancer in a pack of cigarettes.") He opposed cuts in the federal health program in 1969 and 1970 and voted to override the Nixon veto of the 3.2 billion appropriation for hospital construction.

On the various battlefields of the War on Poverty, McGovern supported job training for unemployed youth under the provisions of the Manpower Development and Training Act in 1963 and 1965, opposed efforts to cripple the Manpower Services Act in 1966, and voted to save the Job Corps in 1966, 1967, and 1969. He defended the Office of Economic Opportunity against budget cuts in 1964, 1965, 1966, 1967, and 1969 (including efforts to make poverty programs subject to the veto of state Governors in 1964, 1965, and 1969). He backed Oklahoma Senator Fred

Harris' amendment to extend the Aid to Dependent Children Act in 1969 and Connecticut Senator Abraham Ribicoff's efforts to expand the school lunch program in 1966. In 1970 McGovern himself led the fight to expand the school lunch program and to add a breakfast program for poor children. An aide to one of the Senate's more reactionary members once paid McGovern a high, if inadvertent compliment when he explained to a McGovern man why he never tried to lobby with him. "Oh, we don't bother with you," he said. "We know where you stand."

Interestingly enough, from a liberal standpoint, Edmund Muskie's record has not been nearly as glowing or—the old Muskie bugaboo—as consistent. In 1967 Muskie opposed the Hatfield proposal to gradually introduce a volunteer army and the plan to limit the extension of the Selective Service Act to two years instead of four. In the same year Muskie also opposed the lottery system and the abolition of student deferments. In 1970 he opposed the volunteer army again and voted against the Proxmire amendment to prohibit the use of draftees in Vietnam, Laos, or Cambodia. Muskie voted for space appropriations until 1970, when he reversed his stand and backed cuts in the NASA budget. He voted against the Urban Mass Transit Act in both 1963 and 1964 and in 1970 helped defeat an amendment that would have provided an additional $6.9 billion under the Urban Mass Transportation Assistance Act of 1969. A supporter of the surcharge, both at its passage and at its extension, Muskie has been an opponent of trade liberalization. In the field of civil rights, he voted against an amendment to ban the poll tax as a precondition to voting. It is in national security, though, that Muskie is at his most hardline. He has consistently voted against both overall and line-item reductions in the defense budget. Before McGovern entered the Senate, Muskie backed full funding for the B-52 and B-58 bomber programs, and in 1964 he voted against a cut in funds for the RS-70 bomber project. He has opposed fund reductions for the Air Force medium-range mobile missile (1963), the Nike X ABM (1966), the Sentinel ABM (1968), and Army missile procurement (1968). Muskie voted against limiting the deployment of the Safeguard ABM in 1969. At a time when McGovern began voting against Defense Department weapons authorizations altogether (1969 and 1970), Muskie continued his support. But the most remarkable aspect of Muskie's record is on the environment, supposedly his special field of expertise. There his marks are mixed indeed. He was an early proponent of the SST and in 1970 helped defeat an amendment that would have required the Defense Department to comply with the National Environmental Policy Act of 1969. In addition, Muskie was absent for a number of crucial votes on the environment, including the 1966 Wild and Scenic Rivers Act, the Williams amendment to the 1968 Land and Water Conservation Act, and the 1969 Padre Island National Seashore Act.

McGovern's liberal escutcheon is not completely free of blemishes. It took the murder of Robert Kennedy to change his stand on gun control, which up to that time he had adamantly opposed, both for hand guns and for rifles. After Kennedy's assassination McGovern's mail, which had been running ten to one against control, suddenly shifted to six to one for it. "I don't want on my conscience another murder," McGovern said at the time. "A stronger gun control bill won't prevent another murder, but it will help." Then, as if to atone for his past sins, McGovern wrote a letter to everyone who had ever written him opposing gun control announcing he was now for it and listing the reasons why.

The other major slip from grace as far as liberals and unions were concerned was McGovern's vote against a motion to shut off a conservative filibuster on Section 14B of the Taft-Hartley Act, the "right to work" law. McGovern agonized over the decision for days before finally making it. His liberal instincts commanded him to be against right to work, but his practical sense kept insisting that the National Right to Work Committee was particularly well organized in South Dakota—where "right to work" was a part of the state constitution—and promised dire consequences to anyone who voted on the side of organized labor. McGovern's mail, which usually numbers in the top twenty of the Senate, moved into the first five immediately before the vote, and nearly all of it was antilabor. Finally, he sought out Robert Kennedy's advice. "Since I'm from New York, George, I'm against it," Kennedy told him. "But if I were representing South

Dakota I'd sure as hell be for it." In the end McGovern voted
the way Kennedy advised him. "It was a straight political decision," he says today. "It was the only time in the United States
Senate I voted against my conscience." Ironically, McGovern
did himself no good by voting for right to work. He had wavered
so long that the antilabor forces correctly guessed that he was
something less than a stalwart supporter. Labor, of course, has
never forgiven him, even though the rest of McGovern's record
is traditionally liberal and prolabor. In 1971, as he went about
the country in the first stages of his presidential campaign, Mc-
Govern was invariably asked where he now stood on 14B, and
just as invariably he would answer that he was now against it.
For many union leaders, however, McGovern's return to or-
thodoxy had come too late.* It is one of the paradoxes of Mc-
Govern's public life that despite the fact that as chairman of the
Senate Select Committee on Nutrition and Human Needs (see
p. 222) he has probably done as much or more to alleviate the
suffering of the poor than anyone in the Senate, McGovern
has never been identified, as was Bob Kennedy, as a "civil rights"
candidate.† As the crowds that greet him only too dramatically
attest, his constituency is still the white affluent middle class. In
1967 McGovern had the opportunity to turn this image around.
The Interior Committee, on which McGovern had sat and done
little since first coming to the Senate, had a chairmanship vacancy

----

* The bad blood between McGovern and most of organized labor goes
far deeper than the 14B vote. McGovern originally incurred Labor's wrath
by his 1963 attack on the unions who refused to handle wheat bound for
the U.S.S.R. The real source of animus has been McGovern's stand on the
war, which AFL-CIO President George Meany once implied stopped just
short of treason. In his bid for the presidency McGovern has been able
to attract isolated support from traditionally "liberal" labor leaders and
unions, but by and large the reception is still one of cold hostility.

† McGovern's position becomes all the more ironic when a review
of the record reveals that he was talking about "white racism" as early as
1964, four years before the Kerner Commission put the phrase into public
coin. In a speech that attracted no public notice, McGovern declared on
June 4, 1964: "What is usually referred to as 'the race problem' is, in fact,
. . . the white problem . . . white racism. Although it is more severe in
the Deep South than elsewhere, racism is a prominent feature of the society
and politics of every city and every state in the Union."

on the Subcommittee on Indian Affairs. Committee Chairman Henry "Scoop" Jackson of Washington approached several members and offered them the job. All turned him down. Finally, Jackson asked McGovern. McGovern's staff was dead set against it; they doubted that Jackson, who harbored a personal as well as ideological antipathy for McGovern, would let the subcommittee get anywhere. But McGovern, perhaps thinking of the 30,000 Sioux that live in South Dakota, took the job.

For once it was the staff—and not McGovern's instinct—that was right. Jackson, true to form, refused to let McGovern appoint his own staff man to the committee. Without his own staff, McGovern's chairmanship was practically meaningless. Jackson still called the shots. McGovern's critics concede that Jackson is indeed despotic, but they fault McGovern on two counts. As they see it, McGovern could have demanded a showdown with Jackson, something along the lines of an ultimatum: either he got his staff man or he was through. McGovern himself has fulminated about quitting for more than a year. At one point he even set a deadline. Either Jackson gave him his staff man by January 1, 1971, or he was walking out. The January deadline came and went and McGovern remained as subcommittee chairman, despite his own misgivings. He was either unwilling or unable to confront Jackson directly on the issue. Fine, say the critics, but even without a staff man McGovern could have done more with the subcommittee than he has. As one former legislative aide who watched the controversy at close range puts it: "The most telling point is not what he did on the committee, since no one on Interior would have done any better, but the fact that he had strong intentions and instinct to do something better and didn't." McGovern is quite candid about his failure: "I feel guilty about not having done more for the Indians, and I don't mind being quoted on that." Nonetheless, McGovern has done something. In 1966, before taking on the Interior Committee assignment, he introduced a seven-point resolution on Indian self-determination, which finally won unanimous Senate approval three years later. In gratitude the Oglala Sioux named McGovern "Great White Eagle." ("The eagle flies above everything," explained a chief. "We honor and respect the eagle.") The con-

Left, the Mitchell High Debating Squad, 1940. George McGovern standing left, last row; debate coach Robert Pearson, extreme right. "*He wasn't the pusher type. He was a plugger.*" (MITCHELL HIGH YEARBOOK)

Below, McGovern's bomber crew beside B-24, Cherignola, Italy, 1945 (McGovern, center, second row). "*When you are up there in a bomber, there is nothing you can do except sit there and hope the next burst doesn't hit you.*"

With Eleanor, outside the Progressive Party Convention, Philadelphia, 1948. *It was more than ordinary political support. Intellectually, emotionally, politically, McGovern was committed to Wallace and what he perceived as the cause he stood for.*

Congressional candidate McGovern escorting Vice-Presidential candidate Estes Kefauver, Mitchell Corn Palace, 1956. *"When the results were in, everyone was simply stunned. But not George. He acted like he knew it was going to happen all along."*

Above, with Presidential candidate John Kennedy at the National Plowing Contest, Sioux Falls, S.D., July, 1960. *As he left, Kennedy remarked: "Bobby, I think we just cost that man a seat in the Senate."*

Left, touring a favela in Rio on Food for Peace mission with Arthur Schlesinger, February, 1961. *His thesis, in typical Kennedy style, was a tough, pragmatic one. Food could beat communism.*

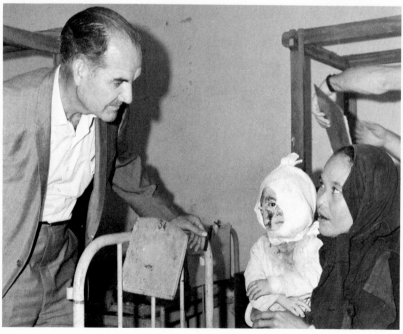

Opposite top, McGovern's first Vietnam trip, November, 1965. "*You have to be a damn fool,*" he said on the long flight home, "*not to know what is going on out there, and not much of it is good.*" (USOM VIETNAM PHOTO)

Opposite bottom, civilian hospital, Da Nang, South Vietnam, 1965. "*They followed us with their eyes in absolute silence. It was like the picture of the wounded deer that is watching the killer close in to take his life.*" (USOM VIETNAM PHOTO)

Left, Robert Kennedy's last campaign in South Dakota, May, 1968. "*As he walked away, . . . he seemed just kind of wistful about the whole thing. I just had such a feeling of sadness as he got on the plane that day, a feeling that he was a lonely figure.*"

Opposite top, with Eugene McCarthy and Hubert Humphrey before the California Caucus, Chicago Convention, August, 1968. *He had decided at that moment if this was the competition, he could beat it.* (BLACK STAR)

Opposite bottom, watching the Chicago Convention riot, while Eleanor, exhausted, collapses. *"Those sons of bitches,"* he kept cursing. *"Do you see what they are doing to those kids down there?"* (DECLAN HAUN, LIFE MAGAZINE)

Below, planning strategy with Pierre Salinger, Chicago Convention (unidentified aide, right). *A campaign without much hope, or resources, or even a clear understanding of how a largely unknown Senator from South Dakota went about becoming President of the United States.* (DECLAN HAUN, LIFE MAGAZINE)

Alone on the prairie. *What faith McGovern has is grounded in the land. He trusts it. He believes in its ability to recover.* (DECLAN HAUN, BLACK STAR)

tinuing credit, however, fell almost by default to another Kennedy, Senator Edward M., chairman of the Labor and Education Subcommittee on Indian Education.

McGovern could not champion every cause that came along. Nor did he want to. At the onset of his Senate term he made a private pledge that he would stop working nights and weekends and devote more time to his family. He was concerned, frankly, that he had been something less than the perfect father. During his second term in the House, Steve, then six, had asked Eleanor: "Mommy, when are we going to move back to that house in Mitchell that we lived in when Daddy used to play with me?" Steve's question was really not so funny. The children were growing up faster than McGovern had a chance to know them. Ann and Susan were at the University of Wisconsin, and soon they would both be married, Susan to James Rowan, a bearded, self-proclaimed "Socialist revolutionary," and Ann as well. It was a time to slow down, to take stock.

In the evenings McGovern would come home from the office and lounge about the Japanese-style home he had recently purchased for $110,000* in northwestern Washington. Occasionally

---

* The relatively expensive price of McGovern's home drew a snide aside from conservative columnist Kevin Phillips, who wondered how supposedly plain folks from South Dakota could afford such affluence. The Phillips column was one of the few pieces of journalism that really got to McGovern. "What the hell kind of crack is that?" he fumed. "Aren't South Dakotans supposed to enjoy nice things like everybody else?" Like most South Dakotans, McGovern is sensitive about his state and defensive about cracks about its lack of social sophistication. He finds particularly tiresome remarks that his new, longer hairstyle and recently adopted modish clothes are somehow "un-Dakotan." When an interviewer asked what the folks at home thought about his new appearance, McGovern shot back testily: "They've all done the same thing. The farmers, the businessmen, everybody out there has sideburns now. They're all moving to the new styles. I noticed the last time I was home that young business and professional people, farmers and others, their styles of clothing, their hairstyles, everything is changing. Conservative Republican bankers have sideburns longer than mine, they have lapels that are wider than mine; so things are changing all over the country, and I think it's fine." To drive home the point, McGovern buys his clothes from a men's shop in Huron. Says one critic: "They look it."

he'd go through the papers he had brought home with him, jotting notes on a yellow legal pad or on any paper that was handy, including the backs of envelopes. He was continually writing little reminders to himself, sketching out his future plans in elaborate charts and constructions, one of the holdovers from his Air Force days. The music appreciation course at Dakota Wesleyan had left him with an amateur taste for classical music. At night he would switch on the stereo, turn it down low, and curl up with one of the books* he continually lugged in his briefcase. (His tastes then as now ran almost exclusively to nonfiction, history, politics, and social criticism.) When he especially wanted to unwind, he would slip out of the house and disappear, just as he had years before, into the womblike dark of the closest movie theater. On the weekends he and Eleanor would take the kids out in the Maryland countryside to the old farmhouse they owned at St. Michael's. The kids were reluctant to go. The place was so lonely, so remote, that it seemed "haunted." For McGovern, of course, remoteness was the farmhouse's charm. As a concession to the children, and to indulge his own passion, he had a swimming pool built. (During the week, McGovern regularly spends an hour a day working out in the Senate gym, most of the time in the pool.)

They took infrequent vacations (though in more recent years

---

* One of his favorites in 1970 was Charles Reich's *The Greening of America*. McGovern wrote in a memo to his staff:

What it all boils down to are the simple old values that my father and my Sunday school teachers taught me forty years ago. It's the best in the Judeo-Christian ethic out of which come the American Declaration of Independence and the Bill of Rights, and I haven't found a new idea in the book. It's an exciting book, one of the most exciting that I have read. It's exciting to me because it is what I have believed in all my life. "Consciousness III" tells us what the youth rebellion is all about. What the kids are saying to us is "Why don't you live in the spirit of the New Testament and why don't you reaffirm the great ethical values of the Old Testament? Why don't you live up to the concepts of the Declaration of Independence and the Pledge of Allegiance?" It's all there. The affirmation of life, the importance of the self—affirming the self, but also loving others as much as you love yourself. No more than that—the Bible never taught me anything more than that.

they have spent a couple of weeks a year in Florida or the Virgin Islands, where McGovern's friend Henry Kimmelman has extensive real estate holdings). Occasionally McGovern would go off on "working trips" to places like Ken Galbraith's summer house in Vermont, for badinage and brandy with Schlesinger, Gloria Steinem, and the clan. Most of the free time, though, was spent back in South Dakota, as was prudent for any man who had been elected by less than a thousand votes. McGovern never missed a state fair, where it was said, in only slight jest, a candidate could shake the hands of most of the voters in the state. He could also be counted on to show up at homecoming parades, Jefferson-Jackson Day dinners, and of course festival week at the Corn Palace. The receptions were not uniformly cordial. The first time he returned to Dakota Wesleyan after being elected to the Senate, McGovern was in a dinner audience while the toastmaster introduced distinguished alumni around the room. McGovern, the school's most famous alumnus, was never mentioned. But McGovern kept coming back, both to South Dakota and to Dakota Wesleyan. In 1967, the year before his reelection, he made twenty-seven trips back to the state, or better than two a month. No matter how many times he came back, McGovern was never able to completely allay the native suspicion that he had somehow "gone Eastern" because of his association with the Kennedys. Matters weren't helped any when McGovern sold the family home in 1964 to the Lutheran Church for use as a parsonage. For a time he maintained an apartment in the Lawler Hotel, but in 1967 he gave even that up. When he came back to South Dakota, which was increasingly rare after 1968, he stayed in a motel.

South Dakota's fears that McGovern was throwing people in the swimming pool at Hickory Hill were unfounded. The McGoverns saw the Kennedys socially only rarely. His relationship with Bobby Kennedy was of a different and deeper kind. Besides, McGovern had little time for socializing. By the mid-1960s his attention—his entire consciousness, some would say—had been seized by something else. It was unrelenting, demanding, at times physically and mentally exhausting. "For a long time," says his wife, "it seems that that was all we talked about here. It got so bad I couldn't watch the eleven o'clock news at night because I was afraid to see it."

Turning off a television dial did not turn off McGovern's mind. There the images persisted, and would persist, as long as the war went on.

8

Magnificent
Obsession

THE SENATE WAS, as usual, nearly deserted when the junior Senator from South Dakota rose to speak. He had, he informed the President of the Senate, a few remarks to make on reversing the arms race. In the press gallery the reporters relaxed. The speech being read into the record that drowsy afternoon in September 1963 could have been—with minor exceptions—a replay of most of the addresses McGovern had delivered before or would deliver hence. "There is potentially a ten- or twenty-ton bomb ticking at the head of every boy and girl," the flat nasal voice intoned, beginning the now familiar litany of horror and overkill. "Both the United States and the Soviet Union can destroy the other several times over. . . . There is nothing in historical record to assure us that awesome weapons can safeguard the peace." For a few polite moments the mind listened, and then began to wander. By the time McGovern was two-thirds finished, most of the brave

souls who had begun to hear him out had departed or sunk into
private thought. Thus it was that five crucial paragraphs—oddly
disconnected from the rest of the speech, included, it seemed, almost as an afterthought—went unheard and unheeded. That day
McGovern said:

> The current dilemma in Vietnam is a clear demonstration
> of the limitations of military power. There in the jungle of
> Asia, our mighty nuclear arsenal—our $50 billion arms budget
> —our costly new "special forces"—have proved powerless to
> cope with a ragged band of illiterate guerrillas fighting with
> homemade weapons.
>
> We cannot even persuade a government financed and
> armed by American taxpayers from tyrannizing its citizens
> and throwing insults at our President when he objects. Al-
> though we have spent $3 billion on the Vietnam war, lost many
> lives, and are continuing to spend $2 million daily, the liberties
> of the Vietnamese people are not expanding. Instead, we find
> them harassed, not only by terrorists in the countryside but
> also by official government troops in the cities. We find Amer-
> ican money and arms used to suppress the very liberties we
> went in to defend.
>
> This is scarcely a policy of "victory"; it is not even a
> policy of "stalemate." It is a policy of moral debacle and po-
> litical defeat. It is a policy that demonstrates that our expendi-
> tures for more and more "special forces" are as useless and dan-
> gerous as our expenditures for more and more nuclear capa-
> bility.
>
> The failure of our Vietnam policy should be a signal for
> every one of us in this chamber to reexamine the roots of that
> policy. Part of those roots are here before us today in the ex-
> cessive portion of the military appropriations bill; and we stand
> derelict before history if we fail to make the examination. For
> the failure in Vietnam will not remain confined to Vietnam.
> The trap we have fallen into there will haunt us in every corner
> of this revolutionary world if we do not properly appraise its
> lessons.
>
> I submit that America will exert a far greater impact for

peace and freedom in Asia and elsewhere if we rely less on armaments and more on the economic, political, and moral sources of our strength.

When McGovern finished, there were none of the ritualistic plaudits from other Senators that accompany almost every speech. The only comment, in fact, was from old Paul Douglas, who said that he wished he could go along with McGovern on disarmament but couldn't "so long as the Soviet Union is so brutal and untrustworthy and does not respond to the outgoing acts of faith." No word was mentioned about Vietnam. No one at all seemed to notice or care that in the space of five short paragraphs George McGovern had become the first man to challenge the war on the floor of the U.S. Senate.

McGovern had not intended to make history. Disarmament was his main concern. The Vietnam portion of the speech was secondary, included in the text, as McGovern puts it, "as only an example of the larger problem, not as any kind of analysis of the war itself." Vietnam had originally come to his attention during the later stages of the first Indochinese war. McGovern had not been sympathetic to the French then. After the debacle at Dien Bien Phu and the signing of the Geneva agreements, McGovern was prepared to accept the inevitable selection of Ho Chi Minh as the popular head of a united Vietnam. When, instead, the United States began dramatically stepping up its assistance to the Diem regime, including the gradual introduction of 16,000 combat "advisers," McGovern was worried. By 1963 a series of events, the most significant of which was the brutal suppression of the Buddhists, deepened his anxiety. Though McGovern was disturbed, he wasn't quite sure what to do. One day in the Senate cloakroom, he approached Arkansas' J. William Fulbright for his opinion. "Vietnam?" said Fulbright, with obvious exaggeration. "God, I don't know anything about it. Do you know anything about it?" But McGovern kept pressing. Fulbright, McGovern remembers, "acted sort of irritated that anyone could even bring up such a peripheral issue when we were all preoccupied with Cuba, Berlin, and the Nuclear Test Ban Treaty." McGovern's staff was even more discouraging when he proposed mentioning Vietnam in a forthcoming Senate speech. "We thought this was pretty dangerous stuff," says Owen Donley, his former administrative assistant. McGovern, however, was looking not for agreement but for ideas. In the end he got most of them from reading Vietnam historian Bernard Fall, who later became a frequent adviser until his death from a Viet Cong booby trap in 1967. The staff was also wrong about the reception that the speech would get in South Dakota. There, as everywhere else, it caused, in McGovern's words, "not a ripple."

Five weeks after McGovern's speech Diem and Nhu were assassinated in Saigon, and three weeks after that John F. Kennedy was gunned down in Dallas. "It was not," says McGovern, "a time to be attacking the White House" about Vietnam or anything else. McGovern's excuse is credible enough; the first priority was, as he points out, "getting the country back together again." But it hardly explains why he kept silent, not only for the remainder of 1963 but for the whole of 1964. Meanwhile, other Senate doves came to the fore. Oregon's Wayne Morse, who McGovern says "had some sort of pipeline to the Pentagon—he knew everything that was going on," delivered his first major indictment of the war on March 4, 1964. Ernest Gruening, the grizzled old warrior from Alaska, followed up with another blast less than a week later. But during the following year theirs were lonely, if determined, voices. The Vietnam debate might have been lent more credibility if they had been joined by a less predictable and irascible figure, especially someone who happened to be a former bomber pilot. McGovern's own explanation for his silence, as he laid it out in *A Time of War, A Time of Peace*, was that "the Morse-Gruening indictments of our Vietnam policy were considered overly harsh and strident by many members of the Senate, although a number of Senators privately agreed with much of what they said. Their own arguments made sense to me, although I feared that the harshness of their approach would create a negative administration reaction and might alienate potential dissenters within the Senate."

McGovern stayed with the Senate's silent majority throughout 1964. He was also on the majority side in August 1964, when the Senate passed the Gulf of Tonkin resolution, which McGovern himself admits was "a kind of blank-check congressional endorsement for the subsequent escalation of the war." McGovern was leery of anything that gave the President such sweeping powers, even if it did stop short of a declaration of war. "I voted against a similar resolution when Eisenhower offered it in the Middle East in 1957, right after the Suez crisis," McGovern explains. "I thought that this was the same kind of thing." McGovern also had questions about "why those American destroyers were up there in the first place," and asked them during the brief debate before the vote on the resolution. His "instinct," he says, was to vote no. In the end he voted yes. His reason, as he explains it, was essentially political: "Fulbright said he had absolute assurance that we weren't involved in any provocative actions. He said [the resolution] wouldn't mean a lot one way or the other. He said we had to get the whole Congress behind the President on this thing. He said if we didn't that Goldwater was going to hammer him [Johnson] over the head for doing nothing. I certainly didn't want to help Goldwater, and what Fulbright was saying made sense. So I voted yes."

Almost immediately, McGovern began having second thoughts. The very next day, he entered his fears into the Senate record:

> I do not wish my vote for the resolution to be interpreted as an endorsement for our longstanding and apparently growing military involvement in Vietnam. I have had serious misgivings about our entanglement in Vietnam since we were first committed to that course ten years ago. . . . Today, ten years after our inheritance of the French responsibility in Southeast Asia, we seem to be faring no better than the French. It is my own judgment that we cannot win a conflict against sustained guerrilla activity in Vietnam without enthusiastic and vigorous action on the part of the people and the government of South Vietnam. I do not think that kind of widespread effort has been demonstrated.

McGovern then warned that an invasion of North Vietnam might well trigger World War III and urged that the United States consider Charles de Gaulle's suggestion that the Geneva Conference be reconvened. "In my judgment," McGovern concluded, "an indefinite continuance of the military conflict in South Vietnam is a hopeless course that will lead in the end either to defeat or to entanglement in the kind of major war which we are ill-prepared to fight in Asia."

When McGovern finished, Morse—who the day before had cast one of two votes against the resolution—couldn't resist the temptation to offer a bitter aside:

> Mr. President, I find the speech of the Senator from South Dakota very interesting, but very belated. . . . His views, of course, are welcome, even under the saying "Better late than never." If Senators who have held the view of the Senator from South Dakota—and many of them have held them privately for these many months—had joined the Senator from Alaska and the Senator from Oregon five or six months ago in urging an economic, political, and diplomatic settlement of the Asiatic strife under the rules of international law, we might have been able to change the war-making course of our government in Asia. But one of the saddest things is that during all those months the talk of many Senators in the cloakroom has been noticeably different from their silence on the floor of the Senate. I hope that the Senator from South Dakota and others who share his views will now proceed with some vigor in trying to make their representations and suggestions known to this administration to see if we can stop the war-making course the United States is taking in Asia.

It was another five months before McGovern took Morse's advice. What finally prompted him was what he calls "certain conversations with my neighbor Hubert Humphrey." Apparently, Humphrey tipped McGovern that while he and Johnson had run on a pledge "not to send American boys to do the job Asian boys should be doing," as the President put it, Johnson had in fact already plotted substantial escalation for the coming year. The revelation ultimately strained McGovern's friendship with Humphrey. Its more immediate impact was to persuade McGovern to make his first major policy address on Vietnam on January 15,

1965, six days before Johnson was to retake the oath of office. McGovern didn't mince many words:

> We are not winning in South Vietnam. We are backing a government there that is incapable of winning a military struggle or of governing its people. We are fighting a determined army of guerrillas that seems to enjoy the cooperation of the countryside and that grows stronger in the face of foreign intervention. . . . We are further away from victory over the guerrilla forces in Vietnam today than we were a decade ago. . . . What has gone wrong? In my judgment, the first answer is that South Vietnam is not basically a military problem but a political one. . . . And it is a South Vietnamese problem. The United States can accomplish much through foreign aid and military support, but we cannot create strong, effective, and popular national leadership where the leadership either does not exist or does not exert itself. That is not only expensive and impractical; it is just plain impossible. . . .
>
> Personally I am very much opposed to the policy, now gaining support in Washington, of extending the war to the North. Attacks on North Vietnam will not seriously weaken guerrilla fighters a thousand miles away, fighters who depend for 80 percent of their weapons on captured U.S. equipment and for food from a sympathetic local peasantry.

In place of bombing and increased U.S. troop commitments, he favored "quiet infiltration and subversion" of the North by South Vietnamese units.* "The aim of any such infiltration," McGovern hastened to add, "should not be military victory, but bringing Ho Chi Minh to the conference table." Once Ho was prepared to negotiate, preferably in a setting similar to the first Geneva Convention, McGovern suggested that five basic terms be worked out. First, there would be "close association or federa-

---

* In fact, the South Vietnamese under U.S. direction had been doing just that even before the Geneva Accords went into effect. Neglecting the fact that such infiltration was in clear violation of international law, the tactic seldom worked. Nearly all the infiltrators were killed or captured, usually within days of landing in the North.

tion between North and South Vietnam, not under a unitary Communist government from the North, but with local autonomy for the South as well as the North." Second, trade and rail links would be renewed between the two Vietnams. Third, cooperative planning would be instituted to enable both North and South to benefit from the development of the Mekong River. Fourth, both North and South Vietnam would be neutralized, with accompanying guarantees of the gradual withdrawal of American combat units. Finally, a UN presence would be set up in Southeast Asia, with the right to enter every country in the area to "guarantee national borders, to offer protection against external aggression, and insofar as possible to insure fair treatment of tribal and other minorities within the boundaries of a given state."

McGovern's plan was a blend drawn from Vietnam historian Bernard Fall (especially points one, two, and four), AID (point three), various liberal academics, and last but certainly not least McGovern himself. The UN idea, which critics scathed as the most glaringly naïve, bore the unmistakable stamp of McGovern's imprimatur. McGovern had never really gotten over his postwar love affair with the United Nations,* nor had his faith substantially diminished in the ultimate practicability of some form of world government. To complete the mélange, there was even a trace of General James Gavin's theory of withdrawal to coastal "enclaves" which for a time during the middle and late 1960s gained popularity with less radical doves, including McGovern. Hinting at the concept, McGovern at one point in his speech declared: "Until such time as negotiation is possible and settlement can be devised which will not surrender South Vietnam to communism, the United States would doubtless not find it feasible to withdraw. If necessary, we can maintain our military position in Vietnam indefinitely, since it is essentially a policy of holding the cities while taking whatever attrition is possible of the guerrillas in the countryside."

It was not so much the precise content of McGovern's speech

---

* For a brief time as a freshman Congressman, McGovern was a member of the United World Federalists. Even today, although his membership has lapsed, McGovern says: "I still go along with a lot of what they say. They have a lot of good ideas."

as the time of its delivery that made the address significant. Now there could be no doubt about McGovern's loyalties; he was clearly on the side of the doves. Another of the new converts was Frank Church of Idaho. The two struck what amounted to an ideological and political alliance on Vietnam. They consulted with the same advisers, coordinated policy with each other, and timed their speeches for mutual maximum effect. They set their first priority as halting, or at least suspending, the bombing of North Vietnam, which had been proceeding with steadily increasing intensity since the supposedly "one shot" retaliatory strikes of 1964. McGovern, however, was still being cautious about attacking Johnson directly. He went out of his way to commend Johnson for "restraint" in ordering "retaliatory" air strikes against North Vietnam, "only after careful consideration of all the factors involved in this complex crisis." By commending Johnson, though, McGovern also meant to warn him not to go any further, or as he tactfully put it: "Doubtless no one recognizes more clearly than the President that bombing attacks on the North will not solve the guerrilla struggle in the South." The deftness of McGovern's approach, while doing little to budge Johnson from his predetermined course, did win McGovern favor among his constituents. As of February 1965 his mail was running fifteen to one in support of his stand for a negotiated settlement.

McGovern's dovishness then gained national attention, especially after he participated in a nationally televised "debate" with two leading hawks, Hanson Baldwin, the military editor of *The New York Times*, and Democratic Senator Gale McGee of Wyoming. Roger Hilsman, former Assistant Secretary of State for the Far East, was introduced as one of McGovern's fellow doves, but the ensuing hour found him almost as much in disagreement with McGovern as the two supposed hawks. The program, moderated by CBS news correspondent Charles Collingwood, was aired early in March. It produced a number of sharp exchanges, with McGovern invariably taking what was then the most radical line.

McGovern: Mr. Baldwin, you quote the famous maxim "We arm to parley." But it seems to me that what you're sug-

gesting here tonight is that "We arm to fight." And you're pre-
scribing a course, as I see it, not to parley, not to negotiate, but
to take us into a major land war on the Asiatic mainland.

BALDWIN: I do not shrink from that, Senator McGovern, if
it's essential. Let's look back at Korea. We undertook there
truce negotiations for twenty-four-months before we were able
to secure a truce. And it took us eighteen months after we decided what the truce line should be. This was our great mistake, when we originally accepted the Communist Chinese
request for a truce, because we did not keep military pressure
on them. My point is that. . . .

HILSMAN: It seems to me that I agree with Mr. Baldwin
that we've got to bite this bullet. We've got to make up our
minds whether or not we intend to save Southeast Asia.

McGOVERN: It seems to me that the basic assumption here
that you gentlemen are making, which I think goes wide of the
mark, is that you're assuming that the struggle in which we're
involved in South Vietnam is primarily a struggle with North
Vietnam and with China, when as a matter of fact this is a
struggle that has been raging in South Vietnam for years, between South Vietnamese and South Vietnamese. It is basically
a civil war that began some years ago for control of a revolutionary situation.

BALDWIN: A civil war supported from the outside.

McGOVERN: To be sure, a civil war supported from the
outside, with our country supporting one side and support
coming in from North Vietnam and China on the other side.
But the basic fact is that some 80 percent of all the equipment,
the armament, and the aid with which the guerrillas are fighting did not come from China, did not come from North Vietnam, but came from our own troops.

A few weeks later McGovern went a step further, when during a speech before the student body of Bucknell University in
Pennsylvania he called on the United States "to refrain from
bombings in North Vietnam for a two-week period to encourage
the possibility of negotiation." "I know something of military
operations," McGovern added. "I was a bomber pilot during

World War II. I saw what B-24s and incendiary bombs could do. But there are some problems bombs can't solve."

By this time McGovern and Church had become more than a minor annoyance to the White House. Each time the United States escalated the war, they seemed to escalate their dissent. The afternoon of April 7, 1965, the President summoned both men to the White House to work some of the old Johnson magic on them. It was not the President's first attempt—twice before he had tried and failed—but it was destined to be the last. As McGovern describes the sessions: "He did most of the talking. He would always close the issue in terms of LeMay versus the pacifists. 'You don't want me to use the nuclear bomb or bomb them back in the Stone Age,' he would say. 'You don't want me to run for the boats either.' Then he would add: 'I'm trying to get this thing squared away so we can negotiate a settlement.' At one point he said to me: 'I don't let those guys even bomb so much as a shithouse without my personal approval. Every target I authorize.' He saw himself as the adroit politician controlling the militarists. He used all sorts of homey expressions to describe what he was doing. Once he said: 'I'm sneaking up their knee an inch at a time, and I'll grab their snatch before they know it.' And I said: 'Mr. President, sometimes, when you start going up a skirt, you get your hand slapped.' He didn't like me saying that, but finally he said: 'Well, I'm watching that.'" During the April 7 meeting, Johnson revealed to McGovern and Church that he was going to make a public offer to negotiate that night at Johns Hopkins University in Baltimore. "He sat us down and read the entire speech to us," says McGovern. "In effect, he was saying: 'Now I'm giving you what you've been asking for, an offer to negotiate. Now I hope you bastards will shut up.'"

But they didn't shut up. Because accompanying Johnson's offer to negotiate came substantially increased American air attacks against the North. As far as McGovern and Church were concerned, that tore it. "When we kept up the drumbeat after the Baltimore speech," says McGovern, "he just didn't understand the nature of our criticism, that offering to negotiate and then accelerating the bombing—which is precisely what he did—was not what we had in mind. We talked about trying to get a negotiated settlement. He was trying to bludgeon them to the negotiating table." As McGovern's and Church's attacks continued, Johnson turned increasingly vindictive. Myer Feldman, who stayed on with the Johnson administration, recalls watching Johnson angrily scratch McGovern's name off an invitation list to a routine White House function. When Johnson finally did order a bombing pause, as the prelude to the so-called thirty-seven-day peace offensive in 1966, he muttered sullenly: "Let McGovern take that and stick it up his ass."

In the months that followed his meeting with Johnson, McGovern came out for a number of alternatives—anything, it seemed, that would lessen the fighting. In June he was calling for the South Vietnamese to negotiate directly with the National Liberation Front. In July, in a major Senate speech entitled "How to Save Lives and Political Face in Vietnam," he endorsed the enclave strategy, as well as a total halt to the bombing of both North and South Vietnam.

McGovern, however, found few takers. Instead, there was either silence or outspoken opposition, especially from the Republican side of the aisle. On one occasion, Everett Dirksen of Illinois rose in the Senate to deplore that fact that Church and McGovern had spoken "in this chamber which echoes with the courageous words of brave men now gone." The bathos of the remark made McGovern lose his temper. He replied acidly:

> There are still brave men in the Senate and the Senator from Illinois isn't the only one. It doesn't require any particular bravery to stand on the floor of the Senate and urge our boys in Vietnam to fight harder, and if this war mushrooms into a major conflict and a hundred thousand young Americans are killed, it won't be U.S. Senators who die. It will be American soldiers who are too young to qualify for the Senate.

For the most part, McGovern remained moderate. At that point he was not urging a withdrawal or anything approaching it, simply that the United States sit down and talk. There were even moments when he could sound almost hawkish. During a home-state visit to the First Methodist Church in Brookings late in

October 1965, he said flatly: "We crossed the bridge long ago in Vietnam. It's too late to turn back now. Our nation has decided that we must stay and fight to stop the Communists from taking over. We have a commitment, and we must stay there until the dispute is resolved." He was also tough on demonstrators. At Brookings he declared: "Recent protests staged serve no useful purpose. If these individuals would put their talents to work helping, the war effort would be greatly aided." At the University of Wisconsin a few days later, he branded draft card burnings as "immature, impractical, and illegal." Today McGovern says that he favored total American withdrawal from Vietnam long before he was saying so publicly. To have taken such a stance in the mid-1960s, he argues, would have turned more people off than it turned on. Or as McGovern phrases it: "I was interested in changing policy, not making speeches." McGovern has a definite point. Still, the statement sounds strange coming from a man who in 1971 was condemning those (meaning Muskie) "who take a position in private and are afraid to defend it in public."

It was inevitable, perhaps, that McGovern would join the growing parade of Congressmen and Senators trooping out to Vietnam for a firsthand inspection of what were advertised as "the front lines" but were actually carefully chosen secure rear areas. McGovern's saving grace is that he went early (November 1965), before it had become entirely the fashion, paid his own way, and kept out a warily skeptical eye and ear for all he was shown and told. The three-week excursion began with an elaborate two-day briefing at the headquarters of the Commander-in-Chief Pacific in Hawaii. From there McGovern and his traveling companion, Joe Floyd, the owner of the largest television station in South Dakota, proceeded to Hong Kong and finally to Vietnam itself. McGovern was subjected to the standard statistic-packed briefings and intelligence reports, all of which concluded with the inevitable assurance that there was indeed light at the end of the tunnel. He met Vietnam Ambassador Henry Cabot Lodge, toured the countryside, visited hospitals, chatted with journalists (apparently the only pessimists in the country), posed for a picture in a fighter plane, and spent one memorable evening in the Saigon villa of the legendary Colonel Edward Lansdale, the CIA's man in Vietnam and the model for both Graham Greene's *The Quiet American* and William Lederer and Eugene Burdick's far less flattering account of American bumbling in Southeast Asia, *The Ugly American*. Lansdale came off as a faintly bizarre character, attended by weird functionaries and surrounded at all times by lissome Vietnamese girls. The supposed highlight of the evening was the screening of a new "psy-war" film that Lansdale's men had just cooked up, which was supposed to win over the peasant population by depicting the Viet Cong as comical Chaplinesque figures. McGovern was less than impressed. "It was the most asinine use of American tax dollars I have ever witnessed," he said later. Indeed, everything about Vietnam only confirmed McGovern's worst impressions. "You know, Joe," he said to Floyd on the long flight home, "you have to be a damn fool not to know what is going on out there, and not much of it is good."

McGovern delivered a kindlier assessment a few weeks later at a $25-a-plate "appreciation dinner" at the Corn Palace in Mitchell. He spoke glowingly of "the superb quality of these fighting men . . . impressive, skillful, well trained." But McGovern noted: "We visited many of them, far too many of them, in their hospital beds in Saigon and in other parts of the country." He recalled one badly wounded Marine captain he had seen in a hospital in Saigon. "His lips were quivering and you could see his fists clenched as he held the edge of that bed in obvious pain. As we walked closer to him to say hello, it became clear that he was one of those many people representing us over there who had stepped on a mine or something of that kind and had lost his feet. I think one foot was blown off entirely and the other one mangled to the point where it was doubtful that it could be saved. A nurse told us that the captain had just been awarded the Purple Heart a few minutes before we came in. Mr. Floyd said: 'Well, Captain, we certainly want to congratulate you on this honor, this award.' And he said: 'Well, sir, it isn't very hard to get the Purple Heart over here.'" In a hospital in Da Nang McGovern saw the shredded remains of Vietnamese civilians. "I will never forget it as long as I live," he told his audience in Mitchell. "As we walked in the door, we saw these long rows of cots, single cots equipped with nothing but a straw mat, and two patients on each of these cots. These were the victims of the war, people with legs blown off, terribly burned by napalm bombs, and they followed us around that room with their eyes in absolute silence. . . . It was like the picture of the wounded deer that is watching the killer close in to take his life."

At Tan Son Nhut Air Force Base in Saigon, McGovern related, his driver made a wrong turn and brought them into the heart of a graves registration area. "As we sat there," said McGovern, "I noticed a whole row of these trucks that were waiting to move into the road; and I suddenly became aware of the fact that every one of those long flat-bed trucks contained neat rows of coffins, each one of them bearing the home address of some American serviceman: a soldier from Oklahoma, whose name I jotted down, a young captain from Minnesota, a Marine corporal from Tennessee, a major from Connecticut—all these American names that one sees in any congregation of Americans—Scandinavian, the Irish, and the Italians and the Germans, and so on. As we sat there in the sun waiting for these trucks to move on so that we could pass by, I thought what a waste, what a tragedy it is; and I wondered, as a member of the United States Senate and as a private citizen, if there is anything that I could have done that I haven't done to try to see that that kind of thing can someday be ended. I wondered if I had spoken out enough or been wise enough in what I had said, just wondering if all of us in the Senate and all of us who are citizens of this country don't have a real obligation to find some better solution for our differences than this."

The questions must have bothered McGovern, because after his return from Vietnam he became noticeably tougher. He called for an indefinite extension of the thirty-seven-day bombing halt and compared the American reluctance to recognize the National Liberation Front as a party to any negotiations to "King George III expressing a willingness to negotiate with our French ally while ignoring George Washington and his rebel Americans." Perhaps most important, he started speaking of the war in more human terms, attacking it not only as an aberration of foreign policy but as a hideous instrument that orphaned children and turned mothers into prostitutes and fathers into Viet Cong. Still, he stopped short of the more radical solutions he would adopt a few years later. He announced on network television that he would vote for the $12 billion Vietnam appropriation for 1967, as he had in 1966 and would again in 1968. "This is a matter," he said, using the precise argument his own critics would turn against him three years later, "of whether you're going to supply equipment to men we've sent overseas or whether you're going to leave them without the means of defending themselves."

As the months moved on and the killing only increased, McGovern's words grew sharper. He also dropped the customary bow to Johnson as "a man of judgment and the highest integrity." By April 1967 the administration was pursuing, in his words, "a policy of madness, which sooner or later will envelop American youth by the millions in a war without end." After Johnson's denunciation of the "nervous Nellies" who would "tuck tail and run," McGovern raked the administration for "trying to blame their failure on those who have warned them all along that they were playing with fire." Vietnam, he said bluntly, "represents the most tragic diplomatic and moral failure in our nation's history."

McGovern's new words did not sit well in some quarters. Back home, he lost some of the editorial support his early, more moderate warnings had won him among normally conservative organs like the *Sioux Falls Argus-Leader* and the *Watertown Public Opinion*. McGovern's statement in April 1967 that he would have to wait and see who the Republican candidate was before deciding whether to back Johnson for a second term brought a warning from some influential South Dakota Democrats that times would be lean in 1968 if McGovern chose to "bolt" the President. McGovern's antiwar stand, according to a poll conducted in June 1967, found favor among only 47 percent of South Dakota's voters, but an overwhelming margin—some 73 percent—defended his right to dissent publicly.

McGovern made it clear that he was not going to back down. As he told a Methodist convention in Aberdeen in the fall of 1967:

To remain silent in the face of policies we believe to be wrong is not patriotism; it is moral cowardice—a form of treason to one's conscience and to the nation. It is not easy to dissent in time of war. . . . I do not know how all this will come out. I do know that the people of a state can easily secure a new Senator, but a Senator cannot easily secure a new conscience. . . . I want to be reelected . . . but I do not want reelection so badly that I will ever sacrifice my convictions to achieve it.

McGovern's rhetorical escalation continued throughout 1967. In April, a few days before the U.S. commander in Vietnam, General William Westmoreland, was to address Congress, McGovern told the Senate: "We seem bent on saving the Vietnamese from Ho Chi Minh even if we have to kill them and demolish their country to do it. . . . After all the dead are counted—American and Vietnamese—and the countryside is laid waste, what will we have accomplished? It would be ironic, indeed, if we devoted so heavy a proportion of our resources to the pacification of Vietnam that we were unable to pacify Los Angeles, Chicago, and Harlem."

At the White House the reaction was silence. The President was beyond words—McGovern's or anyone else's. By the autumn of 1967 he had become remote, resentful, removed from the reality that was taking shape all too quickly. But Johnson was still capable of surprises. Late in September he decided to treat with his enemies, McGovern included, one final time, at a secret stag dinner at the White House. The whole covey of doves was there— McGovern, Church, Morse, and Joe Clark—dining with him on prime ribs, broccoli, and peach melba. Then, as the afterdinner mints were being passed around, the tormentors sat back to listen —half-piteous, half-horrified—as Johnson slowly disintegrated before their eyes. The President was more rambling and incoherent than McGovern had ever seen him. He droned on in response to one question for forty-five minutes. To another, posed by McGovern, he gave no answer at all, but boasted for twenty minutes how he was holding Westmoreland at bay.

McGovern left the Executive Mansion that night shaken from

the performance he had witnessed. "The President is a tortured and confused man—literally tortured by the mess he has gotten into in Vietnam," McGovern wrote when he returned home. "He is restless, almost like a caged lion, as if some great force has overtaken him. He seemed to be almost begging for political advice; yet when we would try to interject, he would immediately break in. . . . He reacts violently to suggestions that our involvement there is immoral or that he is following the Goldwater line or that we can't afford it. . . . [But] he is vulnerable. . . . You almost want to put your hand on his shoulder and say: 'Now, Lyndon, calm down, back away and take a cooler look.' "

Four months later the time had passed for cooler looks. The world awoke to pictures of half-naked Viet Cong guerrillas assaulting the sheltered grounds of the supposedly "impregnable" U.S. Embassy in Saigon. But more than an embassy wall had been breached; the last remaining shreds of Johnson's credibility had been blown apart. Emboldened now, McGovern spoke out even more strongly in the first few months of 1968. In Rhode Island in April, before a cheering throng of Brown University students, he branded the Thieu-Ky regime a "puppet government" and called for its replacement by a coalition—including the NLF—chosen by internationally supervised elections. McGovern also gave the first public indication of where his dissent would lead next. "Frankly," he said, "there are times when I think the only way we are ever going to end the war is simply to get out."

McGovern came very close to saying that during his eighteen-day campaign for the presidency in August 1968. In his August 10 declaration of candidacy, McGovern repeated his call for an immediate end to the bombing, a halt to all search-and-destroy missions, and the election of a coalition government. Before the first week of the campaign was out McGovern had moved even beyond that position, placing himself firmly to the left of anyone, including McCarthy, on the war. McGovern's proposal, which he laid out to the Democratic Convention Platform Committee, was to "end the major portion of the killing and the American military involvement in sixty days on terms acceptable to the majority of the people of both the United States and Vietnam."

To do that, McGovern proposed the immediate withdrawal of 300,000 American troops, leaving in place a force of 250,000 combat troops, which would pull back into coastal enclaves. This remaining force would be withdrawn "as time and events dictate: according to such factors as the willingness of the North Vietnamese to withdraw their forces, the progress of the South Vietnamese in reforming their own government and army, and the progress of the peace talks with the NLF."

Only one step now remained, and in December 1969 he took it, calling for a total phased withdrawal of American troops, beginning with a block of 260,000 men. McGovern also endorsed an immediate end to hostilities. During the cease-fire, McGovern said, remaining American troops would encamp in well-defended coastal enclaves. As they went home, according to the normal twelve-month schedule of rotation, they would not be replaced, meaning that all U.S. troops would be withdrawn in slightly more than a year. If the other side promised "general and complete amnesty" for all South Vietnamese, the withdrawal would be accomplished even more quickly. "Each day the diplomats and politicians use in ending the war," McGovern told his audience, "spells the death of more young men who were never even asked if they wanted to fight. . . . It is long past time to quit saving face and begin saving lives."

McGovern did not immediately introduce his plan on the floor of the Senate. Like other Senate doves, he was giving the newly elected President a period of grace. Shortly before Nixon's inauguration, McGovern publicly said that he expected "that a real effort will be made to liquidate our involvement in Vietnam as soon as feasible by the new administration." As the weeks passed and "the plan" Nixon had talked about during his campaign was not forthcoming, McGovern became increasingly annoyed. His patience snapped altogether the day Adam Walinsky, a former speechwriter for Robert Kennedy, walked into his office with what he claimed was information that the North Vietnamese had withdrawn 80 percent of their troops from the northernmost province of South Vietnam in response to the bombing halt of the previous fall. North Vietnam's withdrawal, according to

Walinsky, was a signal to the United States that it was prepared to begin a step-by-step cease-fire. Nixon, Walinsky went on, had known about the Communist move and ignored it. Instead, his response had been to escalate. During a three-month winter period, the number of battalion-sized operations conducted by South Vietnamese and American troops had climbed from 820 to 1,077. The Marines, meanwhile, had undertaken what was being billed as "the largest amphibious operation since the end of World War II." Most disturbing of all was the first open admission that U.S. troops had occasionally forayed into Laos. The Communist response, inevitably, had been to launch an offensive of their own, a countrywide uprising which was continuing at that very moment.

McGovern decided to check on the authenticity of Walinsky's charges before publicly airing them. He called on Averell Harriman at his Georgetown home and asked if there was anything to the story. Harriman was plainly surprised. "Who told you that?" he demanded. McGovern refused to divulge the source of his information, but Harriman finally admitted that the story was true. But the former ambassador discouraged McGovern from speaking out so early and suggested that he wait until the current fighting died down or the ABM fight was finished in the Senate. Ask questions, he advised McGovern. "Don't go out hammer and tong."

But McGovern was unwilling to wait. Walinsky and Dave Beale, his new legislative aide, were commissioned to prepare a draft of what would be the first public break with the President's war policy since Nixon came to office. The result of their joint effort, which McGovern himself rewrote in part, was characteristically McGovern: tough, plain-worded, to the point. "It is nearly a year since President Johnson announced the first steps to negotiate an end to the war," McGovern told a crowded Senate chamber on March 17:

> Today, the killing continues.
> There is no more time for considering "military options," no more time for "improving the bargaining position." In the the name of decency and common sense, there must be no further continuation of the present war policy, however dis-

guised in rhetoric or more hollow predictions of victory yet
to come. . . . I believe the only acceptable objective now is
an immediate end to the killing.

Alan Cranston of California and Harold Hughes of Iowa, who
had been summoned to the Senate to deliver the customary post-
speech plaudits, sat in their seats in stunned silence. Montana's
Mike Mansfield, who had followed McGovern's words down an
advance copy of the text, bit his lip. Teddy Kennedy pushed his
way to the exit and told waiting reporters that the middle of an
enemy offensive was not the time to attack the Commander in
Chief. The speech, Kennedy concluded, was "precipitate." To
McGovern, the silence of his colleagues was "deafening." But
while there was no credit for him, the spell of the new President
had at least been broken. The next morning in *The Washington
Star* Mary McGrory said it best: "The honeymoon is over."

That may have been the case for Nixon, but for McGovern
and the more radical elements of the peace community it was just
beginning. By his recent public stands—especially the March
17 speech—McGovern had clearly become a Senate dove of major
stature. There were others, like Vance Hartke of Indiana and
Charles Goodell of New York, who shared McGovern's views on
the war, but none could match the time or the passion he had invested in it. It was not surprising, then, that when David Hawk,
Sam Brown, and David Mixner announced plans for a national
"Moratorium" on October 15, they would approach McGovern
to be the principal speaker at what was expected to be the day's
main event, a giant rally on Boston Common. McGovern accepted, in the words of one member of his staff, "instantly."

Besides giving McGovern another opportunity to publicly
express his opposition to the war, the Moratorium date offered
a chance to further McGovern's presidential ambitions, which
even then were running at close to high tide. If McGovern were
to be a credible candidate in 1972, he had to carve out a constituency of his own, much the same as Eugene McCarthy had done
in 1968; the Moratorium was a natural. It turned out that he
would have more than one chance. After the receipt of the Boston
invitation, "an avalanche of offers" poured in from colleges and

local Moratorium committees across the country. McGovern's staff sifted through the pile and ultimately selected two others: American University, whose principal advantage was its Washington, D.C., location, and the University of Maine in Bangor, where McGovern would literally be speaking in Muskie's backyard.

McGovern delivered the same speech before all three gatherings. As a literary and historical document, the speech was a fine effort, filled with facts and statistics and gracefully laced with quotations from Charles Beard, Arthur Miller, and Albert Camus. It went over well enough in the morning appearance in Washington, but when McGovern confronted a singing, chanting, boisterous crowd of 100,000 in Boston that afternoon the scholarly exhortations to "lift the terrible burden of war from his [Nixon's] shoulders and from the American people" fell disconcertingly flat. The crowd shifted uneasily as McGovern began by declaring that the day was not to be "for name-calling or violence and destruction . . . not for the politics of revenge . . . but the politics of reconciliation." By the time he finished telling them not to abandon the ideals of Lincoln and Jefferson, they were bored completely. When the address was over there was polite, if unenthusiastic applause, and McGovern retreated disconsolately to his seat on the speaker's stand, like a boy who had just lost his first big speech tournament. On the plane to Bangor his staff tried to console him. "Nobody could have turned that crowd on," said one of them. "They came to groove on each other, not to listen to speeches." But McGovern brooded gloomily. After six years fighting the war he seemed somehow to have failed, and before the very people who should have loved him most. Happily, things turned up at the University of Maine, where to a thunderous ovation the president of the student body introduced him as "the next President of the United States."

Moratorium was one thing; Mobilization, which was scheduled to follow it a month later in Washington, was quite another. David Dellinger's "New Mobe," the sponsor of the demonstration, was more radical in its attitudes—and in its approach—than it was liberal. Already, the Mobe had the distinction of being labeled by Chicago's Mayor Daley as the instigators of the convention dis-

orders of the summer before. It was a looser, freer, far less predictable bunch than the suburban matrons and fresh-faced divinity
students who had organized the Moratorium, and already the Justice Department was predicting trouble. "There were a lot of
signs that Kleindienst [the deputy Attorney General] was setting
it up for a real thrashing," says Dave Beale. "A lot of people
thought the administration was going to use the backlash from it
to rally support for their war policies."

When the possibility of McGovern participating in the march
from the Capitol to the Washington Monument was first broached,
McGovern's staff split right down the middle. The "non-South
Dakota people," who had been brought in to oversee his forthcoming national campaign, were cautiously enthusiastic. "We
wanted him to do it," says John Stacks, the new press secretary,
"but at the same time we wanted to make it clear that if there was
heavy trashing, this was not his thing." The South Dakotans, however, were, in Beale's words, "nearly hysterical over the very
thought of it." A rumor, floated by George Cunningham, circulated in the office that a group of South Dakotans was planning
to launch a recall petition if McGovern joined the Mobe. Fears
were only slightly eased when research determined that there was
no recall provision in South Dakota law.

McGovern's own instincts were to march. As he put it to one
of his staff members: "If anything happens during the Mobe, we're
all going to go down in the record whether we marched or not."
Sam Brown, who had engineered the invitation for McGovern to
speak at the Moratorium, was at first on the side of the Dakotans.
Eventually, though, he came to the view that if McGovern did
march and speak at the rally, the chances for violence might be
lessened. "He thought we could give a liberal tone to an essentially radical gathering," explains Beale. Early in November Mc-
Govern lunched in the Senate dining room with Cora Weiss of the
Women's Strike for Peace and Yale chaplain William Sloane
Coffin. When they had finished talking, McGovern gave them a
tentative commitment to appear. He firmed up the pledge after a
political trip to California and called in his staff to announce his
decision. The South Dakotans still weren't happy; Cunningham,
in fact, refused to go to the rally to hear his boss speak.

After McGovern had called a press conference to announce that he was marching, Sam Brown burst into the office to tell McGovern that he had to pull out. He had spent the night in meetings with the Mobe, Brown revealed, and had come away convinced that they were nearly as dangerous as Kleindienst said they were. McGovern was unfazed. "Go home and get some sleep, Sam," he advised. "You'll feel better after you think about it." As a final precaution, McGovern called a semisecret meeting between half a dozen Senators and some of the leaders of the Mobe. "He felt the more the Senators knew what was going on, the less trouble there would be," says Beale. Only one of the Senators—Goodell—agreed to march with McGovern. The rest, including Muskie, were content to sit it out on the sidelines.

As it turned out, the Mobe went off virtually without incident. The only violence was a brief spate of rock-throwing at the Justice Department, brought on no doubt by Kleindienst's invitation. The crowd of 350,000 who gathered on the grounds of the Washington Monument in November 1969 heard McGovern deliver what even for him was an unusually temperate speech, with heavy emphasis on peace as the highest form of patriotism:

> We meet today at this historic place because we love America. We love America enough to call her to a higher standard. We love America enough to call her away from the folly of war to the blessings of peace. . . . We are here as American patriots, young and old, to build a country, to build a world, that seeks the ways of peace—that teaches war no more. We meet today to reaffirm those ageless values that gave us birth—"life, liberty, and the pursuit of happiness." We meet to declare peace—to put an end to war, not in some vanishing future, but to end it *now*.

Mobilization did McGovern no good at home. In the polls his stock plummeted to its lowest level. The newspapers turned on him with special vengeance. He was portrayed as the friend of "flag burners and other assorted long-haired peace creeps," to quote one of the kinder critiques. McGovern took the uproar seriously enough to compose an explanatory open letter to the people of South Dakota. "As a careful reader of the newspapers

in my home state, I have noted the recent editorial criticism of
my opposition to the war in Vietnam," the letter said, in master-
ful understatement. "It may be, as some editors have suggested,
that as a Senator I should have rejected the invitation of the students who gathered to protest the war in October and November.
I have mingled feelings about this matter myself. Certainly, no
one with enough political know-how to be elected as a Democrat in Republican South Dakota would be unaware of the political hazards to himself of being identified with long-haired students. But I accepted their invitation in large part because I was
concerned about the growing division between the young and the
old in our country. That division may be more serious than we
yet know. It is my hope that in some way I can remain close
enough to the young to prevent them from dropping out of our
system of government and our way of life."

McGovern didn't say so in the letter, but he had made up his
mind never to participate in a peace demonstration again. In the
following months he seemed to go out of his way to dissociate
himself from the more radical elements of the left. "The rock
throwers, hecklers, and bomb throwers are enemies of us all," Mc-
Govern said in October 1970. "The blunt fact is that the violence-
prone extremists on the left and the inflammatory Agnew-type
orators on the right are natural allies. They feed on each other,
and their target is the moderate and progressive candidates of both
parties." In the spring of 1971 when Rennie Davis' Mayday Movement announced plans for a week-long campaign of nonviolent
civil disobedience in Washington, McGovern was one of the first
to condemn the Maydayers—who included many of the people
he had marched with in the Mobe—as "counterproductive." A
journalist who tried to arrange a secret meeting between Mc-
Govern and some of the Mayday leaders, similar to the one
McGovern himself had arranged two years before with the Mobe,
was informed by an aide: "The Senator doesn't want to have anything to do with those people."

Some saw it as strange, even opportunistic, that a man who in
his youth had been something of a radical would now turn on
those who professed a new brand of radicalism. They were especially disheartened by a speech McGovern delivered in Nebraska

in September in which he attacked several leading radicals by name—including Huey Newton, Tom Hayden, Jerry Rubin, and Abbie Hoffman—and laid down a blanket indictment of the philosophy they espoused. On occasion McGovern sounded like a right wing orator on the stump:

> Reckless political action may provide kicks for affluent youth cut off from the real world, but it is a grave injustice to those who seek an end to the war and misery. The irresponsible militant "doing his thing" at a peace rally or in a courtroom is undermining those dedicated to the long, hard effort to influence public opinion toward peace and justice.

Words like "reckless," and "irresponsible" did not go down easily with the the radical community, many of whose members had done their thing for peace and justice at considerable personal risk. "We don't knock what he is doing," said one leading new-left theoretician. "If he doesn't like the way we're trying to end the war, he should just shut up."

McGovern's own explanation was that peace demonstrations were fine in their day, but that the day was now over. As he put it: "To demonstrate is the easy thing. It is much harder to stay at home and quietly work for peace." With that, McGovern urged those against the war to put away their placards and take up their pens to write their Congressmen. If the war was to be ended, McGovern decided, it would be in the Congress, not in the streets. McGovern's first legislative effort had come in October 1969, when with the co-sponsorship of a handful of other doves he introduced a resolution for the withdrawal of all American forces from Vietnam. "The pace of the withdrawal," the resolution said, "[should] be limited only by steps to insure the safety of our forces, the mutual release of prisoners of war, and the provision of safety, through arrangements for amnesty or asylum in friendly countries, for those Vietnamese who might be endangered by our disengagement." Despite the rather tepid language of the resolution and the fact that it lacked the force of law, McGovern's proposal attracted less than twenty votes. The same month, McGovern watched as a far more radical notion—a bill proposed by Goodell to cut off funds for all Vietnam operations after December 1, 1970—failed by an even larger margin. Though McGovern was one of the few to back the Goodell proposal, he knew it didn't have a ghost of a chance. In 1969 the effectiveness of Nixon's "Vietnamization" alternative had yet to be proved conclusively one way or the other. Until it was, the overwhelming majority of the Senate would be unwilling to attempt anything so bold as a fund cutoff.

In the spring of 1970, however, the time seemed more opportune. That, at least, is what McGovern concluded late in March after talking to Roger Fisher, chairman of the Council for a Liberal World. He instructed John Holum to draft legislation to cut off all funds for Vietnam by June 30, 1971. To give added weight to the legislation—which was to take the form of an amendment to the military procurement bill, thus guaranteeing that it would come up for a Senate vote—McGovern hit upon the idea of getting a Republican dove to lend his name to it. The first and most obvious choice was Goodell, who if nothing else was surely eager. But Goodell had other problems. As one McGovern man explains it: "He's a nice guy, but we wanted to get a Republican with some credibility." So the choice devolved on Mark Hatfield of Oregon, who accepted with delight. In subsequent days Holum's original draft underwent a number of changes, most of them of a technical nature. Sam Brown and some of the Moratorium people lent their ideas, as well as promises of support, as did the Members of Congress for Peace Through Law and other peace and disarmament groups, including SANE.

Meanwhile, McGovern continued to search for co-sponsors. He was especially anxious to land McCarthy. But McCarthy, still smarting over McGovern's late entry into the presidential race in 1968, was playing hard to get. Phone calls to his office went unanswered. Finally, Sam Brown agreed to search him out. In the meantime, Harold Hughes signed on. But still no McCarthy. Then one day, without any urging or solicitation, Alan Cranston called and said he wanted in. With McGovern, Hatfield, Hughes, and Goodell, that made five. For the time being, they would forget about the poet sulking in his tent.

Then on May 1, one day after Amendment 609 was formally introduced on the Senate floor, an event occurred that the Hatfield and McGovern forces hadn't counted on: the United States invaded Cambodia. The invasion and subsequent murder of four students at Kent State momentarily took attention off Vietnam and riveted it on the rest of Indochina. John Sherman Cooper of Kentucky and Frank Church of Idaho introduced an amendment to the military sales bill forbidding U.S. ground troops from entering Cambodia or Laos again. At a strategy session in McGovern's office early in May the priorities were laid out: first concentrate on passing Cooper-Church, then work on pushing McGovern-Hatfield. One of their earliest moves was to mount a publicity campaign. McGovern, Hatfield, Goodell, Church, and Hughes sat in a downtown Washington studio for four hours talking about Vietnam in front of video-tape cameras. Eventually, their remarks were edited to hour length and were aired on prime time by NBC on May 12. At the program's conclusion an appeal was made for funds to further the work of what had by now been dubbed "The Amendment to End the War." McGovern's people were hoping to recoup the program's production costs; to their astonishment, nearly $500,000 poured into the office within the next few days. With the sudden infusion of capital, they were able to set up an organization—the Committee to End the War—and equip it with offices in Washington's Methodist Building. Other committees sprang up, and other offices opened. Unofficial peace lobbyists started to trek toward the Capitol, where they were briefed by professionals on what to say, where their Senator stood, and what approach might move him. The most important lobbying was of Senators by other Senators. The Republicans were the main targets, and none was deemed more crucial than crusty old George Aiken of Vermont, a dove in good standing but also a presidential loyalist. McGovern, it was decided, was not the man to take on Aiken, who was thoroughly exercised by some aspects of McGovern's food stamp program. That was a job for Mike Mansfield, who had agreed to back the amendment but with lukewarm enthusiasm. There is some question whether Mansfield ever asked his old friend to go along, or if he did, just how strongly he tried to persuade him. In any case, in the end Aiken's was perhaps the most important nay. "He was really key," laments one lobbyist. "If we could have gotten him, we could have gotten other

Republican votes." Meanwhile, other Senate offices were enlisted. Church's, Thomas Eagleton's, and Gaylord Nelson's staffs all lent a hand. Cranston hosted a series of lunches for other Senators with former Secretary of Defense Clark Clifford. Clifford was certainly dovish and highly critical of Nixon; the trouble was he didn't agree with the amendment.

As the summer wore on, the McGovern-Hatfield partisans scrambled to prevent their initial support from eroding. "Those few months," says Holum, "were like standing in a pile of marbles." The last draft of the amendment moved the final pullout deadline back six months to December 31, 1971. The President was also given an additional sixty-day escape clause. As a final inducement to wavering Senators, the language of the amendment was sweetened to say that the withdrawal would be made "in accordance with public statements of policy by the President." That change brought over New York's Jacob Javits, who earlier had objected that the amendment seemed to be a club against Nixon. But other Senators remained unmoved. In the spring there was hope of landing William Saxbe, Charles Percy, Jennings Randolph, Len Jordan, Clint Anderson, Aiken and Cooper. By September it was clear that none of them would come aboard. The loss of Cooper, who informed McGovern the day before the vote that he would be against it, was particularly grievous, both for the McGovern-Hatfield forces and, it seemed, for Cooper himself, who had been viciously savaged by the White House during the fight over his own amendment.

When McGovern-Hatfield finally came up for a vote in the Senate in September—almost three months later than McGovern had hoped for—it was clear that the doves had fallen short. McGovern had counted on getting at least forty votes—the margin, he thought, for a moral victory. The intelligence report of the Senate offices, accurate right to the last, told him he would get thirty-nine. Just before the vote McGovern had one last word:

> Every Senator in this chamber is partly responsible for sending 50,000 young Americans to an early grave. This chamber reeks of blood. Every Senator here is partly responsible for that human wreckage at Walter Reed and Bethesda Naval and

all across our land—young boys without legs, or arms, or genitals, or faces, or hopes. There aren't very many of these blasted and broken boys who think this war is a glorious venture. Don't talk to them about bugging out, or national honor, or courage. It doesn't take courage at all for a Congressman, or a Senator, or a President to wrap himself in the flag and say we're staying in Vietnam. Because it isn't our blood that is being shed. But we are responsible for those young men and their lives and their hopes. And if we don't end this foolish, damnable war, those young men will someday curse us for our pitiful willingness to let the Executive carry the burden the Constitution puts on us.

A few minutes later, the Senate of the United States made its decision: 39 aye, 55 nay. The war went on.

If McGovern-Hatfield had passed, and there was never any serious hope that it would, an even stiffer fight would have remained in the far more hawkish House. Even then there would have been nothing to prevent Richard Nixon from using his powers as Commander in Chief to veto the legislation. No one, of course, knew this better than McGovern. What, then, was the profit of all the effort and passion? Mainly it was to put the members of the Senate firmly on the record as to where they stood on war and peace. As McGovern himself said after the vote: "I would have liked to have seen a stronger showing. But I suppose it's the first time in the history of the country that thirty-nine Senators have stood up in the middle of a war and voted to cut off funds." And it would not be the last. "We never expected to win the first time around," says Holum. "We thought of it as a longer campaign." The second time around, in July 1971, there was more cause to be hopeful. The South Vietnamese army had suffered a stunning series of reverses, principally during the American-assisted invasion of Laos the spring before. In 1970 there seemed to have been other choices than simply Vietnamization or withdrawal; now all the other choices had been removed, and Vietnamization did not appear to be faring too well. The most dramatic evidence was a 1971 Gallup poll, which showed that fully

73 percent of all Americans favored an immediate withdrawal from Vietnam. As if to demonstrate the reservoir of support, a quarter of a million demonstrators—older, shorter-haired, and generally more conservative than any group that had preceded them—converged on the Capitol on April 24 to demand an immediate end to the war. The week before, the nation had witnessed the spectacle of a thousand Vietnam veterans hurling back their medals—Purple Hearts, Distinguished Flying Crosses, Silver Stars —in an emotional, sometimes tearful fury of disgust, revulsion, and guilt. Somehow, though, the country seemed inured to it all. When McGovern-Hatfield came up a second time, only three Senators added their ayes. At that rate, the "longer campaign" might take years. And it was questionable whether Vietnam had many years left.

The amendment had done one thing, though. As McGovern pointed out in his speech to the Senate on September 1, 1970, it "helped to keep the nation from exploding this summer. It was the lodestar that inspired more mail, more telegrams, more eager young visitors to our offices, more political action, and more contributions from doctors, lawyers, workers, and housewives than any other initiative of Congress in this summer of discontent." How many of those students, workers, and housewives were permanently embittered when it failed can only be guessed at. The failure partially radicalized at least one person—and that was George McGovern. In the months that followed the defeat of his amendment, he became less tolerant of the posturings of his colleagues. His words—he had startled many with his "This chamber reeks of blood" comment—became even sharper. He accused South Vietnamese Vice President Nguyen Cao Ky, whom he had already labeled "a little tin-horn dictator," of being heavily involved in the heroin traffic that was addicting as many as 10 percent of American GIs in Vietnam. When Mississippi Senator John Stennis suggested that GIs might have to return to Cambodia, McGovern exploded: "I'm fed up to the ears with old men dreaming up wars for young men to die in." With tongue only half in cheek, McGovern suggested that since the Congress seemed so fond of the war, it ought to fight it. He was thinking, he told a frenzied

audience at the University of Wisconsin in March 1971, of proposing an amendment to the pending Selective Service Act that
would require just that and ban the drafting of anyone under
thirty. Those legislators too old for the rigors of combat duty, he
added, would be employed in less strenuous chores—"like clearing
mine fields." To another Wisconsin audience McGovern charged
that "15,000 young Americans have been killed since Richard
Nixon took office, and their blood is on his hands."

McGovern also seemed to grow in his admiration for the
enemy, and he became far less circumspect about saying so. In a
freewheeling interview in the September 1971 issue of *Playboy*,
Washington Star columnist Milton Viorst asked him point blank:
"Do you sympathize with the aspirations of the Viet Cong and
their North Vietnamese allies?" McGovern replied: "In that they
are striving for national independence, yes. I think their posture is
more legitimate than General Thieu's. General Thieu is really a
creature of French and American power. I think he's completely
out of stride with the nationalistic aspirations of the Vietnamese
people, whereas the Viet Cong and Hanoi have been on the side
of expelling first the Japanese and then the French and now us."
The questioning continued:

> VIORST: If we make a historical allegory out of this, what
> similarities do you see with the American Revolution, where
> we Americans were trying to keep a foreign power, Britain,
> and its sympathizers, the Tories, from running the country?
>
> McGOVERN: I think they're very close. I think that Ho Chi
> Minh has copied our Declaration of Independence. He was
> really trying to throw the French out, not invite the Chinese in.
> And as Eisenhower said: "If there had been an election after
> they threw the French out, he would have had 80 percent of
> the vote, at least, in both North and South Vietnam." Simi-
> larly, George Washington was overwhelmingly elected once
> he kicked the British out of our country.
>
> VIORST: I suppose that Nixon would like to make the late
> Ho Chi Minh into the Vietnam Hitler. Are you suggesting he
> might be the North Vietnam George Washington?
>
> McGOVERN: That's right.

McGovern had taken his stand on Vietnam. It was his issue. Indeed, some would say, his only issue. Few colleagues could match his outrage. Only three—Morse, Gruening, and Nelson— could match his persistence. None at all could equal his foresight. McGovern was proud of his record, and rightly so. He boasted that he possessed a "broader and more sensitive perspective than the other candidates on the really crucial problems before the country," and there could be no doubt which "problems" McGovern was referring to. In the public mind, McGovern had become identified—and quite justifiably—as the Senator who had done the "most" to end the war. But the question remained: Was the most enough? Could McGovern have done more?

Those who think he might have point to several instances where, they claim, McGovern's commitment and passion were less than fully engaged. The most publicized is the release of the "Pentagon Papers." Weeks before Dr. Daniel Ellsberg approached *The New York Times* with his purloined copy of the Defense Department's forty-seven-volume study on the history of U.S. involvement in Vietnam, he first offered it to McGovern. McGovern declined on very practical as well as political grounds. For a Senator to knowingly receive stolen property, and property with a "Top Secret" classification at that, would be not only a violation of federal law but the equivalent of political suicide. If, somehow, McGovern escaped arrest or defeat, his security clearance and that of his key staff members would automatically be lifted. McGovern's credibility as a spokesman against the war would probably evaporate.

Those, at least, are the arguments McGovern and his staff present. On the other side is the opinion of the more politically pure, the more radical, and the more bitterly antiwar. Instead of merely advising Ellsberg to take his material to the newspapers, as McGovern apparently did,* the hardliners contend that as a matter

* McGovern insists that he did not directly encourage Ellsberg to go to the *Times*. In his version of the events, he told Ellsberg that the decision whether to break the law was his alone to make, but that *if* he did decide to commit civil disobedience, the most responsible and effective course would be to take the papers to one of the major liberal newspapers, such as the *Times* or the Washington *Post*.

of conscience McGovern should have assumed the responsibility of releasing the papers himself. They note approvingly the example of Alaska Senator Mike Gravel, who did in fact read a portion of the classified material into the Congressional Record and stopped reading only when his voice gave out and he left a Senate hearing room sobbing.

McGovern also puzzled some of his friends by his reaction to the court-martial of Lieutenant William Calley for the massacre at My Lai. At first McGovern (along with the American Civil Liberties Union) was against the trial entirely, saying that its purpose would be to make Calley a scapegoat. Once the guilty verdict was in, McGovern continued to insist, as did most of the left, that Calley was no more culpable than the war itself. "My Lai is just a tiny pimple of the surface of a raging boil," said McGovern. "If you are going to try war criminals, you'd have to try a nation, not just Lieutenant Calley." McGovern found it particularly difficult to differentiate between a murder committed by a pilot and one by an infantryman. "The results," the former bomber pilot observed, "are no more barbaric when you've just eliminated an entire village and perhaps killed several hundred people from 20,000 feet. It's just as devastating as looking down a rifle."

The Ellsberg and Calley incidents did not distress McGovern's critics nearly so much as his statement late in August 1971 that he would have "very little comment on the war from here on out." The war was still the nation's most pressing problem, McGovern hastened to add, but "I am a political realist, and I believe the state of the economy . . . is more decisive politically." McGovern's purpose was plain: he was anxious to divest himself of the "one issue" image. Still, by even suggesting that political expediency had a higher place than personal morality—and morality, McGovern himself stressed, was what Vietnam was ultimately about—McGovern had laid himself open to the charge of opportunism. It seemed odd for someone who had invested so much in the peace movement to "abandon the fight," as some of McGovern's friends bitterly put it, just when he was most needed.

In fact, McGovern was not abandoning any fight, nor was he "shunning" Vietnam, as the press generally reported. Within weeks of his press conference, he was in Paris,* meeting with the North Vietnamese and Provisional Revolutionary Government delegations to the peace talks. He would be willing to go to Hanoi, he said to Xuan Thuy, the chief North Vietnamese delegate, if any useful purpose could be served, especially if there were any hope of bringing American prisoners home with him. But Thuy demurred. The time, he said gently, was not propitious. Instead, McGovern continued on to Saigon, where, during a meeting in a small church with anti-government Buddhist leaders, he and his party were set upon by a gang of rock-throwing Vietnamese secret police. As rocks crashed through the windows, a firebomb suddenly enveloped a truck parked outside, pouring smoke into the church. McGovern, Weil, John Holum, and Mankiewicz retreated to a rear vestibule, seeking shelter from the mob. One of the Buddhists, however, tried to escape. As he stepped from the door of the church, the police pummelled him viciously. This, obviously, was no staged demonstration. McGovern doubted frankly whether any of them would emerge alive. "At the time," he said later, "the only question seemed to be whether they would stone us or burn us."

The rocks kept coming in. Then, mysteriously, a Korean appeared, and, in English, told McGovern and his aides that he would lead them to safety. They had not taken ten steps, when a rock caromed off the wall, inches from McGovern's head. They dove for the floor. An American civilian, who had helped arrange the meeting with the Buddhists, insisted that McGovern could not leave. The lives of the Vietnamese, he said emotionally, were at stake. "Get the hell out of here," Weil shouted. "The life of a Presidential candidate is at stake." When the American refused to budge, Weil knocked him across the room. Finally, Mankiewicz found a telephone and called the American Embassy.

---

* While Vietnam had much to do with McGovern's trip to Paris, the main motivation was China. On and off since 1966, McGovern had been trying to visit mainland China, and renewed his efforts with special intensity after the 1971 visit to Peking by the U.S. Ping-Pong team. After waiting endlessly for a visa, he eventually grew impatient, and decided to leave Asia anyway, hoping that a visa might be available in Paris. Of course, it wasn't.

Within moments, a convoy of American jeeps rolled up, sirens screaming. The police fled.

The next day, McGovern was ushered in to see President Thieu. He came right to the point. "I hold you personally responsible for what happened last night, Mr. President," McGovern said. "It's no wonder this country is in such a mess, if, after ten years of war and 50,000 American lives, the capitol is not safe for a U.S. Senator to visit." U.S. Ambassador Ellsworth Bunker, who was escorting McGovern, blanched. Thieu, disclaiming knowledge of the incident, apologized, and promised an investigation. Later, an official of the Secret Police boasted that he and his men had broken up a meeting of the Viet Cong. McGovern left Saigon a few days later. In six years, he said, as his plane lifted off the runway at Tan Son Nhut, nothing had changed.

In Saigon, as in the well of the Senate, McGovern had always opposed the war by his own tightly defined set of rules. They were hardly establishmentarian guidelines. On the other hand, neither were they a reveille for radicals. McGovern, in his own words, was interested in "changing policy, not making speeches." He was sensitive to the requirements of "credibility" and careful lest he lose his "effectiveness among other Senators." This ruled out making emotional gestures like Gravel or instigating a filibuster, as some of his friends urged him, until the Senate acted on the war—not that emotional gestures were ever a part of his nature. This also ruled out being more than one step ahead of his fellow Senators. That was left to Morse, Gruening, Nelson, and Goodell. The one occasion when McGovern was dramatically out in front on Vietnam was the Mobilization. Then no one, save Goodell—who really had nothing to lose—was willing to join him. But the Mobilization was not only the first time McGovern marched; it was also the last.

McGovern himself would be the first to admit that he could have done more. There was always the extra effort that could have been made, the extra hour that could have been spent, the extra risk that could have been taken. Still, that would not have been enough for some. Because in the end the more radical of McGovern's friends and admirers wanted him to act not as a Senator but as a Gandhi. They demanded not only perception or outrage or even courage but political self-immolation. Whether peace would have been served seemed not to count so much as the spectacle of the burning.

McGovern had little taste for the "kamikaze pacifists," as one of his advisers called them. Without retreating, he moved closer to the mainstream, where his instincts and his strength lay. "If peace is to come," he remarked once, "the people will bring it, not the demonstrations." He believed that, and so he worked at it, quietly, unsensationally, on terms of his own definition. Whatever he would tell a press conference about the economy, it was Vietnam that was on his mind. In its own way the war had become an obsession, and a magnificent obsession it was.

9

A Time to Keep

JANUARY 1, 1968, dawned cold and overcast in Washington, and George McGovern felt much the same way. The year ahead did not promise to be the brightest. There was, first of all, the uncertain matter of his own reelection. To be sure, the early samplings had shown him in no serious trouble with any of several possible Republican contenders. Still, a man who had been elected by the slimmest of margins could never be sure, especially with the war. McGovern had already said that he would wait to see the identity of the Republican candidate before deciding whether to support Johnson. If Johnson continued escalating the war, as McGovern feared, he would put McGovern in something of a bind. If McGovern turned his back on the President, he risked the wrath of his own party. If he continued to support him, even in the face of what he considered an immoral policy, he would suffer the summons of his own conscience. The prospect was not pleasant, personally or politically.

McGovern was still angry with himself for not taking up Allard Lowenstein's invitation to dump Johnson. If he had accepted, it would now be he, not Gene McCarthy, who would be cast as the lonely Galahad trudging through the snows of New Hampshire. McGovern didn't think that McCarthy had a chance, and he wondered at times whether McCarthy really had the stomach for the fight. That left only one hope: Bobby. He had been telling Kennedy to run before anyone else in the Senate, all the way back to 1965. They had chatted about it in a rather light way, but beneath the insouciance both men were deadly serious. The talks continued through 1966 and 1967, as Kennedy increasingly agonized over how he might join McGovern's opposition to the war without making it seem a personal vendetta with Johnson. Kennedy had never claimed a flat disinterest. Of course he wanted to be President, and McGovern knew it. But how? Late in December 1967 Ted Sorensen came to McGovern and put it bluntly: "Now look. You and other people are urging Bob to go. You really ought to know what you are talking about before you do that. Is there support for him? And if there is, you should try to establish that fact. You should call some of the people you know." So McGovern did, tapping a number of Governors and other Senators from the Midwest. The answer came back unanimously: none of them was willing to budge. Reluctantly, McGovern reported back to Sorensen. If there was support out there he, at least, couldn't find it. But, he added later to Kennedy, don't make any decision irrevocably. Not yet. Wait and see what happens by mid-March. So now they were all waiting. And McGovern wasn't hopeful.

Neither, apparently, was Kennedy. At a breakfast meeting with reporters a few weeks later, he allowed them to quote him as saying that he would not run "under any foreseeable circumstances." That sounded final enough. But McGovern was not sure. Kennedy, he was convinced, had said that mainly to free himself to attack Johnson on the war. In his gut, he was sure, Kennedy still wanted to run. McGovern got support for his suspicion when Ted Kennedy stopped him in the Senate gym a month later and in a friendly sort of way said: "Now, you know, let's really think this thing through. 'Cause I think Bobby's going to go, and if just one or two people push him, he'll go." Now McGovern knew; Kennedy was that close, so close that one man could push him over the edge. Perhaps, he reflected to himself, if he had pushed just a bit harder the previous November Kennedy might have been a candidate right then. But he set hindsight aside and resolved to be careful about what he said the next time he encountered Bob Kennedy.

He didn't have long to wait. Two days after McCarthy's victory in the New Hampshire primary, McGovern was scheduled to have lunch with a group of friends from his early days on the Hill, including Lee Metcalf and Gene McCarthy in the Senate and Frank Thompson and Stewart Udall in the House. Unexpectedly, McCarthy failed to show up—busy with answering congratulatory phone calls from New Hampshire, McGovern surmised. Short one luncheon guest, they phoned Kennedy and asked if he would like to come by. He would indeed. For the next two-and-a-half hours Kennedy shared with them his private agony about running, especially now that McCarthy had won in New Hampshire. McGovern and his friends were unanimously against the idea. If he made any statement, they urged him, it should be only that he was going to Wisconsin to campaign for McCarthy. McCarthy, they told him, had just made a great race in New Hampshire, and he now deserved the support of all those who were against the war.* Kennedy listened noncommittally. What they said, he admitted, made sense—and yet? In his expression they could read the torment. "I've never seen his face look so drawn," McGovern said later. The next day Kennedy announced his candidacy.

Kennedy's decision to run, while it pleased McGovern personally, also presented the South Dakotan with very real political problems. Much as he would like to, he could hardly afford to get on the Kennedy bandwagon, not with Eugene McCarthy hailing from next-door Minnesota, and especially not after Hubert Humphrey, who had been born in South Dakota, got into the race. In word if not in fact McGovern had to stay neutral. Indeed, if it were at all possible he wanted to avoid a primary fight altogether in his home state. The obvious course was for

---

* One person whose support McCarthy never got, either before Kennedy's entry or after his assassination, was George McGovern.

McGovern to become a favorite son, which is precisely what all three candidates wanted him to do. None of them wanted to risk being bloodied for the sake of South Dakota's twenty-six convention votes.

McGovern himself, after a period of indecision, was leaning that way. But under South Dakota law it took only one person to file a candidate's name for primary election, and for weeks Bill Dougherty had been itching to do just that. Dougherty was a Kennedy man, and like Kennedy men he could be impulsive, even brash. But for Bobby's sake Dougherty had been on his best behavior. He vowed not to make a move until instructed to do so by the national campaign staff. The trouble was the national staff couldn't seem to make up its mind. "One week," says Dougherty, "they would call and say, 'It's all set. We're going to do it. Just sit tight for a few more days.' The next week they would call and say, 'No, sorry, it's all off. We can't possibly go into there.'" After suffering this treatment for a number of weeks, Dougherty, a man of sharp political instincts but limited patience, decided to act on his own; he filed the name of Robert F. Kennedy in South Dakota as a candidate for the Democratic nomination for President of the United States. When Kennedy got wind of the move, he asked McGovern to persuade Dougherty to call it off. Dougherty refused.

Dougherty's move set off a chain reaction among the candidates. The Kennedy forces immediately rushed the nucleus of a campaign organization to the state. ("You've got us in this, Billy," Kennedy told Dougherty when he arrived in South Dakota. "I hope you can get us out of it.") If Kennedy was going, that meant McCarthy had to go too. Even Humphrey, who had chosen to wait out the primaries, told the state Democratic chairman to gather a slate and announce that he was doing it in Humphrey's name. All of which left George McGovern squarely in the middle. While privately he could lend Kennedy limited assistance (such as his treasured mailing list), publicly he assumed the appearance of a scrupulous neutral. McCarthy did his best to make it difficult. One day McGovern happened to read in the newspapers that McCarthy was planning a trip to South Dakota. Despite his annoyance that McCarthy had not at least called to inform him, Mc-

Govern contacted McCarthy and offered to introduce him during his appearances in the state. McCarthy agreed. McGovern was about to get on a plane for South Dakota when by chance he discovered that McCarthy had decided to cancel his trip. Mc-Carthy, typically, had not bothered to warn him. McGovern was livid. Still, when McCarthy finally did make his way to the state, McGovern was at his side to make a sufficiently fulsome, if artificially enthusiastic introduction. McGovern performed the same chore for Humphrey, though this time with genuine affection; he even agreed to jog with Humphrey for a picture for *Life* magazine. When Kennedy flew into Sioux Falls on April 16th, however, McGovern let out all the stops. If elected, McGovern predicted, Kennedy would become "one of the three or four great Presidents in our national history," greater even than his brother John. "I have heard all the talk about his ruthlessness and his long hair," McGovern declared. "But he isn't as ruthless as the great Theodore Roosevelt, and his hair isn't half as long as Thomas Jefferson's, and unlike Abraham Lincoln he has no beard at all. What he does have is the absolute personal honesty of Woodrow Wilson, the stirring passion for leadership of Andrew Jackson, and the profound acquaintance with personal tragedy of Lincoln."

Kennedy responded in kind. To an overflow crowd at the Corn Palace in Mitchell, he proclaimed: "There is no one I feel more genuinely about, whether we are in politics together or not—about the importance of their contribution and the importance of their understanding and feeling than George McGovern. Of all my colleagues in the United States Senate, the person who has the most feeling and does things in the most genuine way, without affecting his life, is George McGovern. He is so highly admired by all his colleagues, not just for his ability but because of the kind of man he is. That is truer of him than of any man in the United States Senate."

Kennedy returned to South Dakota once more, to speak at the Corn Palace on May 10. It was not one of his better performances. Plainly fatigued from the recently completed primary in neighboring Nebraska, Kennedy stumbled through his prepared text. He was so tired that without realizing it he repeated his trademark quotation from George Bernard Shaw three times. That night, Kennedy slept in the Lawler Hotel. The next morning, refreshed and full of life, he took a run with his dog Freckles, then joined McGovern for breakfast. "Do you really think it is impossible?" Kennedy asked earnestly. "No," McGovern answered, "I don't think it's impossible. I just think you're willing to try something that's awfully hard. It's worth making the effort —whether you win or lose." "Well," said Kennedy, "that's what I think." But there was a note in Kennedy's voice that signaled he was less than totally convinced. At that moment he seemed very low, uncertain and worried about South Dakota, California, and what lay ahead. McGovern went to the airport to see him off. As Kennedy walked toward the light plane that was to take him to Brookings, McGovern suddenly felt a chill. He said later: "I remember that morning being seized with a feeling of sadness. For some reason he looked so small. Bob, at various times, appeared different sizes to me. Sometimes he looked like a large man . . . I mean physically. At other times he seemed very slight, small. But as he walked away, he looked frail, and stooped and tired. And he seemed just kind of wistful about the whole thing. I just had such a feeling of sadness as he got on the plane that day, and a kind of a feeling that he was a lonely figure." McGovern never saw his friend again.

Kennedy needn't have worried about South Dakota. On June 5 South Dakotans gave him the biggest victory of his campaign. In some Indian precincts Kennedy literally got 100 percent of the vote. The farmers went for him too, despite the fact that he had summed up his acquaintance with agriculture in one line: "New York is first in the production of sour cherries!" In the end the tally read Kennedy 49 percent, McCarthy 20 percent, Humphrey 30 percent. When the shape of the vote was apparent, McGovern called Teddy Kennedy in San Francisco, where he was overseeing his brother's northern California primary campaign. McGovern explained that he wanted to relay the results, but he didn't want to disturb Bob in Los Angeles, because he knew he would be busy that night watching the returns come in from the Golden State. "No," Teddy assured McGovern, "give him a call. He'd love to talk to you." So McGovern did, and the two men talked together a few moments. Finally, Kennedy had to break away. The television cameras were ready, and there was a crowd waiting in the Ambassador Hotel ballroom, chanting to hear his victory speech. They said good-by, and McGovern went to bed.

George and Eleanor rode the funeral train back from New York. The last seventy-two hours had been the most emotionally upsetting McGovern had ever known, and at that moment he wanted more than anything else simply to be alone. For a long while he and Eleanor sat on opposite sides of the car, staring out the windows at the people who lined the right of way to pay their last respects. There was a tap on his shoulder, and McGovern turned around in irritation. It was Bill Dougherty. "I'm sorry to bother you, especially at a time like this," Dougherty began, "but we gotta start thinking about what is going to happen from here." McGovern shrugged in resignation while Dougherty laid out his idea. With Bobby dead, someone was needed to hold his delegates together. McCarthy was out of the question. While Humphrey was more acceptable personally, ideological reasons ruled him out. "And that," Dougherty concluded, "leaves you." McGovern was more irritated now; talking politics on a train bearing Bobby's coffin seemed somehow sacrilegious. Besides, what Dougherty was saying didn't make sense. If anyone was to take up the Kennedy mantle, Ted—not he—should. And there was one other reason: McGovern just didn't want to do it. "No," he said firmly, "no, no."

But Dougherty was not about to be put off so easily, nor was Jesse Unruh, the leader of the California delegation, who had the same idea. There were others who pressed the proposal on him, both that afternoon on the train and in the days that immediately followed. Adam Walinsky called on him, and so did Frank Mankiewicz, Bobby Kennedy's press secretary, as well as Joe Dolan, the Senator's administrative assistant. Mankiewicz and Dolan were especially insistent. Still McGovern resisted.

Then, several weeks after the assassination, McGovern spotted McCarthy on the Senate floor and went over to talk to him. A report had been circulating that McCarthy was intending to depart shortly for Hanoi and a face-to-face meeting with North

Vietnamese leaders. If the report was true, McGovern wanted to talk him out of it. "Gene," he said, "in the present climate, if you were to go over there to Hanoi as a presidential candidate, I think it would just kill you. I think that if anything goes wrong, they [the Johnson administration] will blame it on you. These guys will stop at nothing." McCarthy shrugged. "It really doesn't make any difference," he said, "because the nomination is all over now. Hubert's got it. I'm going to go through with the deal because I don't want to let my supporters down, but it's all over with." McGovern was flabbergasted. He was also furious that any man could so cynically play with the idealistic allegiance of a whole generation of young Americans. The truth of what Bobby had always said about McCarthy now became starkly evident. McGovern turned on his heel and walked back to his office, more sad and confused than ever.*

Through June and into July a quiet momentum built behind the idea of a McGovern candidacy. McGovern himself had reached the point where he could joke about it with his staff, who as usual were none too amused with anything they regarded as jeopardizing his chances for reelection to the Senate. Back in South Dakota, though, the irrepressible Dougherty had other ideas. His first one was to organize an RFK memorial dinner in Huron on July 13. The dinner would not only bring together the Kennedy delegation and all the leading Democrats in the state —with the notable exception of McGovern, who would con-

---

* McGovern and McCarthy have one of the strangest relationships in American politics. Though they have known each other for some time, having first become acquainted when they were both members of the House, they have never been personally close. They were at least cordial, however, until McGovern announced for the presidency, a move that McCarthy regarded as a personal affront. Their friendship has never been the same since. "Talking to McGovern," says McCarthy in one of his famous waspish epigrams, "is like eating a Chinese dinner. You're still hungry when you're finished with both." McGovern has never been able to match McCarthy's wit or his clever cuts. He no longer particularly likes McCarthy, regarding him as something of a spoiled brat. But there remains a certain amount of envy for the man. "You know," he said to one of his staffers after the election, "whatever you say about the way McCarthy ran, they never laid a glove on the son of a bitch."

veniently be in Uppsala, Sweden, as a guest of the annual conference of the World Council of Churches—it would also provide
the natural focal point for Kennedy leaders to organize a Mc-
Govern candidacy.

The plan came off exactly as Dougherty expected. There on
the dais on July 13 sat no less than Ted Sorensen, Jesse Unruh,
Pat Lucey of Wisconsin, and Kennedy wordsmith Dick Goodwin. When a reporter asked Dougherty what was going on, he
played dumb. "I'm just a country boy with hayseeds in my hair,"
Dougherty said, shaking his head as if to prove it. "But it seems to
me it must be important or all you big-time reporters wouldn't
have come all this way." It was, all right. That night after dinner
Sorensen met with the Kennedy delegation and extracted a promise that they would remain united and uncommitted—to anyone
but McGovern, should he decide to run—until the convention
balloting. It was not an easy pledge to get; both the McCarthy
and Humphrey camps were pressing hard for the South Dakotans
to come their way. But with invocations of the memory of RFK,
Sorensen got their word. Now only one thing remained: to convince McGovern.

McGovern was fast heading in that direction already. He
moved even faster after a trip to Los Angeles late in July to
speak to a group of young Kennedy volunteers, who after the
assassination had organized themselves into a loosely political
group called the Kennedy Action Corps. Though McGovern did
not know it, the meeting of the volunteers had been specifically
organized to persuade him to run for President. But instead of
politics McGovern talked of Kennedy's work and what they all
must do to further it, especially ending the war. "Let us clearly
understand," he said, "I do not speak for Robert Kennedy, as
none of us can; as I am not even the man I would have been had
he lived, because all of us were enriched and ennobled by the
grace of his presence. But perhaps from the meaning of his life
we can take a new measure of conviction, a new courage, a new
resolve that he shall not have died in vain; and that in our calm
and implacable determination we can yet serve the end he so
tenderly sought for us all—'to tame the savageness of man, and

make gentle the life of the world.' " To McGovern's surprise, the
words brought the Kennedy workers to their feet, shouting "We
want McGovern, we want McGovern."

They could not have him, not just then. For shortly before
McGovern made his speech, word had come from South Dakota
that his second-youngest daughter, Terry, had been arrested near
Rapid City on a charge of possession of marijuana. He had to
hurry home as soon as possible. Terry, a pretty girl of nineteen,
with long, straight blonde hair, held a special place in her father's
heart. He had shared a thousand gay and kidding moments with
her. But in her late teens, she had begun to withdraw from her
parents. Late in July, she had gone with eight of her friends to
Rapid City to canvass for her father's reelection campaign. They
were out finishing the last few precincts when the manager of
their motel discovered marijuana in Terry's belongings while
cleaning her room. The woman, who happened to be a Republican, knew marijuana when she saw it and also knew that the
McGovern girl registered in her motel was the daughter of the
state's Democratic Senator. She did what all her instincts told her:
called the cops. Terry spent the night in the Rapid City jail before Archie Bangs, the family lawyer, was able to get her out.
But her prospects didn't look bright. A few weeks before, the
South Dakota legislature had passed a tough new marijuana law
calling for a prison term of not less than five years for the first
offense. Even if Terry were fortunate enough to get off with a
light or suspended sentence, her father's political chances would
hardly be enhanced. (Indeed, there were suspicions among a
number of the state's Democrats that the arrest was politically
inspired, especially after an assistant state's attorney, a Republican,
reportedly boasted that he had had his "eye on that girl for
months.") Luckily, a quirk of the law saved Terry. On the day
of her arrest the regular judge was out of town. An interim
judge, whose authority expired at five in the afternoon, signed
the arrest warrant two hours and twenty-eight minutes too late,
thus making the arrest technically invalid. Before Terry came up
for trial, her case was thrown out of court on grounds of "in-
admissible evidence." As for its political impact, after some

clucking of tongues, both the publicity and the clamor died down, and if anything something of a sympathy vote resulted. The Republicans, perhaps fearing just such an occurrence, never mentioned the arrest publicly.

The resolution of political and legal difficulties, however, did not solve Terry's very real personal difficulties. McGovern, feeling a bit guilty that he had not spent as much time with his family as he might have, decided that the best thing for all of them would be to get away for a few days. They chose Hisega, a resort hidden away in the Black Hills, close to Mount Rushmore and about as remote from the politics of Washington as any spot in the country. Only the closest members of McGovern's staff knew where he had gone. He didn't want to be bothered with interruptions from politicians. He wanted time with his family, and time to think.

The moment of decision, McGovern knew, was approaching. He had stalled for as long as he could, hoping that Ted Kennedy would climb into the breach. Teddy, however, was not about to budge. That, at least, was the opinion of his brother-in-law, Steve Smith, who seemed to know the surviving Kennedy brother's mind best. McGovern had called Smith a few days before and asked directly: "Do you think he's going to go?" "No, I don't," Smith had answered. "Do you think I should?" McGovern said. Smith had been far less definite on that one. "Well," he said hesitatingly, "I'm not sure. I think I would stop short at the favorite-son role. But I'm not at all sure, if I were you, whether I would press beyond that." Of course, Smith hastened to add, that was merely his personal opinion; he was not speaking for the Kennedys.

So from the Kennedy family there had been no discouragement, but then no encouragement either. The situation had been almost the same during a supposedly secret meeting that McGovern had had on August 4 with a number of important liberal Democrats, including Jack Gilligan of Ohio, Claiborne Pell of Rhode Island, Harold Hughes of Iowa, Jesse Unruh of California, Philip Hoff of Vermont, and Pat Lucey of Wisconsin. The gathering, held at the O'Hare Inn in Chicago, was organized by Dough-

erty and Don O'Brien, who had run the Nebraska primary for
Kennedy, and co-hosted by Hughes and McGovern. It was supposed to be an informal talk session about how to unite the Kennedy and McCarthy anti-war delegates. Its other purpose, at least
as Dougherty and McGovern saw it, was to drum up support for
a McGovern candidacy. None, however, was forthcoming.
Hughes said frankly: "I love you, George, but you can't do anything for me." By the end of the meeting the participants had
decided only, as Dougherty puts it, "that if Humphrey got the
nomination we would all go down the tubes." To forestall that
possibility, they were prepared to do only one thing: form a
Committee for an Open Convention, of which McGovern was
elected chairman. They were not ready to commit themselves
further than that, to George McGovern or any man. Once again
there had been no discouragement, but no encouragement either.
The choice was squarely up to McGovern.

By the time he arrived at Hisega, McGovern had all but made
up his mind to run. Terry's problems had given him momentary
pause, but finally he had decided that even that was one more
reason for running. "If the country is so mixed up that even our
daughter is playing with drugs," he told Eleanor, "maybe I ought
to do it." What he needed was a final shove to push him over
the edge. He got it from an unexpected quarter during a dinner
with Karl Burgess, a wealthy Republican friend. McGovern
shared his thoughts with Burgess, then asked him, as he had asked
so many others: "What would you do?" "I'll give you a concrete
answer," said Burgess, pulling out his checkbook and writing out
a check to "McGovern for President" in the sum of $5,000. "If
you run, you can cash that check. If you don't, give it back to
me." McGovern took the check.

McGovern went back to his cabin and started making the
necessary calls to prepare the announcement. When his administrative assistant Owen Donley received the instructions to call a
Saturday news conference, he gasped. "Are you sure you are
calling me from Hisega? Or by any chance are you calling from
Mount Rushmore?" McCarthy took the news almost without
comment. He did not dispute the contention that McGovern's

candidacy, rather than taking votes away from him, would in fact hold those Kennedy voters who were on the verge of bolting to Humphrey. Privately, though, McCarthy was incensed. As he saw it, McGovern was merely playing the pawn for the Kennedys, who meant to deny him the nomination no matter what it meant—to the party, to the war, or to the country.

McGovern had considered the risks. Undoubtedly the odds were long, almost but not quite, he thought, impossible. Dave Harrison, the astute Kennedy political operative in Massachusetts, had assured him of a rock-bottom base of 225 delegates. That left 1,025 to go for the nomination, and most if not all of those, McGovern knew, Humphrey had already locked up. Nor could he count on all the Kennedy delegates automatically transferring their allegiance. Jesse Unruh had been skittish about committing himself. He faced a tough Governor's race in 1970, and if he were to have even a ghost of a chance he needed the state's large McCarthy faction behind him. Already he was having trouble holding his own delegation together. Since the assassination, thirty-two of the delegates had resigned rather than face the choice of voting for McCarthy or Humphrey. Without all of California behind McGovern, the going would be rough. An endorsement from the Kennedy family would certainly help, but that too could not be counted on. Had he approached McCarthy earlier and talked to him longer, McGovern felt, he might have persuaded him to withdraw in his favor. Now that possibility, however remote, was gone too. Al Lowenstein, who was among the first to be informed of his decision, was not optimistic. All McGovern could do, he told him, was hold the convention long enough for Teddy to enter. He should get any notions of winning out of his mind. Frank Mankiewicz, who had agreed to come on as press secretary after McGovern publicly announced that he would run, was cold-bloodedly realistic. Their only chance, he felt—and it was an exceedingly slim one at that—was to provoke Humphrey into committing a fatal gaffe, namely, disowning the Johnson war policy. Unlikely as that was, Mankiewicz thought that if it happened the ego of Lyndon Johnson would be so wounded that he would "pull the rug out from under Hubert" and turn the uncommitted Southern favorite sons to a candidate more of his liking, say, Governor John Connally of Texas. Whatever the scenario—waiting for Teddy or waiting for Hubert—it all seemed as fruitful as waiting for Godot. But McGovern thought it was worth a try, if for no other reason than one: he wanted to be President.

On the morning of Saturday, August 10—a bare sixteen days before the Democratic National Convention was to convene in Chicago—standing in the Senate caucus room, where a few months before Robert Kennedy had thrown down his challenge to the President, and surrounded by his family, his friends, and the nation's press, George McGovern, forty-six, announced his intention of becoming President of the United States:

> I wear no claim to the Kennedy mantle, but I believe deeply in the twin goals for which Robert Kennedy gave his life—an end to the war in Vietnam and a passionate commitment to heal the divisions in our own society. . . . If I have any special asset for national leadership, it is, I believe, a sense of history—an understanding of the forces that have brought this country to a position of power and influence in the world and an appreciation of what is important in our own time. For five years I have warned against our deepening involvement in Vietnam— the most disastrous political and military blunder in our national experience. That war must be ended now—not next year or the year following, but now. . . . Beyond this, we need to harness the full spiritual and political resources of this nation to put an end to the shameful remnants of racism and poverty that still afflict our land. Just as brotherhood is the condition of survival in a nuclear world, so it is the condition of peace in America. . . . It is for these purposes that I declare myself a candidate for the presidential nomination.

And so it began, without much hope or resources or even a clear understanding of how a largely unknown Senator from South Dakota went about becoming President of the United States. But there was grit—and there were also the Kennedys.

They began arriving within hours of the announcement, the people to whom the fact that McGovern had been a friend of Bobby's was enough. Frank Mankiewicz, who had taken over press chores, was soon joined by Pierre Salinger—which left McGovern's nominal press secretary, George Cunningham, somewhat stunned. "I feel like a Baptist preacher working with Jesus Christ and John the Baptist," he mumbled dazedly. A bank of eight phones was installed in McGovern's Senate office, and a cadre of Kennedy political operatives began making calls to old political friends all over the United States, cajoling them to sit tight until the convention. In Chicago Bill Dougherty and Don O'Brien set up a national campaign headquarters in one room of the Sheraton-Blackstone Hotel, the first installment of an organization that would eventually occupy forty-two more rooms, plus the Blackstone's grand ballroom. Dave Harrison came in from Massachusetts to oversee the vote-counting operation and announced that their first task would be to telephone every one of the 2,500 delegates in the country. In Harrison's wake came scores of lesser volunteers. The first to walk through the door was a pretty girl with short blonde hair from Bobby's "boiler room" operation named Mary Jo Kopechne. The beautiful people also enlisted. Gloria Steinem phoned McGovern, asked what she could do, and was told in two words: "Bring money." A few days later she arrived in Chicago with $17,000 in her purse.

Meanwhile, McGovern tried to put together the semblance of a campaign. It was not easy. He chartered a prop-jet Electra from American Airlines, figuring that it could take him into smaller fields than the larger pure jets on which the other candidates were blitzing the country. But for all the good he accomplished during his public appearances, McGovern might just as well have stayed at home. In Kearney, Nebraska, where he went to deliver what was billed as a major address on farm policy, a desultory crowd of 250 looked down on him from the nearly deserted grandstands. "I looked up at the grandstands, and I had to look again," says Cunningham. "I couldn't believe there were so few people there. I think you could have gotten that many people out to see a champion hog caller as anybody. They just didn't care. We had fifty press people with us, and I remember how afraid we were that they would turn their cameras around and pan on the empty stands. My God, it was terrible."

More trouble lay ahead. In Valparaiso, Indiana, a convention of college newspaper editors, many of them radical, listened to McGovern for the better part of an hour and left unimpressed. A speech on urban problems before the National Press Club in Washington seemed to bore more reporters than it inspired. A well-researched address on foreign policy delivered to the Cleveland Club was similarly received. For a fleeting moment McGovern seemed to have a chance to pick up significant black support, enough perhaps to influence the Washington, D.C., delegate the Reverend Channing Phillips or the Mississippi Loyalist delegation. A meeting on the second day of the campaign in Brooklyn's Bedford-Stuyvesant section had gone well; if it could be repeated, it might be possible to get some momentum going. But on Saturday morning of the preconvention weekend, before 4,000 people at a weekly meeting of the Reverend Jesse Jackson's Operation Breadbasket on Chicago's South Side, all hope went aglimmering. Jackson, showing the honky who was boss, kept McGovern waiting nearly two hours in the ninety-degree-plus heat of the massive Tabernacle Baptist Church. When McGovern was finally asked to speak, he did so without passion for a total of five minutes—to a revivalist audience that was expecting hours of hellfire and brimstone.

A major part of the problem was sheer time; the McGovern campaign simply did not have enough of it to lay on the kind of advance work that was the hallmark of a Kennedy blitz. Instead, McGovern's staff relied on word of mouth or hurried telephone calls to plan when and where the candidate should go. With new people shuttling into the campaign every day, announcing they knew so and so and had been told to do this and that, it was impossible to focus McGovern's efforts organizationally. The South Dakotans resented the outsiders, and the outsiders were contemptuous of the South Dakotans. In the process the fact that both groups were working to elect the same man President sometimes got lost. To complicate matters Washington lawyer Ed McDermott, nominally McGovern's campaign director, announced after the first week that he was leaving to see a client in Mexico City. McDermott's departure, while meaning little in the practical sense, was indicative of the larger problem. "I don't think anyone was ever in charge," says Cunningham. "There were just a lot of people running around. It was like grabbing ahold of Jello in a bowl. You'd squeeze it and it would just squish between your fingers." McGovern and his staff joked with each other to maintain their spirits. "Here comes the ruthless McGovern machine," Cunningham bellowed through the campaign plane. To which McGovern would respond: "By announcing when we did, we have at least eliminated the possibility of peaking early."

Somehow McGovern had to position himself between McCarthy and Humphrey without seeming to toady to either one of them. Except on the war: there McGovern was to the left of everyone, even many of his own supporters. For the rest of the issues he had to maintain a delicate balance. On the cities and race he adopted Humphrey's old-fashioned liberalism, with a measure of Bobby's personal passion and concern. On the issue of Humphrey himself—namely, whether he would support him if the Vice President became the nominee—McGovern faced a more difficult quandary. In the first place, McGovern had a lasting and deep affection for his old neighbor and friend, Humphrey. In the second, he had to retain his acceptability to potential Humphrey crossovers as the more "regular" of the candidates on the left. This, however, placed him in direct opposition to many of the Kennedy and McCarthy men, for whom the unacceptability of the Vice President under any conditions was fast becoming one of the most emotional issues of the convention.

Torn and seemingly afraid to offend either side, McGovern at first waffled. The day he declared his candidacy he also announced his intention of supporting the party nominee, whoever he might be. Ten days later McGovern told reporters that he was no longer sure he could support Humphrey if he didn't change his views on the war. McGovern was stung by Humphrey's claims that the Humphrey and Kennedy views on the war were identical. McGovern was also angered by Humphrey's opposition to including a specific plank in the party platform outlining a way out of Vietnam, as well as his refusal to include in the document an admission of past error. "To correct error," McGovern said, "it is first necessary to admit it—to admit it frankly, without recrimination, but with a quiet determination to put an end to it." Two days later McGovern altered his position once again, for an apparently final time. He would now support Humphrey against Nixon. But, he added, if Humphrey didn't make some move to get himself from under Johnson's Vietnam shadow, he would do so "completely unenthusiastically." "I might not even mention him in my campaign," he warned.

By the time the campaign encamped in Chicago, McGovern knew that he was in a losing effort. Humphrey, he admitted, could not be stopped. Still, he had committed himself and the energy of others, and he was bound to go through with it, even the distasteful ritual of seeking out the favor of Mayor Richard J. Daley. "There is something almost obscene," he confided to a reporter before going into the Saturday morning meeting, "about presidential candidates going hat in hand to one man to ask what a hundred delegates are going to do." But McGovern went along. With him were Connecticut Senator Abraham Ribicoff, who had agreed to nominate him, and Dick Wade, a history professor at the University of Chicago with close ties to both the Kennedys and Daley. A few minutes past noon they were ushered into the Mayor's presence. Ribicoff started talking at once, assuring Daley that he would be the one to elect the next President of the United States, telling him what a wonderful city he had, and complimenting him on what a great Mayor he was. Daley listened impassively. When McGovern finally spoke, he laid out what he had to say simply and directly: how he would make a good candidate, what he could do for the rest of the ticket, and finally why he would make the best President of the United States. McGovern talked for ten minutes, and then he and his party got up to leave. As they were going out the door, Daley pulled Wade aside and told him that the Illinois delegation, breaking convention tradition, would wait until Wednesday before making its decision. When Mankiewicz got the news, he exulted: "We just got ourselves a three-day hunting license."

But was there game for the taking? Not in the Pennsylvania

delegation certainly, where the union bosses and party wheel-horses were solidly locked up for Humphrey. Joe Clark, the most notable exception, brought only his vote to McGovern. William Clark, another McGovern endorser, whom Daley had selected as the sacrificial lamb before the electoral altar of Everett Dirksen, was one of the few chips off the Illinois block. Even Ribicoff came to McGovern as a way out of the tough conflict between the regulars and the McCarthyites in Connecticut. Ribicoff, Clark, and the rest of the endorsers were bringing themselves, adding marginal prestige but delivering nothing. Here and there bright spots flickered, then almost as quickly died. McGovern's appearance before the Mississippi Loyalist group had delegate Fannie Lou Hamer on her feet clapping the whole time. But when the moment came for the roll call, only four Mississippi delegates announced themselves for McGovern. It was a dispiriting process. Everywhere McGovern turned Humphrey had been ahead of him. Many of the delegates, he discovered, had been committed to Johnson-Humphrey as long as two years before the convention. Others told him that they would vote for him, if only they weren't bound by the unit rule. The allegedly uncommitted favorite sons of the South turned out only to be waiting for a call from Humphrey. And now he had made it. Obviously, McGovern was going nowhere fast. Nowhere, that is, until California.

The huge 174-member California delegation—second only in size to New York's—was crucial to McGovern's hopes. Without all or nearly all of it, he could forget about being a serious contender. Indeed, without California he might even have to start worrying about looking foolish. Humphrey didn't need California; moreover, he couldn't get it. Within this the most liberal of the delegations his supporters numbered precisely two: Eugene Wyman, the Democratic national committeeman, and San Francisco Mayor Joseph Alioto, both of whom had been admitted to the delegation only as a token of the personal largesse of Jesse Unruh. McCarthy, on the other hand, had considerable strength within the delegation and assuredly could have gained more had he worked for it. But would he? McCarthy would, at least to the extent of appearing in a nationally televised "debate" with the other two candidates at a Tuesday morning caucus of the delegation in the LaSalle Hotel.

It was the showdown everyone had been waiting for, the only time in the long campaign that the three protagonists would face each other head to head. The room was jammed. All the networks were there. The delegates leaned forward expectantly, hoping for, however, they would be disappointed. McCarthy waiting for the candidates to speak. If it was a debate they were wasn't going to go along. Instead, he treated them to an exposition of his private character at its most haughty and vain. McCarthy's target was McGovern. Though he plainly no longer coveted the nomination for himself, McCarthy had been piqued by the sudden appearance of the upstart South Dakotan, who dared to challenge him for the allegiance of the antiwar liberals. McCarthy's mood had not been improved by McGovern's remarks of recent days, which seemed almost calculated to present the greatest offense. When asked how his candidacy differed from McCarthy's, McGovern had replied: "Well, Gene doesn't really want to be President and I do." After McCarthy had dismissed the Soviet invasion of Czechoslovakia as "not a major world crisis," McGovern had joined the chorus denouncing McCarthy's "lack of compassion." McCarthy, McGovern told reporters, "lacked a sense of moral outrage."

Now it was McCarthy's turn to settle accounts. "Well," he began, "I think a little passivity in that office is all right, a kind of balance, I think. I have never quite known what active compassion is. Actually, compassion in my mind is to suffer *with* someone, not in advance of him. Or not in public necessarily." When a questioner pressed McCarthy for his position on the war, McCarthy replied coldly: "The people know where I stand on that."

If McCarthy was contemptuous, Humphrey seemed almost blithely indifferent. To this the most dovish of delegations he presented a standard defense of the Johnson line. Democracy was on trial in Southeast Asia, and by all accounts it appeared to be winning. Why, Humphrey boasted, "when you look over the world scene, those elections [in Saigon] stand up pretty well. The government today is a broad-based government." The reason there wasn't peace, Humphrey went on, sinking deeper into the rhetorical quagmire, was the "road block" in Hanoi. The United States, he insisted, had intervened in Vietnam only to "resist aggression." Then, to boos and hisses from the audience, Humphrey proclaimed: "I did not come here to repudiate the President of the United States. I want to make that quite clear."

Humphrey's performance, however brave, was a setup for McGovern. And like a batter drawing a bead on a big fat softball, McGovern stood up and knocked it out of the park. On the Vietnamese elections of which Humphrey had spoken so glowingly, McGovern said it was only too bad that the man who happened to come in second was quickly sentenced to five years at hard labor for advocating precisely what he and McCarthy were calling for: a negotiated end to the war. McGovern continued to bore in on the war, then switched his attack to the citadel of Johnsonian power itself, the state of Texas, where, McGovern noted, the percentage of blacks serving in Vietnam was much higher than the percentage of blacks serving on the delegation to the Democratic convention. Where Humphrey had defended the compromise Georgia delegation, McGovern supported the rebel leadership of Julian Bond. "Bond is being attacked not because of his position on Vietnam," McGovern declared. "Why should that have anything to do with it? Make no mistake about it. He is being attacked because of a decision he had nothing to do with. The fact that he was born with a black skin."

The Californians loved it, and their cheers only inspired McGovern more. He was in his element now, joking and jostling, serious at the right times, gay at others. About things—the war, racism and poverty—he could be tough. About people—notably Hubert Humphrey, whom he lauded for his service to "human and civil justice"—he could be magnanimous. The contrast with McCarthy could not have been more explicit. McGovern carried the day. As he walked from the room, the applause still ringing in his ears, a reporter asked him how he thought Humphrey had done. "He came in fourth," McGovern grinned. McCarthy was not so amused. As the limousine carried him back to his hotel, he sank into his seat and muttered only one word: "Demagogue."

But winning a debate, however satisfying that might be, was not winning a convention, or for that matter even a delegation. After the California caucus, McGovern, assuming the rule of winner take all, dramatically revised his predictions of first-ballot votes upward. Where he had been saying 150 to 200, he now talked to reporters of a 300-vote minimum. McGovern presumed that because the Californians had clapped for him they would also vote for him. What he failed to realize was that Unruh, no matter what he personally felt about McGovern, had political obligations to fulfill. That meant reserving a certain percentage of the votes—the largest portion as it turned out—for McCarthy.

No one could predict—until it was too late—the sudden emergence of District of Columbia delegate Channing Phillips as a black-protest candidate, or that he would garner 67½ votes, nearly all of which would have otherwise gone to McGovern. Phillips' candidacy bothered McGovern, not only because it took away votes that would have been his—dipping him dangerously close to the 150 mark, below which he did not want to go—but more important, because it further blurred the possibility of a clear test on the peace issue. The McCarthy-McGovern minority plank on the war—which itself was more of a compromise than McGovern would have liked—had already been ruled unacceptable by the Johnson regulars, who were in indisputable control of the convention. With the peace plank dead, McGovern hoped that the final convention vote would serve as a symbolic referendum on the war. McGovern briefly toyed with the idea of asking Phillips to withdraw. In the end, though, he decided that if blacks felt so strongly about a token candidate they should have him. Besides, by midweek there was more to worry about— namely, Ted Kennedy.

The short-lived boomlet for Teddy Kennedy hit hardest in the McGovern camp, where some volunteers began sporting "Kennedy for President" pins right next to their "McGovern for President" buttons. Signs appeared in McGovern's headquarters urging Kennedy's nomination. By Tuesday night, at the peak of the Kennedy speculation, there were so many Kennedy signs that a visitor to the Blackstone wondered whose campaign this was, Kennedy's or McGovern's. The South Dakotans, all but shut out of the campaign since coming to Chicago, were particularly disheartened. "They're all Kennedy people wearing McGovern masks," said one aide. "When the time comes, they'll change faces." Owen Donley was so upset by all the talk wafting up and down the corridors of the Blackstone that he accosted Pierre Salinger, who was clad only in "his red silk bathrobe and his big black cigar," pinned him against a wall, and stuck his finger in his stomach. "Look, you son of a bitch," Donley exploded. "Everybody's talking about what Teddy is going to do. If anyone has got a right to know what your guy is going to do, George McGovern does." Salinger could only agree. "I'll have an answer for him by ten tomorrow morning," he promised, and headed for the telephone.

McGovern kept telling reporters that "Ted won't get into it." Still, he could hardly have missed hearing all the speculation to the contrary. By Wednesday morning McGovern was growing increasingly curious, to say the least. His curiosity was finally satisfied by a telephone call that reached him at 8:30 A.M., as he prepared to meet with a group in the Chicago Club. It was Kennedy on the line, assuring him he would not be a candidate for anything under any circumstances. By that afternoon all the McGovern volunteers had returned to wearing only one button.

With Kennedy's candidacy and lesser concerns out of the way, it was time to sit back and watch the main event. But where did one look—to the convention floor or to the streets? All day and night Wednesday McGovern tried to do both. From his fourth-floor suite in the Blackstone he looked down on the chaos below, as the Chicago police proceeded to systematically brutalize anyone who didn't meet their standards. One of the victims was a McGovern worker, who had volunteered to carry a Telex message across the street to the Hilton. She had barely stepped off the curb when a cop hit her across the face with a truncheon, breaking her jaw and knocking out her front teeth. McGovern himself watched as several police knocked Mobilization organizer

Sidney Peck to the ground, then dragged him by his heels through the street, viciously bouncing his body on the concrete.

Friends of McGovern had never seen him more angry. "Those sons of bitches," he kept cursing. "Do you see what those sons of bitches are doing to those kids down there? Those bastards." * Every new visitor to McGovern's suite had to watch while he went through a reenactment of the beatings he had witnessed on the streets below. "This one guy," he said, demonstrating by throwing his own body into it, "took this kid and knocked him down for no reason. He kept hitting him with his club like this and like this." Gloria Steinem made her way into McGovern's presence and begged him to go into the streets. "Those are your people," she beseeched him. "You've got to go down there and do something." Theodore White was just as emphatic that he do nothing. "Don't go down there," he warned. "There are ten people who are causing the trouble. They're all Communists from New York." Once again McGovern was torn. The kids who were being beaten really weren't his followers, or for that matter McCarthy's either. Still, the violence revolted him. If there were something he could have done, he might have tried it. But in the face of a catastrophe so large he felt powerless. Meanwhile, his aides were bustling in and out, trying to scotch any thought that he might have about going into the streets. Donley, who had already reduced Gloria Steinem to tears, told McGovern bluntly: "None of those people down there are going to vote for you in South Dakota." McGovern paced back and forth, agonizing over what to do. Finally, he came away from the window, poured a

---

* McGovern was still boiling when he met with the press on Thursday morning. Of the Chicago police, McGovern said:

> Let me say it has been the first time that I have been in a position where I could clearly see with my own eyes beyond a shadow of a doubt a naked example of what I would call police brutality. . . . When young people or old people or people of any age assemble to peacefully protest policies over which they have no voice, it seems to me that it is well within the American constitutional system. I don't come here to encourage lawlessness, but I do remind you that this country began with the Boston Tea Party, and I think what happened out on Michigan Avenue was a case of police power getting out of hand. Police for a period of time were literally going berserk.

drink, lit a cigar, and sat down in front of a television to watch the larger disaster taking place on the floor of the amphitheater.

One of the things he watched with special attention was the nominating speech of Abe Ribicoff. Ribicoff started off with all the predictable clichés—"George McGovern, an extraordinary man for such extraordinary responsibility." Then, midway through his text, Ribicoff took the advice Mankiewicz had given him as they sat together waiting to address the convention in a small room behind the podium. Ribicoff, a liberal up for reelection, had been troubled. "What should I say, Frank?" "I'd throw away that speech and say something about what is going on in the streets," Mankiewicz had answered. So now Ribicoff did. "With George McGovern," he declared, "we wouldn't have Gestapo tactics in the streets of Chicago." For a moment there was stunned silence. Then the great hall filled with a roar. Daley cupped his hands around his mouth to shout what appeared to be "Fuck you, fuck you," over and over again. Ribicoff gazed down at the man he had a few days before tried to appease and said patronizingly: "How hard it is to accept the truth. How hard it is."

How hard it was. A few hours later, in the early morning moments of Thursday, the delegates cast their ballots. McGovern's pessimism had been well founded. The totals read: Humphrey 1,760¼, McCarthy 601, McGovern 146½, Channing Phillips 67½, Governor Dan Moore of North Carolina (the only favorite son not to break for Humphrey) 17½, Edward Kennedy 12¾, abstentions and others 16½. In his hotel room McGovern drew on a final cigar and went to bed.

Early the next morning there was a call from Hubert Humphrey, requesting that McGovern meet him at five o'clock that afternoon. McGovern, fearing the worst, called Frank Mankiewicz. "Look," he said. "Hubert's just called me and wants to see me this afternoon. I think he might want me to be on the ticket. I want you to go with me in case I have to say no." With McGovern's stand on the war, a vice presidential offer seemed doubtful. In any case, McGovern was determined to reject it if it came along. There was no doubt in his own mind that Humphrey was coming out of the convention a loser. He would far rather be a Senator than a defeated candidate for the vice presidency; for that matter, he would rather be a Senator than the Vice President period. As it developed, McGovern had nothing to worry about. If there had been something on Humphrey's mind, it was gone by 5 P.M. McGovern and Mankiewicz passed several awkward minutes of conversation with Humphrey, whose legendary gift of gab seemed for once to have failed him. Finally, Humphrey said: "What do you think I ought to say tonight?" Mankiewicz had an answer: "You should say something about the violence and security in the convention hall." Humphrey beamed. "Can you put that on paper?" Mankiewicz said he could and retired to a typewriter in another room to pound out a three-page statement. "Here," said Mankiewicz, when he had finished. "You can just put this right ahead of your prepared text." "That's just fine, Frank, that's just fine," said Humphrey. "I'll do just that." Naturally, he didn't.

Only the final rituals now separated McGovern from South Dakota. Humphrey's people wanted him on the platform that evening with his arm around the nominees. There were many more people, including some of McGovern's closest friends, who wanted him to have no part of what they regarded as a betrayal. The pressure from the antiwar liberals was intense. They wouldn't forget, they promised him. Neither could he, answered McGovern, which was precisely the reason he was endorsing Humphrey. "I didn't see in conscience how I had much choice," he said later. "You compare the records of the two men [Humphrey and Nixon] the last twenty years, and there isn't any question who is deserving of support." The antiwar forces were true to their word, though; they didn't forget. Three years later, at every liberal stop along the way, the question was virtually identical: How could he have supported *that* man? Each time McGovern's answer came back the same: Hubert Humphrey was a good and decent man; the same could not be said of Nixon. But the true believers weren't interested; by this time most of them had stopped listening.

"I hope we won't have any dropouts from the effort to end

the war in Vietnam," McGovern told his last press conference, shortly before he left Chicago. "I hope we won't withdraw to the sidelines in despair because we didn't get the plank that we wanted in our platform . . . or the presidential nominee." "Is Mayor Daley still an asset to the Democratic party?" a reporter asked. "He's apparently an asset to those who want to get the nomination," McGovern shot back. Had the violence hurt the party? "I think all of America has suffered from what has taken place," said McGovern. "Every citizen in this land wants to see law and order restored, but we can't do it by the kind of methods that were used on the streets of Michigan Avenue here last night. I hope and pray that kind of exhibition will not be repeated anywhere else in America, because if it is, instead of contributing to the cause of law and order and hope in this country, it will contribute to disorder and despair." The reporters stood as McGovern left the room, and a number of them did what men who make their living by detachment aren't supposed to do: they broke into applause.

Back home, McGovern feared, a different reception awaited him. For all his new national reputation he was still instinctively a South Dakotan, and he didn't need to be told how his fellow South Dakotans regarded the spectacle of Chicago. Already, the Republicans were hard at work scissoring his quotations out of newspapers and press accounts. Even before the Convention started, Archie Gubbrud, the former Governor and his senatorial opponent, had charged him with the responsibility for the riot in Cleveland that killed 13 people. "This," said Gubbrud, "is a manifestation of the lawlessness and disorder that has arisen from the spirit fostered by such people as Johnson, Humphrey and McGovern." As McGovern flew back to South Dakota late Friday night of convention week, he knew a hard autumn was ahead of him.

He left immediately for Huron, site of the state fair, and his first political test. When he walked into the arena, the grandstand crowd of 10,000 stood as a body and gave him a deafening ovation. For the rest of that day and the two days that followed McGovern was rarely off his feet, as he shook hands with literally thousands of his constituents. Across the way, at the nearly deserted Republican pavilion, one of his antagonists looked over enviously. "When I saw what was happening," he said disgustedly, "I knew right then and there we didn't have a chance." McGovern felt exactly the same way: "Whatever the polls showed and whatever the political writers were saying, there was considerable pride in what we had done. Maybe people didn't say so, but they were glad that one of their own had run for President. I knew when we left there that we were going to win that campaign. It would be tough, but I knew we were going to win."

Tough it would be, all right. According to a poll taken shortly after the convention, McGovern's popularity, which at one point had reached the 70 percent mark, plunged to 48 percent, just two points above Gubbrud. Even at the fair, while the voters had been friendly enough, there had been a persistent questioning about what had *really* gone on at Chicago. McGovern had tried to explain, but it was clear that his listeners were not in the mood for complex answers. "Mayor Daley," as one political observer put it, "could have been elected Governor." McGovern could not ignore that fact, distasteful as he found it. So in mid-September, to the distress of some of his liberal friends, he started backing and filling on his press conference remarks in Chicago. Now it was only 5 percent of the police who had gotten out of hand. The rest, he said, comported themselves with commendable discipline in the face of the 5 percent of the demonstrators who had come to Chicago spoiling for trouble. The ultimate sellout, as the hardline liberals saw it, was McGovern's journey to Chicago on September 19 for an hour-long summit meeting with Daley; afterward he sat at the Mayor's elbow during a fund-raising luncheon at which he was the featured speaker. From their talks, McGovern told the press, "came . . . a recognition on my part and on the part of the Mayor that most of the police at the convention conducted themselves in a responsible and proper manner. We also agreed that most of the demonstrators were peaceful and well-behaved."

Though it was done in a fashion to please everyone, Mc-

Govern's apparent change of heart succeeded in fully satisfying no one. His old liberal friends, many of whom had been beaten at the hands of the "responsible" and "proper" Chicago police, were furious. "What McGovern says about Daley," fumed Sanford Gottlieb, "shows no acquaintance with reality, except perhaps what he perceives as political reality." The right wing was not appeased either. If anything, the volume and ferocity of its attacks only increased. McGovern was depicted as a spokesman for the "ultraliberal fringe," as Gubbrud always put it, someone who not only would fire the director of the FBI but would let criminals run free through the streets, while taking away the rifles and shotguns of South Dakota "sportsmen." The most sensational charge was that McGovern advocated the shipment of "50,000 unemployed Negroes to South Dakota."

The Republicans' mistake, as usual, was equating the South Dakotans' lack of social sophistication with lack of intelligence. It showed up in their ads and their public statements—in short, in the way they approached the entire campaign. Nowhere, though, did it reveal itself more than in their choice of a candidate. Even Archie Gubbrud's friends found it hard to be kind about the hulking (six-feet four) farmer from Alcester. "He's a deep thinker," said one friend helpfully, trying to explain some of his more nonsensical public statements, like his proposal to install a "hot line" between Pierre and Washington. McGovern, in one of his less Christian moments, likened debating Gubbrud intellectually to "kicking a dog." Gubbrud, who had won the governorship in 1960 in a surprise upset, suffered from a chronic case of wandering syntax. Which perhaps was just as well, since it helped fuzz his thinking on the major issues. ("I'm going to give them a lot of study when I get to Washington," he promised.) He was reluctant to commit himself on such things as Vietnam, he said, because he didn't want to "influence the outcome of the Paris talks." Gubbrud appealed instead to South Dakota's chauvinist instincts. His, he pledged, would be the real voice of South Dakota in Washington. One of his qualifications for office, he said, was the fact that "we have never had a farmer or a rancher in the Congress." When Charles Guggenheim brought his documentary film crews back into the state for Mc-

Govern, Gubbrud boasted that his own film was being shot "inside South Dakota with South Dakota crews," *and* at one-third the cost. That, said Gubbrud, was an example of "South Dakota thinking."

McGovern meanwhile was running the kind of energetic person-to-person campaign he had always run, only this time with more money, more media, and more organization. He played down his left wing associations—"I'm a liberal in the Theodore Roosevelt sense," he told one interviewer; "I believe in the use of federal power to advance positive programs"—and carefully kept the rest of the party at arm's distance while playing up his service to South Dakota, particularly on behalf of agriculture. It did not hurt him to have battled with the Secretary of Agriculture and the President of the United States;* in South Dakota, as one farmer put it, the Democratic administration was "about as popular as a plague of grasshoppers." Nor did McGovern's supposedly radical solution to the burgeoning Pentagon budget and the Vietnam war damage him with the voters. "Taking money away from the Pentagon and staying home minding our own business is pretty conservative talk out here," explains one former state legislator.

Where McGovern was in trouble he applied heavy doses of personal charm laid over with an awesome organizational skill. Gubbrud, by contrast, conducted an almost leisurely campaign. "By the time Election Day rolled around," says Cunningham, "Archie was twenty-seven counties and 500 meetings behind." McGovern also had the services of ten busloads of college students, most of them from neighboring states, who were brought in

---

* A confidential survey by the John Kraft organization late in 1967 confirmed that Freeman and Johnson were the two most unpopular figures in the state. The survey also found that McGovern's stand on Vietnam did not seem to have appreciably hurt him; on the contrary, by opposing Johnson on the issue, McGovern may have actually helped himself. The survey revealed, among other things, that McGovern did far better on the farm than he did in the city, was better thought of by men than by women, and was decidedly more popular among the poor than he was among the rich. McGovern's strengths, according to the survey, were the job he had done as Senator and the image he portrayed of courage and conviction. His greatest weakness apparently was something he had little control over: he was a Democrat.

for an Election Day get-out-the-vote blitz. There were moments when Gubbrud must have felt that even God was on McGovern's side, like the day late in October when Chief Eagle Feather of the Rosebud Sioux returned from a week of meditation atop Azi Paha Mesa to announce at a political rally that he had seen a vision of Chief White Eagle—otherwise known as George Stanley Mc-Govern—standing on the largest rock, an omen signifying victory. In a state where the bloc vote of 10,000 to 15,000 registered Indians can mean the margin of victory, Eagle Feather's words were not to be taken lightly.*

By Election Day the polls showed McGovern edging over the 50 percent mark once again. But Gubbrud too was climbing, and the state's psephologists officially certified the race as "too close to call." They should have listened to Eagle Feather. McGovern won handily with 57 percent of the vote. Gubbrud even failed to carry his hometown.

Back in Washington a few months later, McGovern stared out the picture window of his home at the blowing winter snow. Soon the year would be over. It was hard to believe that in twelve months so much had happened. The mind didn't have to reflect on the events. The good and the bad—they were all too much a part of recent memory. And now, finally, it was ending. "For everything there is a season, and a time to every purpose under heaven," the author of Ecclesiastes had written. The words were among

---

* Certainly McGovern's organization didn't think so. Early in August Chief Eagle Feather, who until six years before had been Bill Schweigeman, a Los Angeles electrician, had experienced another vision. This one showed a big image of Hubert Humphrey and a small image of McGovern. Word of the bad sign produced a minor crisis in McGovern's headquarters, and Jeff Smith, a twenty-four-year-old Bostonian who had organized the Indians for Robert Kennedy's campaign, was dispatched to powwow with the chief. The chief was open to persuasion—and to the $20 bill that Smith offered him—and once again climbed Azi Paha (Tit Butte) for another vision. Smith remained behind to organize the rest of the Indians in traditional Democratic style. On Election Day buffalo and steak feeds were held on all the reservations, free to any Indian who appeared with a sticker reading "I have voted." (Translation: "I have just voted for George McGovern.") Smith marveled: "My God, it's just like Massachusetts."

McGovern's favorites from the Bible. He had quoted them in his statement of reelection to the Senate. "A time to kill and a time to heal . . . a time to weep, and a time to laugh . . . a time to mourn, and a time to dance . . . a time of war, and a time of peace . . . a time to keep, and a time to lose. . . ." Bobby, Terry, the presidency, and the Senate. Nineteen sixty-eight truly was a time to keep.

10

Their Daily Bread

IT HAD NEVER BEEN any secret that some Americans went to bed hungry every night. John Kennedy, in his first Executive Order as President, had directed that surplus U.S. commodities first be distributed to the needy at home before being sent abroad under the Food for Peace program. Later the Congress and the Department of Agriculture refined the technique with the creation of food stamps, certificates sold to the poor to enable them to buy more with their food dollar. But who were the hungry? And how hungry were they? Not many people thought or cared about such questions until one day in April 1967 when two Northern Senators wandered into the small delta town of Cleveland, Mississippi, and found people who were hungry—very, very hungry.

One of the Senators, wrote the Pulitzer Prize-winning journalist Nick Kotz in his book *Let Them Eat Promises*, "felt his way through a dark, windowless shack, fighting nausea at the strong smell of aging mildew, sickness, and urine. In the early afternoon shadows, he saw a child sitting on the floor of a tiny back room. Barely two years old, wearing only a filthy undershirt, she sat rubbing several grains of rice round and round on the floor. The Senator knelt beside her. 'Hello . . . Hi . . .Hi, baby . . . ,' he murmured, touching her cheeks and her hair as he would his own child's. As he sat on the dirty floor, he placed his hand gently on the child's swollen stomach. But the little girl sat as if in a trance, her sad eyes turned downward, and rubbed the gritty rice. For five minutes he tried: talking, caressing, tickling, poking—demanding that the child respond. The baby never looked up." When the Senator walked outside the hut, he "stood alone, controlling his feelings, which were exposed to the press entourage outside the house. Then he whispered to a companion: 'I've seen bad things in West Virginia, but I've never seen anything like this anywhere in the United States.' " Because the last name of the Senator who came and saw the people of Cleveland, Mississippi, that day was Kennedy, a nation discovered overnight that there was indeed hunger in its midst.

It remained for others, however, to document the nature and extent of that hunger. Within weeks after the trip of Robert Kennedy and Joe Clark of Pennsylvania, the Field Foundation dispatched a team of doctors to examine hunger in several Mississippi counties. The researchers found the same evidence of disease and deficiency. In their report for the Field Foundation, "Children in Mississippi," they wrote: "We saw children fed communally—that is, by neighbors who give scraps of food to children whose own parents have nothing to give them." The hungry children of Mississippi, the doctors concluded, "are out of sight and ignored. They are living under such primitive conditions that we found it hard to believe that we were examining American children of the twentieth century!"

Meanwhile, the Citizens Crusade Against Poverty, a liberal pressure group whose major backers include the United Auto Workers, the National Council of Churches, and the Ford Foundation, formed a twenty-five-member Citizens Board of Inquiry into Hunger and Malnutrition in the United States to focus public attention on the problem. They succeeded a year later with the publication of *Hunger USA*, which reported among other horrors the existence of the most severe protein diseases—including kwashiorkor (a Ghanaian word meaning "the disease of one who has left the breast") and marasmus—which previously were thought to afflict only those in underdeveloped countries. In addition, *Hunger USA* found:

—that substantial numbers of newborn, who survived the hazards of birth and live through the first month, die between the second month and their second birthday from causes which can be traced directly and primarily to malnutrition.

—that protein deprivation between the ages of six months and a year and one-half causes permanent and irreversible brain damage to some young infants.

—that nutritional anemia, stemming primarily from protein deficiency and iron deficiency, was commonly found in percentages ranging from 30 to 70 percent among children from poverty backgrounds.

—that teachers report children who come to school without breakfast, who are too hungry to learn and in such pain that they must be taken home or sent to the school nurse.

—that mother after mother in region after region reported that the cupboard was bare, sometimes at the beginning and throughout the month, sometimes only the last week of the month.

—that doctors personally testified to seeing case after case of premature death, infant deaths, and vulnerability to secondary infection, all of which were attributable to or indicative of malnutrition.

—that in some communities people band together to share the little food they have, living from hand to mouth.

—that the aged living alone subsist on liquid foods that provide inadequate sustenance.

The release of *Hunger USA*'s findings, which were sharply critical of existing government efforts to cope with want—including commodity distribution, food stamps, and the national school lunch and school milk programs—provoked more public attention and triggered other exposés, the most powerful of which

was the CBS special "Hunger in America." The effort to highlight hunger, with programs like the CBS show and reports like
Hunger USA and "Children in Mississippi," plus the continuing
agitation of Senators Kennedy and Clark and the other members
of the Senate Subcommittee on Employment, Manpower, and
Poverty, hardly pleased those officials who were lawfully charged
with ending it. Secretary of Agriculture Orville Freeman, who
perhaps had the most to lose by the sudden emergence of hunger
as a political issue, dismissed "Hunger in America" as "shockingly
irresponsible." To Freeman, the newly focused attention on
hunger was part of a "pattern" to discredit the administration, a
plot furthered by CBS, the liberals, and the "tactics and efforts
of so-called poor people." On Capitol Hill the conservative heads
of the House and Senate Agriculture committees at first denied
that hunger existed, and when that ploy proved fruitless they held
that if it did exist there was nothing that the U.S. government
could or should do about it. Five months after the release of
Hunger USA in 1968, Texas Congressman Bob Poage, the mossbacked chairman of the House Agriculture Committee, issued his
own rebuttal:

> The basic problem is one of ignorance as to what consti-
> tutes a balanced diet, coupled with indifference by a great
> many persons who should and probably do not know . . . de-
> liberate parental neglect. . . . Relief clients are virtually un-
> educable. . . . Mentally retarded parents are blamed in a great
> many instances for the neglect of children. . . . Fatherless
> households, with children born out of wedlock, are blamed for
> distressing conditions. . . . Children suffered because a father
> spent disproportionately large sums either on liquor or on ex-
> tramarital relations. . . . Jobs were available in the community
> but rejected by able-bodied men who apparently preferred to
> live on welfare rolls. . . .

When it became apparent that hunger could not be attributed
exclusively to these racist theories, Senator Strom Thurmond
shrugged: "There has been hunger since the time of Jesus Christ
and there always will be." Besides, as Allen Ellender, chairman of
the Senate Agriculture Committee, homily put it: "I know that

in my state we had a number of fishermen who were unable to catch fish. Do you expect the government, because they cannot catch fish, to feed them until the fish are there?"

George McGovern's response, expectably, was precisely the opposite. The day after the Citizens Board of Inquiry report was issued, McGovern took the Senate floor with a copy of *Hunger USA* in his hand. He remarked that the report was "a little long on criticism of the adequacy of the human *welfare* job agriculture has done and short on praise of the agricultural sector for doing all that it has done." However, said McGovern, "history will allocate credit and place blame, and it is not really important to allocate it now. What is important is that there is a serious food gap in the United States today. We need to meet it just as speedily as humanly possible. It is long past time that we quit relying on diversion of unplanned surpluses to provide food for people trapped in poverty and want. It is time that we took a look at our programs to meet basic human needs for food, clothing, and other necessities of life and health and useful citizenship from the standpoint of our obligations as a civilized people toward our fellow men." With that, McGovern introduced a resolution creating a select committee to examine hunger and how it was being solved, a committee that would develop "a coordinated program or programs to meet basic human requirements for food, clothing, and other necessities of life among our disadvantaged people."

At first glance, it looked as if McGovern was proposing the usual bureaucratic remedy for any social ill: appoint a commission to study it. But hunger was one of those rare instances where study really was needed. At the moment, there was only the vaguest guess as to how many people were truly hungry or undernourished. The Department of Agriculture had determined that one-fifth of all the households in the United States were subsisting on diets officially listed as "poor." But who was to decide what "poor" was? Like the standard for poverty, the definition could be juggled at bureaucratic whim, one moment proving a problem, the next moment disproving it. What was needed was some hard-headed analysis of just what hunger was, how widely it had spread, and what could be done to bring it under control. More than that, if good was to be done, hunger needed its own lobby on Capitol Hill to defend it against the slings and arrows of indifferent Congressmen and defensive bureaucrats. Up to then Kennedy and Clark—the two Senators who had "discovered" hunger in 1967—had been performing much of that function. But in the spring of 1968 Kennedy was away from Washington for long periods campaigning for the presidency, and soon Clark would have to return to Pennsylvania, where he faced a stiff test for reelection. That left the hunger forces looking for a champion. And early in 1968 McGovern decided he wanted to be it.

McGovern was no stranger to hunger. Among his most vivid memories of the Depression were the gaunt-faced men who regularly appeared at the family dinner table to share the Reverend McGovern's meager fare. As a young airman arriving in Italy, McGovern had been appalled as he watched scrawny street urchins risk their lives to swim out to the arriving troop ships, begging for the GIs to throw them a candy bar. On his first day at the base McGovern awoke to the sound of peasant women scrounging in the garbage heap behind his tent for scraps of bread and meat that the Americans had thrown away the night before. Later Food for Peace had offered an intimate acquaintance with hunger on a world scale, as well as with the possibilities of using U.S. abundance to combat it. In the Senate McGovern was an early critic of the Department of Agriculture's surplus disposal policies, both at home and abroad. That is not to say that McGovern was a principal leader in the earliest stages of the fight against domestic hunger. But he was concerned, and with the continuing revelations of the dimension of the problem, his concern increased steadily. By early in 1968, his feelings were every bit as high as Kennedy's and Clark's, even if they drew much less notice in the press.

The original idea for a congressional committee to probe hunger had been Robert Choate's, of the Citizens Board of Inquiry. Choate had been meeting daily with Kennedy legislative aide Peter Edelman, poverty subcommittee counsel Bill Smith, and Ben Stong, McGovern's legislative assistant, to plot strategy for getting hunger legislation through Congress. Choate's proposal was for a joint congressional committee to probe the problem. McGovern liked the idea, but thought that a committee might move more quickly and with more impact if confined to the more liberal Senate. Stong, a wily veteran of congressional politics, was commissioned to draft the resolution. McGovern feared for their chances if they were forced to take the resolution through the Senate Agriculture Committee, which was dominated by conservative Southern interests. Instead, he wanted the resolution referred to the more liberal Education and Labor Committee, where it had a far better chance of getting a friendly reception. Stong carefully worded the resolution "so agriculture was as far down as possible and health, education, and welfare was as far up as possible." To avoid the Senate Rules Committee, another conservative pitfall, Stong's resolution omitted the usual mention of subpoena powers and financial authorization. By the time McGovern brought the resolution to the Senate late in April, he had been able to round up thirty-eight co-sponsors. With backing like that, the resolution quickly passed the Senate.

So now the Senate Select Committee on Nutrition and Human Needs existed—on paper, at any rate. Without money or staff, however, its existence was meaningless. When the new committee requested interim funding of $150,000 to keep it going from October through January, the Rules Committee appropriated a paltry $25,000, barely enough to hire Bill Smith as general counsel and install him and his secretary in a penurious suite of offices in the Senate Annex. In February, when the Nutrition and Human Needs Committee went up for full funding, this time for $250,000, the Rules Committee slashed $100,000 from its budget. The cutback prompted McGovern, who had been elected chairman of the committee at a preliminary session early in the fall, to take the almost unprecedented step of challenging the Rules Committee's decision on the Senate floor. The Senate, for its part, responded in an even more unheard-of way, by restoring the full $100,000 to McGovern's authorization. "That," boasts Stong, "was the first goddamn licking anybody has given the Rules Committee in twenty-five years."

It was one thing to get funding for a congressional committee; it was quite another to secure the financial commitment necessary to end hunger in the United States. McGovern and the committee got their first break on January 20, 1969, two days after Richard Nixon took office. The opening was the release of preliminary findings of the National Nutrition Survey, which Congress had authorized in 1967 to collect concrete physical data on the existence and extent of hunger. The report, based on physical examinations of 12,000 people from low-income areas in Texas, Louisiana, New York, and Kentucky, revealed little about hunger that was not already known. What it did do was for the first time confirm officially what the private agencies had been saying all along: that "the phenomenon of hunger and malnutrition," as *The New York Times* phrased it in a front-page story, "[exists] in a land fat with agricultural surpluses." "We did not expect to find such cases in the United States," admitted Dr. Arnold E. Schaefer, a Public Health Service official, referring to the discovery of marasmus, kwashiorkor, rickets, and goiter. "In many of the developing areas where we have worked—Africa, Latin America, and Asia—these severe cases of malnutrition only rarely are found. They are either hospitalized or have died." Between 16 and 17 percent of the people the survey examined, said Schaefer, were considered "real risks" and needed medical attention. The toll was particularly vicious among the children. Physically they lagged from six months to two and a half years behind their better-fed peers: 34 percent were badly anemic, 33 percent suffered from a severe shortage of vitamin A (of which fortified milk is the primary source), and 16 percent lacked adequate amounts of vitamin C. Schaefer admitted that the deficiencies in nutrients were "the same or higher" than the Department of Health, Education, and Welfare had found in a similar study of six Central American countries.

Armed now with the data he had been waiting for, McGovern moved to dramatize the findings in much the same fashion as Kennedy and Clark had done two years earlier—by taking his committee to the scene of hunger itself. Immokalee, Florida, was the first target chosen. As a case study in racism, misery, and indifference, Immokalee—"The New World of Opportunity," as the signs at the city limits proclaimed it—played out its role only too well. Home base for 20,000 migrant workers, nearly all of them black or Chicano, who spent eight months of every year working the vegetables and watermelons in the surrounding area, Immokalee had for years been resisting any and all federal food programs. Its reason, in the words of a lawyer for the Florida Rural Services, was simple: "They don't like 'nigras' and they think free food will keep the 'nigras' around." The commissioners of Collier County put it more delicately: they took care of their own, they insisted (meaning an allocation of $7,500 of the county welfare budget, enough to feed twenty-four people on an adequate diet for a year), but the migrants were not theirs. They were "federal people, not Immokalee people. They're not Collier people, they're not Florida people."

The leading citizens of Immokalee denied that hunger existed. Stanley Wrisley, the wizened, white-haired editor of the *Immokalee Bulletin* ("The Light of the Everglades"), challenged the committee to "produce a child who is actually emaciated and who is actually suffering from malnutrition." If people were going hungry, Wrisley said, it was only because they didn't spend their money on the right kinds of food. Anyway, he knew "these kind of people" and they were not the sort who deserved the Senate's sympathy. They were the kind of people who "didn't really want to work, because it will damage their welfare standard." They were the kind of people who broke windows in their homes, threw garbage into their yards, had one illegitimate child after another, used their commodes as outhouses and then moved on in the middle of the night without paying their rent. That's the kind of people they were, and Stanley Wrisley knew every one of them. Joseph Brown, a bald, beefy crop-dusting pilot for the local farmers, went further than Wrisley. The whole thing was being blown out of proportion, he said. There was no need for any government food program for the migrant workers of Immokalee. "They're a gypsy type of person who like that kind of life, who pay no withholding taxes, no social security, and contribute nothing to the society in which they live.

We need people who don't run out and buy wine at the end of the working day," he boomed. Then Brown provided the clincher. "Gentlemen," he told the Senators, "the Bible says the poor you shall have with you always." "My God," gasped Senator Walter Mondale, when the first day of testimony was over. "How could they talk about human beings like that? Why, it was just as though they were talking about a monkey or a giraffe."

Early the next morning McGovern and Mondale, along with Senators Ellender, Javits, and Marlow Cook, went out to see for themselves. One of their first stops was "Booker's Alley," a clutter of twenty-four shacks housing thirty families, who paid an average of $52 a month rent to a landlord who also happened to be chairman of the board of the local bank. It was not a bad investment: $1,560 a month for a few shacks with neither water nor heat. In the doorway of one hovel stood a child whose legs were so badly bowed with rickets that they almost formed a circle from his hips to his feet. His mother, Mrs. Katie Dell Murphy, told McGovern that she, her husband, and their eight children lived in the two-room hut, which had only three beds, on an income of $125 a month—"if there's work"—$65 of which went to the bank chairman as rent. Her children seldom ate meat. They never drank milk.

The Senators moved on. They stopped a few yards later to peer into what appeared to be a storage shed; it was the home of another family of ten. Their evening meal that night consisted of exactly one loaf of bread. Again the Senators moved on, this time to the house of George and Mary Adderson. He was sixty-eight and she was sixty-five, but they looked even older. A few months before Mrs. Adderson had lost her leg to gangrene. Now she slowly pitched back and forth in a rocking chair, staring at McGovern, seeing him and not seeing him. "Are you hungry?" he asked. "No, I'm not hungry," she answered, rocking in her chair. "What did you eat today?" McGovern pressed gently. "Some peas and beans," she said. "What will you have for lunch?" asked McGovern. "Oh, maybe some peas." Was that all she ever had? "Sometimes," she said, "I has a little fat back with some greens." McGovern and Javits opened the refrigerator door. There was the fat back, a few peas, and some greens. Nothing else. They apologized for intruding and moved out into the sunlight. McGovern brushed past the newsmen. "It's obvious that the woman doesn't even know what good nutrition or a decent standard of life is." he said to someone. Then he added almost under his breath: "I don't even think they're aware they're poor."

Next on the tour was a dingy two-story block of buildings which housed black families, most of them farm workers. There Rosalee Bryant, an unmarried mother of four, held her five-month-old son in her arms. His head was covered with scabs, sores, and lumps. His mother told McGovern that he suffered from water on the brain; the doctor wasn't sure, but she thought the condition was caused by malnutrition during her pregnancy. She and her children lived in a 10-by-14-foot room divided by an old refrigerator. Like all the refrigerators the Senators had seen that day, it was nearly empty. Rosalee tried, she said, to buy milk for her children, but it was hard; sometimes at the end of the month she had to borrow money for food. As they left, McGovern noticed three pictures on the wall. One was of Christ. The others were of John F. Kennedy and Martin Luther King.

It had not been a happy day in Immokalee. Claude Kirk, the Republican Governor, flew in to express his rage at not being informed that the committee was coming. "I wish my office had been asked so I could have supplied you with information about my previous trips here," he huffed. The local business community wasn't pleased either. Frederick Edenfield, a town grocer, muttered: "This is going to kill us for local industry. There should be some way we can sue them." The chairman of the county commissioners, who had been dogging the inspection team all day, told reporters: "We knew we had three strikes against us. We had Senator McGovern, an ultraliberal; Senator Javits, who in my thinking is a Socialist; and Senator Mondale, who I understand was hand-picked by Hubert Humphrey." The only Senator on the commissioners' side, it seemed, was Allen Ellender, who protested that the committee was touring only the worst areas. "The people we talked to here today seemed to be happy," Ellender protested. "I haven't seen anyone who isn't contented."

Not even the reporters were entirely happy. Senators Mondale and Javits had both acted properly outraged, but McGovern, the man they had come to see, seemed unwilling to express his emotions in front of a TV camera. He had few comments for the press, but the ones he made were blunt. "Most of the cattle and hogs in America are better fed and sheltered than the families we have visited in these two counties," he said at the end of the tour. But the drama of a Kennedy was missing. Overt emotion seemed foreign to the man. It didn't make good copy or good film, but it delighted a white poverty worker who guided McGovern and was at first suspicious of his motives. "I thought this would be a political circus," he said later. "But I didn't know McGovern. He doesn't show public emotions, but what he saw really got to him. If you look closely at him, look at his eyes, you can see it. All the pain is there."

McGovern hadn't been back in Washington twenty-four hours before the political skirmishing began. To a group of Young Republicans, Herbert Klein, the communications director for the Nixon administration, declared: "I think one disgrace of the moment is for Senator McGovern and others to make hunger a political cause, by traipsing around the country with television cameras." Claude Kirk, still smarting over the bad publicity his state had received in the wake of McGovern's visit, advised him to "stop talking about hunger and do something to end it." "I for one will not stop talking," McGovern replied on the floor of the Senate. "Our committee will continue to put the problems of hunger before the American people and expose the good and the bad in our food assistance programs. . . . Hunger knows no politics."

If McGovern really believed that, he was either being terribly naïve or overestimating the Nixon administration. Nixon and his aides—particularly Secretaries Clifford Hardin in Agriculture and Robert Finch in HEW—had been jolted by the public impact of the National Nutrition Survey's findings and were further chagrined when McGovern blasted an offer of free food stamps for two counties in South Carolina as "inadequate." On March 17, less than a week after McGovern's attention-getting foray into southwestern Florida, Nixon, Finch and Hardin met in the White House to consider a recommendation from counselor Daniel Moynihan's staff for a billion dollar reform of the food stamp program. The following colloquy, taken from the official White House notes of the meeting and reprinted in *Let Them Eat Promises*, shows just how politically sensitive the issue of hunger had become:

NIXON: The most troublesome question is, how wide is the hunger problem in fact?

HARDIN: We know there are 6 million persons in families with less than $300 per capita income, 25 million with less than $3,000 family income, and probably one-half have nutritional problems, give or take 1 or 2 million. We're absolutely convinced this is a serious problem and one that with our abundance shouldn't be permitted to exist.

NIXON: To what extent does our report reflect or respond to the Senate hearings? I've been on that side as a Congressman or Senator. Are we allowing their propaganda to pull us?

HARDIN: No. We've been very cold in our analysis. The absolute minimum a family of four can get by on is $100 a month for food.

NIXON: For $100 a month, you can't even pay the interest on a bill at Gristede's [an expensive New York grocery chain]. You might see less of a problem than the McGovern group, you might see more. All I hope is that we are really analyzing this for ourselves.

FINCH: Let's take the play away from the McGovern committee and send a couple of your guys [White House aides] in a helicopter to southern Virginia, for example.

NIXON: Good. Don't be props for McGovern.

HARDIN: I feel very much on the spot.

NIXON: How soon do you have to move? This week?

HARDIN: I have three speeches to give this week, the first one tomorrow night. And what I need to do when I speak is to say that I'm speaking within the policy of this administration.

NIXON: You can say that this administration will have the first complete, far-ranging attack on the problem of hunger in

history. Use all the rhetoric, so long as it doesn't cost any
money. Now is the time to get right into it. Make a speech tomorrow night and say you favor flexible price supports to pay
for this. *Some* administration must grapple with the farm problem and limiting payments.

HARDIN: This is specific, direct, and basic. We can make
this the showplace in the whole poverty area.

McGovern, however, saw it quite differently. When word
leaked out that the administration was considering a $100 million
food reform package, to be spread out over four years, Mc-
Govern retorted: "This is precisely the sort of half-hearted
tinkering with the needs of our poor that we have seen time and
time again in recent years—underfinanced poverty programs,
underfinanced food programs, all with the decimal points in the
wrong place."

Actually, by the time McGovern spoke Nixon had all but
decided to give the hunger campaign far less than the $100
million boost—in fact, little if anything at all. Attention had
shifted to welfare reform and Moynihan's pet, the family assistance program.

Meanwhile, pressures were building in the opposite direction.
The work of the McGovern committee and the findings of the
National Nutrition Survey had not gone unnoticed. Fifteen
Governors formally requested the National Nutrition Survey to
come into their states. Hunger lobbyists, notably nutritionist
Jean Mayer of the National Council on Hunger and Malnutrition,
buzzed in and out of offices on Capitol Hill demanding action.
On April 29 McGovern introduced his own food stamp bill
providing for free food stamps for families with incomes of less
than $80 a month. McGovern's bill lowered the price of food
stamps for families with incomes above $80 from the current
range of 30 to 50 percent of the family's income to between 15
and 25 percent. Under McGovern's plan, the value of the food
stamps received by all participants would be raised to a minimum
of $120 a month. If they wished, families could also purchase
less than a month's supply of food stamps, and the stamps could
be used to buy soap and other products "necessary for personal

and home sanitation." Finally, McGovern's bill permitted the distribution of surplus commodities in counties where a food stamp program was in operation, a duplication that previously had been forbidden. "The day has come," McGovern said, in introducing his bill to the Senate, "when most of us would like to see more of our tax dollars invested in people—to help hungry Americans get enough to eat—instead of spending additional billions for more missiles and tanks when we already have enough to blow up the world many times over."

Still, the White House resisted. "The hunger program is on the shelf," said one senior administration official. "There may be malnutrition in America, but real hunger on a substantial scale—I don't believe it." Then, early in May, serendipity stepped in. From a friendly source inside the White House Bill Smith had secured a copy of a confidential Moynihan memo contending that there was no evidence linking brain damage in children to hunger. The basis for Moynihan's assertion seemed primarily to have been his desire to kill food stamp reform once and for all. Smith leaked the memo to the *Post*, which gave the story prominent play. Two days later Smith leaked another White House memo, this one describing in detail the Finch-Hardin plan to end hunger. The *Post* placed it on page one. On May 7 Secretaries Hardin and Finch were scheduled to appear before McGovern's committee, the same committee that seemed to know all their plans almost the moment they made them. The confrontation would be uncomfortable, to say the least. No one knew this better than Richard Nixon, still the ablest politician within his own administration. On May 6 Nixon acted. "The moment is at hand," he declared, "to put an end to hunger in America for all time. . . . It is a moment to act with vigor; it is a moment to be recalled with pride."

Nixon's notion of ending hunger "for all time" was to increase the food stamp allocation by $270 million for fiscal 1970 and to raise that figure to a billion dollars for 1971. McGovern's reaction came one day later. "Two hundred seventy million in fiscal year 1970 is not enough," he said, moments before Finch and Hardin were to testify before his committee. "A billion dollars in the year after that is probably less than a third of what is needed." The Nixon plan did, in truth, fall far short of what McGovern's own bill provided. Where McGovern wanted families with a monthly income of less than $80 to receive food stamps free, Nixon would set the limit at $30 a month.

The difference in costs between the two plans was enormous. The Nixon proposal "saved" $384 million. By so doing, it also denied free food stamps to 3.5 million families who would have received them under McGovern's plan. Nixon's plan cut the minimum food stamp allotment for a family of four to $100 a month, despite the fact that his own Department of Agriculture had pegged the amount needed to maintain a minimum nutritional standard at $120. In overall cost, the Nixon program had a price tag of $2.1 billion to feed 11 million poor—about half the estimated poverty population in 1969. McGovern's bill, by contrast, would have fed the same 11 million with $4 billion, and all the poor with $6.5 billion.

As promised, McGovern fought the Nixon plan, and with the aid of key Senators—Percy, Javits, and Cook—rammed his bill through the Senate.

A meaner fate awaited it in the House, where compared to Texas' Bob Poage and Mississippi's Jamie Whitten (who informed McGovern that food stamps were useless because "nigras" were "too lazy to work"), the twin pillars of the House Agriculture Committee, Louisiana's Ellender came off as a flaming liberal. At first, Poage and Whitten simply ignored food stamp reform. When the bill was finally reported to the floor late in the year, it was a pale shadow of the proposal McGovern had successfully pushed through the Senate. Not only did it fall far short of the funding provided in McGovern's bill; it also imposed a work requirement on anyone receiving food stamps. At the conference committee set up to resolve the differences between the House and Senate versions, McGovern was the only one of eight legislators to vote for his own bill. The committee finally left in the work requirement and substantially less funding than the Senate version. McGovern refused to sign the conference report. Shortly thereafter both Houses of Congress passed the bill into law. Though McGovern had lost on a number of points, the principles of free food stamps and a national eligibility standard had been established.

After the passage of the expanded Food Stamp Act, it would have been easy, as one staff member of the Senate Select Committee on Nutrition and Human Needs noted, for McGovern "to declare a victory and then get out." Instead, he stayed and continued to pressure throughout 1970 for more and cheaper food stamps. But the battle was getting lonelier. The enactment of food stamp reform had cooled public passions about hunger. Despite the fact that the job was literally left half undone, hunger had lost much of its political sex appeal.

A memorable editorial column in *The New Republic* early in May 1970 summed up the mood:

> It's a big room paneled in pine with cork floors and hardly anybody in it. The TV camera lights are on but the crew is reading newspapers. The witness is Dr. Arnold Schaefer, head of the government's National Nutrition Survey that Congress ordered two and one-half years ago. A couple of experts sit behind him, one of them seemingly intent on keeping him from saying anything dramatic about hunger. Last year Dr. Schaefer spoke his mind and probably cost the government several million dollars in extra food grants. He is short, sober, middle-aged, prosaic, and obviously watching his step. This year he sticks to graphs, tables, and a dull text.
>
> Normally a dozen Senators sit behind the semicircular dais up front that looks down on the witness, but this time there is only one man there, George McGovern of South Dakota. He is all alone.
>
> All the drama has gone out of it. The country was shocked and incredulous when McGovern and others went out a couple of years ago and showed there is hunger, malnutrition, and even starvation in affluent America. But a lot of other excitements have come up since then. Congress ordered a National Nutrition Survey and this is part of it; today we will hear about two of the ten states surveyed, Louisiana and Texas. But it's like

counting the ballots when the election is already conceded—old stuff. . . .

Sitting up there alone, McGovern keeps asking questions. He never quits. He lacks the drama of McCarthy, the glamor of Kennedy. He's got no style or wealth. Somewhere out in the Adriatic one time he crash-landed a collapsed B-24 and got the Distinguished Flying Cross. But his clothes aren't Fifth Avenue. He's got a slight Midwest nasal accent and a kind manner. He doesn't look like a hero. He went to Dakota Wesleyan and got into politics as a history teacher. He looks like a YMCA secretary.

It is awfully hard to stop men like McGovern. They have iron in them. When they think about hungry children, it bothers them. When they go out and find the facts and then come back with them, then, by golly, before the Senate knows what it's doing it appropriates money—as much as $200 million of it, because McGovern and others won't let up. Will he get his bill through Congress? I don't know. Mr. Nixon had his celebrated "White House Conference on Hunger," which rode off in all directions as expected, and that was *that*. Now the President has more sensational things to spend money on, like Cambodia. But McGovern is still there. "For a quarter of a century," he says in his mild voice, "America has been caring for the rest of the world. The time has come for America to take care of its own."

Don't underestimate him.

McGovern was not to be underestimated; nor, however, was Nixon. Even as McGovern continued to escalate his attacks on hunger—climaxing in May 1971 with a flat call for a nationwide food stamp program by July 1, 1972, his "deadline" to end hunger—the Nixon administration continued to retreat from its own goal of eradicating hunger in America.

One of the first signs that all was not right was a report from two professors at West Point on federal food distribution in four states. When the officers completed their report, the White House, which had commissioned it in the first place, attempted to suppress it. Eventually, McGovern succeeded in getting both the report and the officers before his committee. When the officers told their story, it was obvious why the White House had tried to silence them. Theirs was a tale of official defiance of the law, of "paper programs" and "absurdly low participation rates." In Natchez, Mississippi, the officers reported, black women who refused to sit in the segregated waiting room of the local welfare office were either ignored or told that they failed to meet "recently amended regulations." In Adams County, Mississippi, the welfare director "emphasized her benevolent attitude toward the 'poor colored,' but indicated . . . that they lead morally disgusting lives and that her primary concern is to 'educate' them to proper forms of behavior." She did that, she told the officers, by removing pregnant women from the welfare rolls "for a month or so." In Mendocino, California, a person with any income at all was considered "employable and hence unqualified to receive free food." That interpretation of the law, the officers noted, excluded all the working poor and most welfare mothers. In California there was none of the harassment, but food was almost equally impossible to get. In four California counties there was only one food distribution point, even though one of the counties was as large as the state of Connecticut. In Missouri, the officers found, "food shipments to Vietnam often affected the availability of flour for local distribution."

A few weeks after the West Point officers appeared before the committee, a Department of Agriculture official admitted under McGovern's questioning that independent cities and counties wishing to adopt food stamp programs might "have to be denied" after the conclusion of the 1970 fiscal year. The threat became more specific on April 15, 1971, when the Department of Agriculture posted new regulations basing the eligibility for food stamps on income. The third installment of the National Nutrition Survey, presented to McGovern's committee late in April 1971, was suspiciously far less pessimistic than the first two, and it found less disease attributable to hunger—not surprisingly, since its criteria were now much narrower. The reason was only too plain: Dr. Arnold Schaefer, the tough-minded author of the first two reports, had been suddenly detached for duty to the

Pan American Health Organization less than a month before the third report was due to be published.

Shaefer could at least defend himself (and he did, buttressing McGovern's contention that the survey's " 'evidence' was tailored to blunt the harsh edges of what the collected information may actually have revealed"). The same was not true of the several million children who depended on the national school lunch and special school milk programs.* On Christmas Eve 1969 Nixon had promised that every poor American child would receive a free or reduced-price school lunch by Thanksgiving Day 1970. But by Thanksgiving even the Department of Agriculture was admitting that 17,000 schools with more than 6 million students were still outside the program. The President's pledge, McGovern said bitterly, "has turned out to be 3 percent food and 97 percent promise." What especially upset McGovern was that although Congress had authorized $33 million for the program—much of it at his urging—the administration's Office of Management and Budget had requested only $16 million to fund it. "At that rate," said McGovern, "it will be 1980 before every school in the nation has adequate facilities, and every child a meal that is legally his."

By promising food and then going back on that promise, Nixon and his administration were playing with fire—and they were apparently getting away with it. Though the funds for the summer lunch program were eventually restored, each new charge of administration irresponsibility, of promises made and unkept, of figures bounced and distorted, seemed to get less attention, both from the press and from the public. Even McGovern's rhetoric began to get predictable. After being outraged for so

---

* Deficient as these programs are, they are markedly better than they might have been, thanks to a crucial series of amendments introduced by McGovern. One of McGovern's amendments created a national standard of eligibility for the lunch and milk programs. Another equally important addition was "self-certification" of need to qualify for the program. Self-certification eliminates the need for parents to submit an often humiliating financial statement to attest to their child's need. A simple declaration now suffices.

long, he found difficult to find new ways to express indignation. The very scenes of hunger began to have a numbing quality. Nick Kotz said it best in March 1971, when after yet another set of hunger statistics was presented to the McGovern committee he wrote in the *Washington Post*: "Last week marked the fourth annual performance of a horror show on Capitol Hill. The Senate hearing room lights dimmed. The color slides flashed on the screen . . . and the members of the Senate Select Committee on Nutrition and Human Needs gasped and grimaced."

Much remained to be done, and Nixon was clearly unwilling to do it. But it was hard to fault an administration, no matter how half-hearted its performance, that had at least done something. And Nixon had done more than something. In less than two years the food stamp budget had been effectively tripled, while the number of people benefiting from the program had increased by a multiple of four. During the same period, the school lunch program had more than doubled. Perhaps most important, the existence of hunger in America had been recognized —grudgingly perhaps, certainly under pressure, and no doubt for the wrong motives, but at least the admission had been made. Lyndon Johnson and Orville Freeman had been unwilling to concede even that.

Much, if not most, of the credit for the progress that had been made in ending hunger went to the Senate Select Committee on Nutrition and Human Needs and its chairman. There were those in the Senate, especially on the Republican side of the aisle, who were anxious to have McGovern take his bows and to have the committee over and done with before it became a further springboard for his presidential ambitions. The partisan pressures on both sides had been mounting since the committee was less than six months old. Kansas Senator Robert Dole was especially strident. Dole complained that the committee was going out of its way to see the "worst side of America," ignoring the fact that that was precisely its mission. He zeroed in on McGovern. Once when McGovern was a few minutes late for a hearing on the White House Conference on Hunger, Dole groused: "Why should we have to wait for him just because he's running for President?" On another occasion, during a debate on the Senate floor, McGovern rose to challenge something that Dole had said. Dole contemptuously turned his back on him, a violation of every rule of senatorial courtesy. When Jesse Jackson appeared before the committee to testify against the family assistance program, Dole said scornfully: "I suppose next we'll be having hearings on the space program." McGovern stared back coldly at him and replied: "Do you think it could use improvement?"

The sniping continued all through 1970. By the time the committee came up for renewal at the end of the year, there were rumors that it was finished, and if not the committee then certainly its chairman, who was momentarily expected to announce his candidacy for President. There were stories that White House political operative Harry Dent was calling for McGovern's scalp, a tale that Bill Smith, an expert by now at leaking things to the press, promptly passed on to columnist Jack Anderson. Fearing that there might be some substance to the gossip, McGovern privately announced that he was ready to step down if it meant the continuance of the committee. In the end, it never came to that. No one made a direct challenge to McGovern's leadership, and after the committee flogged some of its own members into line—notably Chuck Percy, who would have preferred to see the committee ended but was convinced by Jesse Jackson that it would be politically fortuitous in Illinois to have it continue—the bill for its renewal sailed through the Rules Committee and past the Senate.

In its second life the committee would have a broader focus than in its first, which had necessarily concentrated on bread-and-butter issues like food stamps and school lunches. Now nutrition and human needs were defined to encompass such things as the environmental conditions that encouraged good eating habits. McGovern toured the apparently bombed-out blocks of the Bronx, where hundreds of apartment buildings had been abandoned by their owners to rats, decay, and disease. The failure, he charged, belonged to no less than the Federal Housing Authority, the government agency charged with promoting new housing. In a scorching report on the agency released in February 1971, McGovern's committee accused the FHA of tearing down more houses than it helped to build and subsidizing more squalid homes than decent ones. In the name of urban renewal, the government, according to the report, had demolished 440,000 housing units—or about three and a half times as many units as it had built to replace them. The FHA, the report continued, refused to insure loans in inner-city neighborhoods, where the housing need was most critical, while lavishing money on suburban home construction, the area that needed it least. McGovern himself said that the government had built only 1.5 million housing units in the thirty-three years since the first federal housing legislation had been adopted. "The real need," he said, "requires that level of output each year, not each third of a century."

From housing the committee moved to the study of lead poisoning, and then to a whole variety of urban ills, all of them at least loosely related to human needs. The committee also looked into the nutritional value of various foods, like hot dogs, which McGovern joined Ralph Nader in condemning for their high fat content, which in some cases reached as much as 33 percent. What made the lowly hot dogs particularly villainous was that the poor looked to them as a cheap source of meat and protein. McGovern revealed that they had little of either. But if the committee was willing to attack such culturally sacred things as the hot dog, it steered clear of others. Shortly before McGovern was to depart Washington for a campaign swing through Wisconsin, the committee staff scheduled hearings on the relationship between high cholesterol content in dairy products and heart disease. A call from McGovern's friend Gaylord Nelson quickly put at least a temporary end to that. The hearings, McGovern announced to a disbelieving press, were being postponed to the fall to give the dairy industry time to prepare its defense. The real reason, as all the reporters knew, was presidential politics.

Such instances of political log-rolling were rare. Despite Dole's insinuations, McGovern kept the committee remarkably free of partisan politics. Committee staffers, all of them fiercely loyal to McGovern, estimated that they spent no more than 10 percent of their time on "noncommittee work," the code words for politics. By nature, of course, the committee could not help being politically controversial. Every critique of the Department

of Agriculture, the Office of Management and Budget, or the
FHA was also an aspersion on the Nixon administration. Certainly McGovern was alive to these possibilities, as well as to
the personal opportunity that the chairmanship of an emotional,
high-visibility committee like Nutrition and Human Needs presented. But in large measure—far too large a measure for the
tastes of some of his political advisers—McGovern resisted turning the committee into a vehicle of personal publicity. He seemed
to regard the baying press corps that attended each of his field
trips as a necessary evil, and sometimes more evil than necessary.
"I wish he would do something," moaned one reporter who accompanied McGovern through West Virginia. But McGovern
wouldn't. "I sometimes wish he would do something too," commented one of his aides, "but that's not him. He thinks obvious
display is phony and cheap." For much the same reason
McGovern could never bring himself to pursue witnesses, even
obviously hostile ones, with the zeal of a prosecuting attorney or
a Robert Kennedy stalking a Jimmy Hoffa. "He won't make
points at other people's expense," said one admiring, if exasperated
adviser. "It'll be right out in front or him and he just won't do
it. He won't ask the damning or embarrassing question."

That trait, if it hampered McGovern's political exposure,
measurably improved the general regard for his committee. By
being calm and undogmatic, McGovern managed to bring
around tough men like Ellender and Herman Talmadge, the hard-
bitten Georgia segregationist. "They never write him off as a
hopeless urban welfare type," comments one congressional observer. "They've worked with him on farm legislation and a
certain understanding and trust has developed." McGovern's low-
key style was in marked contrast to that of some of his equally
liberal but more abrasive colleagues, one of whom chaired a Senate subcommittee on hunger in 1967. The test of the two different
approaches was the fate of the two committees. The Senate subcommittee, thanks to the volatility of its chairman, who managed
to offend all the conservative members, got nowhere on hunger,
and after a brief period of bitter wrangling, in the words of one
commentator, it "dissolved in chaos." Late in 1971 the Senate
Select Committee on Nutrition and Human Needs was still very

much alive and useful, with a record of achievement that few committees in recent congressional history could match.

Which is not to say that McGovern could not have done more. Indeed by general agreement, even among his supporters, he could have. The food stamp reform bill, for instance, might have fared better in the House if McGovern had pursued it more closely and brought more public pressure to bear. Several lesser issues too might have come to full fruition if McGovern had had more staying power or, in the minds of some of his critics, simply more interest. "McGovern has worked as hard as anyone could have hoped or wanted," explained one staff man. "But face it, Senators—all Senators—have an interest in some things and lesser interest in others. They pick up things and they drop them. McGovern has an overriding interest in the war. We are stuck with that." McGovern has never turned down a staff request or refused to do or say something that staff members felt was important. On the other hand, he has not, especially in recent months, pushed them or the committee as far perhaps as they are capable of going. "This is a weakness in all liberal men," explains a former committee staffer, himself a decidedly liberal man. "After you knock your head against the wall for eighteen months and a lot appears to have been done, you get a little bored and anxious to move on to the next crusade. It's easy to convince yourself of this, especially after something dramatic has been accomplished, like was accomplished with food stamps and school lunch. In reality, of course, there is a helluva lot more to be done, and a helluva long way to go before we reach the ultimate goal of getting everyone fed."

It might well be that neither McGovern nor anyone else could prevent, in the words of Albert Camus, "this world from being a world in which children must suffer." But Camus also said: "We can reduce the number of suffering children." That incontestably George McGovern had done. And for the rest, the ones who still went to bed hungry every night, no one man could be responsible. "Who is to blame for this?" a reporter had demanded outside one of the shacks in Immokalee. McGovern had looked back at him and said slowly: "We're all to blame."

11

Toward 1972

THERE WAS NEVER any question, after the battle of Chicago, that George McGovern would again run for President. If there had been any lingering doubts, he had resolved them by January 1969. Now only two things needed to be answered: when and how.

McGovern's first move was to bolster his staff, which for all its loyalty was determinedly South Dakotan in outlook. Dave Beale, a young Yale-educated lawyer who had been working on Wayne Morse's unsuccessful reelection campaign for the Senate, was brought in to work on legislative matters, especially national security. Beale had a clear understanding that he would be doing more than tinkering with bills and amendments. He was there as underpinning for the presidential campaign. Six months later, John Stacks, who had covered McGovern's 1968 campaign for *Time* magazine and who, as it happened, was Beale's roommate at Yale, signed on as press secretary. Before Stacks's arrival, McGovern's limited press needs were handled by George Cunningham as a sideline to his normal constituency chores. Stacks too came aboard with the understanding that he was to be a press secretary for a presidential candidate.

Meanwhile, McGovern had secured an agent in New York to book his speaking engagements, which beginning early in 1969 had escalated enormously. Within a few months McGovern was making an average of three appearances a week, mostly before church groups and college audiences. "He was out of town so much," says Beale, "it became hard to involve him in legislative matters." A larger concern was the money that poured into the office in the form of honorariums. In 1969 alone McGovern collected nearly $70,000 in speaking fees, second only in the Senate to Edmund Muskie. There were fears among some of the staff that such munificence would not go down well in South Dakota.

Aside from the money, with which McGovern was able to retire his 1968 campaign debt, there was the question of how much political good the frenzied speaking pace was doing him. To a large extent McGovern spoke simply because there was a date open and people wanted to hear him. An overall master plan was lacking. He wasn't being scheduled into the cities and states that would bring him the maximum profit in 1972. The notion of going out and developing speaking opportunities in key areas was almost entirely ignored. McGovern's strategy, if it could be called that, could not have been more basic: get the maximum public exposure in the minimum amount of time. But was this any way to run for the presidency?

The old Kennedy hands told him no. If he was serious about running for the presidency—and McGovern had already made clear to Ted Kennedy that he was, no matter what Kennedy decided to do*—then McGovern had to begin developing a coherent strategy right then, four years in advance of the election, just as John Kennedy had done in 1957. The first part of that strategy, they advised McGovern, was getting his affairs in order, his "ducks in a row," as Joe Dolan put it. And that meant hiring a

* As McGovern put it to Kennedy, and others, with unwitting prescience: "We should have a number of candidates. After all, you never know what can happen. The leading contender could be driving home from a speech one night and run into a light pole."

full-time political operative to handle McGovern's schedule, some-one who would make sure that he went to all the right places, saw all the right people, and made all the right phone calls. What McGovern needed was a guy with savvy.

McGovern took the advice. The man he eventually tapped, after conversations with several candidates, was Dick Leone, an intense, self-assured, and somewhat abrasive political operator who was as tough and pragmatic as he was liberal—and Leone was very liberal. He packed an uncommon lot of political experi-ence and know-how into his thirty-odd years of life. Leone had come up with Richard Hughes, two-fisted Democratic Gover-nor of New Jersey, and had then signed on with Robert Ken-nedy's national staff for the 1968 campaign. His reputation was such that when it came time for McGovern to run on his own, Leone was one of the few people he went out of his way to ask for help. Leone was also one of the few who refused. He had had his candidate in 1968, he said, and now he was dead. The two men remained in close contact, however, and after several preliminary sessions, during which McGovern all but promised Leone that he would run, Leone was hired as senior political technician and tactician early in the summer of 1969.

In the meantime, McGovern had involved himself in what at first seemed a highly dubious political enterprise: the chairman-ship of the Commission on Party Structure and Delegate Selec-tion, otherwise known as the Democratic Reform Commission. McGovern had not wanted the job; few people did, except Harold Hughes of Iowa, who had been studying the possibilities of party reform since early in June 1968, when he chaired a rump liberal commission on the subject. Hughes, however, was a McCarthy man, and like McCarthy he had refused to support the nominee of the convention. Since the nominee was Hubert Humphrey, who was also titular head of the Democratic party, that meant Hughes was out. In his place Humphrey and Fred Harris of Oklahoma, the newly appointed chairman of the Democratic National Commit-tee, wanted McGovern. McGovern had all the right credentials. He was liberal, strong on reform (at his last convention press conference he had made a point of endorsing the idea not once but several times), and at least equally important willing—as Hughes definitely was not—to go along with the old conservative bulls of the party for the sake of a point.

But McGovern resisted. What with the war, the Committee on Nutrition and Human Needs, and the looming prospect of his own campaign, he certainly did not lack for things to do. Besides, he couldn't see the profit in taking the job. "I thought it was a thankless task," he said later. "All I could see you getting out of it was irritating a number of people." But Harris was persistent—by some accounts, almost desperate. So reluctantly McGovern finally accepted, but not before extracting from Harris a number of painful concessions. Hughes, he insisted, would have to be on the commission; moreover, he would have to be vice chairman. Harris fought both points, but McGovern was emphatic. "Take it or leave it," he said bluntly. Harris finally took it, but he refused to personally name Hughes vice chairman. McGovern, he said, would have to take that responsibility himself.

Thus in February 1969 was the Democratic Reform Commission born. Its real roots, however, went back much further, all the way to the early days of the McCarthy campaign and the work of a young liberal lawyer from Brooklyn named Eli Segal. The McCarthy campaign was full of young liberal lawyers, but Segal was one of the brightest, as well as one of the most politically astute. As director of McCarthy's campaign in the nonprimary states, Segal soon discovered that the delegate selection process had started two years before, and in some cases—notably the selection of Democratic national committeemen, a position that brought with it automatic delegate status—a full four years before the convention. Segal noted these facts to a few of his friends in the campaign, and eventually they brought them to the attention of Harold Hughes, perhaps McCarthy's most important political backer.

The result of Segal's conversations with Hughes was the creation of the Commission on the Democratic Selection of Presidential Nominees. For three weeks in June and one week in July 1968 Segal and his friends worked feverishly to compile data for inclusion in a report to the Democratic Convention Rules Committee.

Eventually the Credentials Committee under Governor Richard Hughes of New Jersey proposed that a committee be appointed to "aid the state Democratic parties" by enacting reforms and report its "efforts and findings" to the 1972 convention.

Neither Illinois Governor Sam Shapiro, chairman of the Rules Committee, nor Richard Hughes went as far as the reformers wanted to go. Instead of the vague "serious consideration" of reform they proposed, Segal and his co-workers demanded that the 1972 convention "shall require" that "all Democratic voters . . . [have] full and timely opportunity to participate" in nominating candidates. Further, the reformers insisted that the unit rule be eliminated from all stages of the convention process, and that "all feasible efforts [be] made to assure that delegates are selected through party primary, convention, or committee procedures open to public participation within the calendar year of the national convention." Their recommendations, put in the form of a minority report of the Rules Committee, passed by a razor-thin margin—1,350 to 1,206—the only minority report in the long, bitter convention to do so.

The reformers were disappointed and suspicious when Harris named McGovern chairman of the Reform Commission early the next year. They guessed correctly that in style McGovern was considerably less radical than Harold Hughes. They assumed that McGovern would also be less radical in action, that he would, as one of the more zealous reformers put it, "use party reform as his proof that he could be one of the boys too." They were only slightly more cheered by the composition of the twenty-eight-member commission, which, as Segal describes it, was "a half-step to the left of the Humphrey constituency and a big step to the left of Johnson." Whatever its precise ideology, it certainly was a varied lot. Sitting alongside figures like I. W. Abel of the Steelworkers Union and John Hooker, president of the chicken dinner franchise, Minnie Pearl International, were Aaron Henry of the Mississippi NAACP and David Mixner of the Moratorium Committee. Fred Dutton was there from the Kennedy camp, as well as Will Davis from Texas and former Florida Governor Leroy Collins to guard the interests of the Deep South. Humphrey had his people, and so did Muskie. Birch Bayh was present to look out for himself—though, in the words of one observer, "he never seemed to understand what was going on."

Not many people did. Of all the members on the commission, not more than half a dozen had any clear idea of what was at stake. And for the sake of reform their ignorance was just as well, because McGovern made it clear from the start that he had not taken the chairmanship as a token gesture. As he put it at the commission's first meeting on March 1, 1969: "When parties have been given the choice of reform or death in the past, they have always chosen death. We are going to be the first to live." Two weeks later McGovern stood before the Women's National Democratic Club and in plain terms warned them that unless the party changed, and changed quickly, they could look forward to wholesale defections to third- and fourth-party movements, like the New Democratic Coalition, which had sprung up in the wake of the Chicago disaster. "We have seen the end of the loyal, faithful, and innocent electorate," he declared. "People will no longer let decisions be made for them—even if the professional managers can make more efficient ones. These people want to participate—as Democrats, Republicans, or something new." A few days after that McGovern addressed the Maryland legislature and said in equally blunt language that unless the state party reformed itself by the next convention, its credentials would be challenged. "We will not be weak-kneed on the hard questions of political reform," McGovern also told of members of the commission. "We have a clear mandate to fulfill without weakening either its letter or its spirit. . . . I do not ever again want to see another convention like the one in 1968."

McGovern's words impressed the doubters. They were even more impressed by the people he brought in to run the commission. Though Bob Nelson, his old South Dakota crony, was named staff director, the real direction was in the hands of Eli Segal, who became chief counsel, and Ken Bode, who assumed the position of director of research—both uncompromising McCarthyites. To finance their work, which would soon be supplemented by the arrival of ten summer interns, McGovern lent the commission $15,000 of his own money.

The commission set up shop in the offices of the Democratic National Committee in the Watergate apartment complex in Washington. Almost immediately it set to work planning field hearings in seventeen cities across the country. With equal swiftness, the flak began to fly. Organized labor provided most of it. I. W. Abel never did show up at a commission meeting, and his fill-in stopped coming after the opening session. The attitude of most of the other unions—with the notable exception of the United Auto Workers—was similarly hostile. Word was passed up to the Democratic National Committee that George Meany was "livid" over the very notion that the party was in need of reform. "Any party that produced a Roosevelt, a Truman, a Kennedy, and a Johnson doesn't need reform," humphed one labor official. So saying, the unions proceeded to boycott the commission's hearings—an odd decision, considering that Union representation at the 1968 convention was only 4 percent of the delegates.

Once the commission ventured into the field, the pressure mounted. "The whole atmosphere," wrote conservative columnist William S. White after one hearing, "is . . . somewhat reminiscent of the Moscow purge trials of some years ago, when Communists who had strayed from the one true faith vied with each other in self-abasement in proclaiming their own total wickedness." In Texas *The Dallas Times-Herald* warned that the state was being invaded by "the 'new left' duo, Hughes and McGovern." Texas Governor Preston Smith, who did not know that the commission was coming until he read it in the newspapers, exploded: "This is an absurd way of going about this." Smith then announced that he was absenting himself from the hearings. Most of the state's leading Democratic officeholders followed suit. South Carolina Governor Robert McNair, a moderate by Southern standards, complained that "the commission is headed and staffed by a minority" which was trying to impose its will on the majority. Mississippi Governor John Bell Williams, after boycotting the hearings in Jackson, fulminated: "This group isn't going to accomplish anything." In Louisiana the national committeeman, J. Marshall Brown, distributed 500 copies of a "private and confidential" letter to Fred Harris demanding that he resign and that the Reform Commission be kept out of Louisiana. McGovern lashed back: "We're holding hearings whether you like it or not."

That didn't soothe Tennessee Governor Buford Ellington, who was incensed that the commission came into his state without first informing him. Not to be outdone, Governor Lester Maddox of Georgia labeled McGovern the leader of the "Socialist" arm of the party. Maddox kept his distance from the hearings, as did state officials in Virginia, Florida, and both of the Carolinas. In Chicago Mayor Daley was cordial enough, until McGovern, hoping to head off a far sterner assault by Mixner, suggested that the Mayor might salve some of the "raw wounds" opened up during the convention by dropping indictments against those arrested during the demonstrations. Daley cut McGovern off and huffed angrily: "People came here, not to hold a convention, but to destroy Johnson because they thought he would be a candidate. If you are asking for amnesty, I don't agree. In knowingly violating the law, they must take the consequences." McGovern replied: "What is important is that we put that chapter behind us. It is not a question of amnesty. It is a question of judgment. It's charity and humanism I am asking for." But Daley was not impressed. Nor were some of McGovern's Democratic colleagues in Washington. Kennedy and Muskie began keeping McGovern at arm's length, while McCarthy voiced skepticism about what McGovern was accomplishing. Some former aides to Humphrey were even more direct. The Reform Commission, they charged, was a disaster. McGovern wasn't healing the party; he was irreparably splitting it.

For a time McGovern himself was deeply disheartened. The advice of Eleanor, his staff, and his closest friends seemed to have been right: the Reform Commission job was suicide. Privately, he talked of resigning and might well have if Hughes hadn't talked him out of it. Eventually, McGovern straightened out some of the staff problems that had been responsible for much of the needless friction with party leaders. He also made a point of henceforth calling party officials to personally alert them of his approach. McGovern was not, however, about to be pushed around by anyone. "We can't let any state decide where we go," he assured his staff. "And we don't intend to."

It was well that McGovern stayed with it, because the commission was beginning to have an impact. In six months' time it took testimony from more than 500 witnesses, the great majority of them endorsing drastic reform. ("It seems the outs always want to bitch about the ins," says one commission staff member, explaining the disproportionate number of reformers to standpatters. "But the ins had their chance. They made their mistake in not showing up.") Some of the most remarkable ideas came from what seemed to be the least likely sources. No less than Richard J. Daley urged that every state be required to hold a presidential preference primary, and that candidates enter at least one-third of the primaries to be eligible to compete for the nomination at the national convention. Those who chose to sit out the primaries, Daley suggested, should be required to attain a two-thirds majority in order to win the nomination. Before a commission hearing in Denver, Colorado, Senator Frank Moss proposed that instead of selecting the nominees, future conventions pick the top two or three vote getters, who would then go before a national primary for final approval. McGovern himself leaned to some sort of national primary, or at the very least to primaries in every state. "I would feel uncomfortable as a delegate to any future national convention if I were not there by the direct vote of the people of my state or district," he said. "It is most reassuring to the delegate and to the democratic process to know that one has an authentic constituency."

In 1968, however, there seemed to be few "authentic constituencies" and precious little regard for the niceties of the "democratic process." In state after state the commission gathered examples of the most cynical contempt for the principles for which the party supposedly stood. They discovered that fully one-third of all the delegates to the 1968 convention had been selected more than two years in advance, long before the issues— not to mention the candidates—had been clearly focused. Youth, for all the noise it made during 1968, had been glaringly underrepresented. In eighteen state delegations there were no voting delegates under thirty years of age. In thirteen other delegations there was only one voting delegate under thirty. The average age of one delegation—Delaware—was fifty-three. Women and blacks were similarly shut out. Women, who comprise a majority of the voting-age population in the United States, accounted for only 13 percent of the convention's delegates. Ten state delegations did not have the statutory four women required to fill the places assigned them on the four standing committees of the convention. Only one delegation out of fifty-five—had a woman as its leader. Blacks, despite the fact that they provided 20 percent of the Democratic presidential vote, constituted only about 5.5 percent of the convention's delegates. Thirteen states and three territories had no black delegates or alternates at all, and fifteen had no black voting delegates. Another eleven states had only one black member, and six had three or less. The selection process also discriminated economically. In one state insurgent Democrats wishing to challenge for all delegate positions in the primary had to put up more than $14,000 in filing fees—payable before they could even begin canvassing for petition signatures, which were also required to get on the ballot. In several other states the party assessed each delegate from $15 to $250 to cover "hospitality costs" at the convention. In one state such "hospitality costs" were $500—more than enough to discourage the poor from trying to join the delegation. As a result, the median income of delegates attending the 1964 convention was $18,000. Which is to say that the typical delegate to the Democratic convention was white, male, middle-aged and relatively affluent, a profile more fitting perhaps for the Republicans.

More outrageous than the end product of the delegate selection process was the means by which it was conducted. By use of such devices as unit rule, proxy voting, laughably lenient quorum requirements, the vagaries of state law, and various other Byzantine selection quirks known only to God and the county chairmen, party regulars in 1968 were remarkably successful in keeping the insurgents out. In one Missouri county the chairmen of four township conventions refused to disclose where the delegate selection meetings were being held. In another county the chairman refused to disclose the place of the meeting until the afternoon of the preceding day. In some counties the required meetings were simply done away with. The designated chairman merely forwarded the list of "approved" delegates to the next level in the nominating process. In most instances, though, meetings were at least held, no matter how rigged.

The Reform Commission—or more accurately, a few members of the commission plus the commission staff—set out to right these wrongs with a vengeance. From the beginning, says Segal, they were determined not to be "like the Kerner Commission—long on recommendations, even courage, but very short on follow-through. We weren't interested in recommendations; we were interested in standards." For a long time, though, their resolve remained hidden, from both the press and the party regulars. "The party regulars woke up too late. No one appreciated what we were doing," says one staff member. "Humphrey and the others, they always felt that this was going to be another of those commissions, like the Richard Hughes commission in 1964 that investigated discrimination on the basis of race and did almost nothing, didn't even have any staff until the end and conducted no field hearings. A lot of people thought that the appointment of [Bob] Nelson was a signal that the commission was going to do nothing, because here was this professional party bureaucrat. But they didn't know what was involved. They didn't know what we were up to." What they were up to, says Segal, was "not a revolutionary thing that would move the Democratic party ten steps to the left. The purpose was to lend credibility to the party's institutions." Or as McGovern put it after one field hearing: "What we want to do is present a hopeful alternative to going into the streets."

If the commission was to be credible, though, it had to be tough—and tough it was. Much of the credit went to McGovern. "From beginning to end," says Segal, who later became director of Harold Hughes's short-lived presidential campaign, "whenever we laid out alternatives, he always took the tougher one, the one that meant the most work for the state committees." Most of the alternatives McGovern approved ultimately became the commission's official guidelines.* Eighteen in number, they listed a variety

* The commission's guidelines "required" state parties to publish explicit rules governing delegate selection (some twenty states had no rules at all in 1968); eliminate devices like proxy voting, unit rule, and delegate instruction; set a quorum standard of not less than 40 percent at all party committee meetings; remove all mandatory assessments of convention delegates; limit mandatory participation fees to $10 and petition require-

of reforms, from prohibiting proxies and unit rules to banning discrimination against blacks, women, and the young. In no sense were they merely a set of high-sounding recommendations to be looked at and just as quickly ignored. "We regard our guidelines for delegate selection," the final commission report stated firmly, "as binding on the states."

In September a draft of the commission's findings was circulated among 6,000 "interested Democrats." Their comments resulted in some very minor technical changes in the final commission document, which went before the whole commission during a lengthy, sometimes acrimonious meeting on November 19 and 20. The chief bone of contention was the guideline calling for the elimination of the winner-take-all primary and its replacement by an election that would give losing candidates a share of the delegates on a proportional basis. Under the existing system, the winner of a single primary—California—would have more delegates than the twenty-five smallest states combined. Dutton, a Californian, was determined to keep it that way. The staff, joined by Yale law professor Alexander Bickel, who had been brought in at McGovern's suggestion as a special consultant, was equally determined to make the system fairer to the smaller states. Far more than principle was at stake; the real issue, as both sides knew only

---

ments to no more than 1 percent of the standard used to measure Democratic strength; insure adequate public notice of all party meetings involved in the delegate selection process; provide that all party meetings, except those in rural areas, be held on uniform dates at uniform times and in public places of easy access; encourage representation on delegations of minority groups, young people, and women "in reasonable relationship to their presence in the population of the state"; select alternates in the same way as delegates; pick no more than 10 percent of the delegation by the state committee; designate adequate procedures by which slates are prepared and challenged; apportion all delegates to the convention not selected at large on the basis of representation, giving equal weight to population and Democratic voting strength based on the previous presidential election; choose, in convention systems, no less than 75 percent of the total delegation at a level no higher than the congressional district and adopt an apportionment formula based on population and/or some standard measure of Democratic strength; ban the ex officio designation of delegates to the convention; and conduct the entire process of delegate selection within the calendar year of the convention.

too well, was raw political power. "We must have spent 60 percent of our time debating that one issue alone," says a commission staffer. Eventually, McGovern struck a compromise by which the commission would "urge" the states to have proportional representation by 1972 and "recommend" that the convention adopt a proportional representation scheme for all conventions thereafter.

McGovern would brook no compromise at all, however, on the issue of representation for blacks, women, and youth. His hard line on near-proportional representation for minorities prompted a threat from Maine National Committeeman George Mitchell, Muskie's man on the commission, that he would write a minority report condemning the commission for setting racial "quotas." Mitchell never carried through with his plans, however; nor did Dave Mixner, who was intransigent on the proportional representation issue.

The commission published its findings publicly on February 1, 1970. The same month the Democratic National Committee, at the recommendation of its chairman, Larry O'Brien, approved the guidelines and included them in its call to the 1972 convention. Any state ignoring the guidelines, the committee warned, would be subject to a credentials challenge in 1972.

Apparently, the state parties took the committee at its word, because almost immediately a number of them undertook reforms. In many cases, the worst offenders were the quickest to improve. Alabama, for example, reapportioned its state committee on a one-man, one-vote basis, a move which guaranteed that 15 to 20 percent of the committee's membership would be black. The Florida Democratic Advisory Committee provided for ex officio representation of blacks and young people on the state committee. North Carolina went a step further, appointing a black, a woman, and a youth as vice chairmen of the state party. In Colorado the state committee adopted a proposal to insure proportional representation at the 1972 convention. New Mexico became the first state to opt for a primary that insured proportional representation for supporters of minority presidential candidates. Many other states took the shortest path to reform by passing presidential primary laws.

Whatever the ultimate outcome of these changes, a significant start toward reform had at least been made.* That it got anywhere at all came as a shock to a number of people, especially some of the more cynical observers on the left. "The spectacle of Larry O'Brien saying he was wrong on the war, wrong on repression, wrong on kids, and wrong on the convention was something I frankly did not expect to see," confessed one baffled critic. "I still don't know how McGovern pulled it off." The answer was a combination of enlightened self-interest on the part of the regulars and initial disinterest and disbelief from the commission's potential opponents, right and left. "We backed into it because no one watched us," says one commission staffer. "We were operating in a complete vacuum. Without anyone really realizing it, we were allowed to build up a considerable head of steam and assemble an enormous constituency for reform. After the momentum took over, it was impossible to stop." A likelier explanation perhaps is the one McGovern offered at the very start of the commission's work: when faced with reform or death, the Democrats would choose reform.

Not everyone emerged a winner. Among a number of political observers there were strong suspicions that if anyone suffered especially, it was George McGovern. "He killed himself in the South. His name has become almost an epithet down there," notes one liberal journalist for a national publication. "They'd even take Teddy before they'd take him. Teddy comes off as a Populist. But McGovern, especially after those hearings, comes off as a radical, someone who wanted to end the war two years ago."

One benefit, though, could not be discounted, whatever the ultimate accounting. The Reform Commission had made it demonstrably easier for all insurgents, McGovern included, to go after

---

* Not everyone agreed that the start had been all that significant. A survey by the Democratic National Committee in June 1971 revealed that more than 70 percent of the states had yet to comply with the commission's guidelines on representation for racial minorities. Another 75 percent had failed to compel party officials to issue written rules for the selection of convention delegates, as the guidelines required. Only eight states—totaling about 10 percent of the 1972 delegates—had complied fully with the commission's guidelines. Minnesota Congressman Donald Fraser, McGovern's successor as commission chairman, admitted: "We're going to fall short in some states."

the presidency. And by midsummer of 1969 there was not the slightest doubt that this was precisely what McGovern intended. He might have been willing to defer to Teddy Kennedy in 1968, but not in 1972. The youngest Kennedy had always been friendly enough, sometimes—such as the moment he called McGovern from his yacht to console him about his daughter Terry's arrest—touchingly thoughtful. But Teddy, whatever else he might be, was not Bob. "McGovern," says one man who worked closely with him, "never trusted Teddy to hold up the left wing of the party. He just didn't have confidence in him personally." Deeply sympathetic to Kennedy, fond of him personally, and still a little reverential about the family name, McGovern nonetheless seemed to regard Kennedy as something less than a whole man. To at least one person he suggested that Kennedy was the prisoner, and in some respects the creation, of his staff. "I never want to be like Teddy," he remarked, "so dependent on my staff that I couldn't even write my own press release."

McGovern was in the Virgin Islands relaxing at the estate of his friend real estate developer Henry Kimmelman* the day the

---

* McGovern's friendship with Kimmelman, to whom he was introduced in 1967, is one of the stranger relationships in U.S. politics. "I'd compare it to Nixon and Bebe Rebozo," says a man who knows both of them well, "but it's weirder than that." At first the relationship was strictly social. The McGoverns and the Kimmelmans exchanged a number of dinner invitations, and they vacationed together on Kimmelman's properties in Florida and the Virgin Islands. Kimmelman, who dresses rather modishly, also provided McGovern with sartorial counsel after McGovern abandoned his "shiny brown suits from Sears" for more elegant clothes. Gradually their friendship evolved into a political relationship as well. In 1970 Kimmelman was named finance chairman of McGovern's campaign, though to some people the title appeared to be largely honorific. Kimmelman himself is one of McGovern's biggest contributors, donating somewhere in the neighborhood of $40,000 to the campaign as of late in the summer of 1971. From time to time Kimmelman has offered McGovern advice on political issues, especially the Middle East. By all accounts, McGovern listens but doesn't take what Kimmelman has to say too seriously.

The source of Kimmelman's fortune, which he modestly puts between $5 and $15 million, while others estimate it at closer to $50 million, is almost entirely derived from his real estate holdings in the Virgin Islands and Florida. Kimmelman credits his success to hard work, steady application, and a few breaks. One of his biggest breaks, say some, was his marriage race for the Democratic presidential nomination changed unalterably. July 19, 1969 was a big day in many ways for McGovern. It was, in the first place, his forty-seventh birthday, and the Kimmelmans had planned a small party in celebration. Over dinner, they had chatted about the impending first landing of men on the moon. If there had to be a race to the moon, McGovern said, he was glad that the United States had won it. But he doubted the wisdom of such an expensive contest and wondered aloud whether manned exploration of space was really a smart idea. Couldn't machines do it just as well, he argued, and more safely and inexpensively in the bargain? Maybe, Kimmelman countered, but there was something special about having a man up there on the moon. Well, perhaps, McGovern admitted. He didn't want to argue the point, not on so pleasant a day.

And as it turned out, such a fateful one. For unknown to McGovern and all but a handful of Americans, a drama was at that moment unfolding in the chill waters beneath Chappaquiddick bridge. When McGovern heard the news the next day, his reaction was one of concern for Ted Kennedy. His worry deepened as more press accounts continued to come in. Mike Mansfield was reported issuing a statement of support for Kennedy. McGovern thought that perhaps he should do the same. But first he decided to check it out with one of Kennedy's senior advisers. The reaction was ominous. "You can do that, George, if you want to," he was told over the phone. "But you ought to know that when the facts come out, you may have to retract it." McGovern sent off a telegram of personal sympathy. The public statement of support was forgotten.

A few days later McGovern was back in Washington, talking with Dick Leone, who had just come to work for him. Already it was apparent that Kennedy's position as a serious presidential contender was either untenable or badly compromised. "It's a whole

---

to the daughter of a very rich man. Kimmelman is chairman of the board of the West Indies Corporation, which he describes as a "mini-conglomerate." He is also co-owner of the Virgin Islands Hilton in St. Thomas. Among his other major interests is Overview Corporation, an environmental consulting firm, of which he is president and Stewart Udall chairman.

new ballgame," McGovern summed it up. Both men concluded that they ought to be in and pitching before too many innings were over. But first they should get the opinion of the pros and, if they were lucky, their pledges of support. McGovern contacted Kimmelman and asked whether he would be willing to host a small dinner party for a dozen or so of McGovern's friends. Kimmelman replied that he would indeed, and the invitations went out.

In seeking advice, McGovern turned both to his friends and to those with whom he was not personally close but felt "should be there." Abe Ribicoff was asked to come, and so were the Udall brothers, Stewart and Morris. Fred Dutton and Charles Guggenheim were on the list, along with Blair Clark, Allard Lowenstein, and Myer Feldman. Cunningham, Leone, and Mixner rounded out the bunch. McGovern wanted to invite Gloria Steinem, but Ribicoff vetoed the suggestion. "No broads," he said emphatically.

It was not the most auspicious of beginnings. Talk around the dinner table tended to ramble. Lowenstein offered a defense of his 1968 strategy. Ribicoff frankly couldn't see why anyone wanted to be President. "If you run, George," he said, "you have to be willing to give up your life, your fortune, your family, even some of your ideals." To insure that McGovern didn't miss the point, Ribicoff repeated it several times during the meeting. Clark quietly observed that if McGovern were to have any chance at all, his would have to be a "high risk" candidacy, out front—meaning furthest left—on all the issues. Dutton talked about where McGovern should travel, and Guggenheim mentioned how he could improve his TV style. The media were going to be crucial in 1972, he insisted, and McGovern had better prepare for it. Feldman agreed; he knew a voice coach in New York who could remedy McGovern's nasal twang. And so it went. There was general agreement that Kennedy was "out of it" and considerable speculation about the new faces that might come forward to take his place. Maryland Senator Joe Tydings, who would shortly be defeated for reelection, was mentioned as one likely possibility. McGovern, of course, was the certainty. But no one in the room, with the exception of the people who worked for him and perhaps one or two others, was prepared to commit himself to McGovern then and there. Somewhat disappointed, McGovern thanked them for coming and asked everyone send him a short memo of his impressions. Few did.

In the future, McGovern decided, he would not waste his time on the unconvinced. He wanted advice from those who were willing to back it up with work. Meanwhile, the political "guns for hire," as Leone called them, began knocking on McGovern's Washington door. Ted Van Dyk, Humphrey's top speechwriter and tactician during the 1968 campaign, stopped by to visit and later sent along a memo with some of his ideas. ("Avoid 'Meet the Press' type programs" was one of them, apparently reflecting his memory of Humphrey's unhappy confrontations with reporters before television cameras.) Eventually, Van Dyk became one of the McGovern campaign triumvirs. For the moment, though, he wanted to limit his help to advice, and informal advice at that. That was the attitude of most of the others who came calling, like Curtis Gans, who ran McCarthy's student volunteer operation. Gans, Dutton, and the others who lunched with McGovern in the far corner of the Senate dining room were merely paying their respects, letting him know that they were interested, even encouraging him, but still a little wary. McGovern, though, read far more into their visits. Then, as later, he had a tendency to take people, especially politicians, at their most generous. Another trait that sometimes led him into trouble was his readiness to offer a man a job if he liked him. McGovern did this to Steve Schlesinger, then embarrassingly had to retract the offer when Arthur's son arrived in Washington to find that there was nothing to do. An unhappier incident was McGovern's seeming job tender to a *Chicago Sun-Times* reporter, who delightedly quit his job, told off his bosses, and caught a plane for Washington, only to discover, as had Schlesinger, that the supposed job did not exist.

The false starts were a sign of McGovern's growing exuberance. He was impatient to begin. His already crowded speaking schedule was jammed still further, to the point that he was spending half his time on the road. California, his advisers told him, would be critical, and McGovern made a point of getting out to the coast at least one weekend every two months. Kennedy, now self-certified as out of it, suggested that McGovern visit Wisconsin once a month, which ate another weekend. Leone, for his part, told McGovern that he had to go anywhere outside Washington if he expected to get press coverage. The Washington press corps, he decided early on, was "death." All of which added up to one conclusion: Run, run, run.

The constant travel put strains on his staff; the South Dakotans were naturally jealous of new arrivals like Leone, Beale, and Stacks, while the out-of-staters seemed a bit contemptuous of the way the veterans operated, especially how they protected their boss, shielding him from potential controversy, resenting the intrusion of outsiders, defending him, or so they thought, from the unreasonable demands of young hotspurs who seemed to think only of the presidency. Leone, who had very definite ideas about how to do things and tended to demand rather than ask, hardly helped matters. Before long, staff members weren't speaking to one another. McGovern tried to solve the problem by switching desks, and when that didn't work he switched desks again, and then again. He refused, however, to intervene personally, saying that he liked "creative tension." There was tension aplenty, but it was highly questionable how much of it was creative.

The real trouble, though, was not so much McGovern's staff as McGovern himself. The weeks raced by in a blur. He was here, there, and everywhere without any real plan or concept of what he was doing except going for the big prize. Finally, in November, his system gave out and he returned to Washington for a few weeks' rest and reflection. Awaiting him was a sharply critical memo from Fred Dutton warning him that he was "turning too political . . . reaching out and straining too hungrily at this stage as a matter of political form." McGovern, Dutton wrote, was "not coming through as the strong solitary figure . . . but rather [was] becoming a more calculating person." "You seem to keep trying to generate momentum by letting out what should be going on behind the scenes," Dutton concluded. "The net effect is that you leave an impression of being self-reaching, premature, contriving. . . . Your entire forthcoming efforts should be built on what personal qualities are already deeply engrained in you, [which are] to be dramatized and emphasized, so that the country knows you as a human being—who is also of presidential dimensions."

McGovern could only agree with Dutton's analysis. Thinking of the presidency, he admitted, was "pretty heady stuff." Perhaps he had been carried away by the thought of it. (Looking back on the period two years later, he was even more self-critical. "I suppose," he confessed, "there is a certain amount of greed in wanting to make a lot of money, and a certain amount of pride in wanting to get well known.") That didn't deter his fundamental enthusiasm for the project. If anything, he was even more keen about coming into the open about his plans and desires. He was tired of being coy with reporters' questions. "Of course, I want to run for President," he said in exasperation. "How can I keep bullshitting people about it?"

If McGovern had followed his instincts, he would have stopped pretending then. Late in the fall of 1969, pushed on by friends like Galbraith, he was on the brink of announcing his candidacy. In fact, at one December lunch with Haynes Johnson of *The Washington Star* he admitted that he was running. Thinking that he had an exclusive, Johnson rushed back to his office and prepared a major story, only to have McGovern call him a day later to request that what had been said on the record twenty-four hours before now be kept off. McGovern had drawn back, but only because staff members had beseeched him to. They correctly pointed out that an announcement of candidacy at that time would make a shambles of his work on the Reform Commission, seriously jeopardize his chances of getting major legislation through the Congress, undo the Committee on Nutrition and Human Needs, which was then up for refunding, and most damaging of all, create the impression that his opposition to the war was politically inspired. Reluctantly McGovern gave in. It was clear, though, that the manner in which he was pursuing the presidency demanded a major reevaluation.

The personnel changes came first. For Stacks, who had grown increasingly unhappy with the intraoffice wrangling, the Haynes Johnson episode was the breaking point. He left in December. Beale followed two months later. The most predictable departure was Leone's. Temperamentally, he and McGovern were poles apart. Leone sought to direct McGovern, and McGovern was not about to be directed by anyone, even if it was for his own good.

Leone's fatal mistake, though, was regarding McGovern like Bob
Kennedy, expecting him to do the things Kennedy would have
done, act the way Kennedy would have acted. As the South Dakotans could have told Leone, if only he had bothered to ask,
George McGovern acted like George McGovern. Leone himself
was tight-lipped about his reasons for quitting. As he put it nearly
two years later: "Let's just say I was spoiled by other people I
had worked for."

Alone now, and a bit shaken by the suddenness of events, Mc-
Govern paused to take stock. He had been running loose at top
speed for the better part of a year, and if he had made much
progress it was hard to notice. Certainly the polls didn't show it.
Muskie seemed more entrenched as the front runner than ever.
Even his bread-and-butter issue—the war—seemed to have failed
him. The indifferent reception at the Moratorium and the hostility
growing out of the Mobilization were the first faint hints that he
might be "wearing a little thin," as one of his staffers put it, as a
spokesman against the war. A new course was called for, a slower
and more thoughtful course, that would permit him to weigh
and consider what he did even as he did it. He cut his speaking
schedule down drastically and disciplined himself to spend more
time in Washington, where after the Cambodian invasion, his
presence was increasingly demanded. McGovern, in short, was
weighing his priorities: the war or himself. Not surprisingly, the
war won out.

McGovern did not quit campaigning entirely. Several times a
month he managed to slip out of Washington for a brief speech
or party function. It was on one of these occasional forays late in
March 1970 that he met Gary Hart, a 31-year-old Denver lawyer
who had worked on Robert Kennedy's campaign in 1968. Hart
had much of Leone's expertise and none of his personal drawbacks.
Easygoing, personable, and warm, he suited McGovern's tempera-
mental requirements perfectly. And Hart knew what he was doing
—as well as what McGovern was doing wrong. McGovern's
initial proposal was that Hart oversee his political affairs in the
Western States. That arrangement lasted until May, when Hart,
now McGovern's national campaign director, began dividing his
time between Washington and his Colorado law practice. The

transcontinental commuting continued all summer, with the law practice predictably getting shorter and shorter shrift. Finally, late in August, Hart came to Washington permanently and opened McGovern's first campaign office a few blocks from the Capitol. The staff consisted of Hart, Rick Stearns, a Rhodes scholar in political philosophy who the winter before had made a confidential study of McGovern's voting record, and Yancey Martin, a black man who had worked on the minority affairs staff of the Democratic National Committee.

The McGovern presidential campaign, having gone through one life and death, was reincarnated on July 25, 1970, at a meeting at McGovern's Cedar Point Farm in St. Michael's, Maryland. None of the big-name pros were there. Instead, McGovern assembled people who were indisputably for him: Pat Donovan, his personal secretary; George Cunningham, his administrative assistant; Dick Wade, who had recently moved to New York; and Stearns and Hart. There was no fencing about the wisdom of McGovern's running. The main topic on the agenda was when. McGovern, as always, was for the earliest possible declaration, if for no other reason than to head off New York Mayor John Lindsay, who he figured might switch parties at any moment. He should announce early, McGovern argued, before Lindsay had the chance to become "the white hope of the more rational elements in the party." Announcing soon might also discourage other contenders, notably Harold Hughes. McGovern's strongest argument was that the people he encountered on his travels across the country were urging him to go, more now than ever before. "There is no Adlai Stevenson as titular party head," McGovern said. "We don't have the White House speaking for the party. The national organization is floundering in debt. For all those reasons, the first person who announces loud and clear is going to receive support from the people, who are going to be relieved that somebody will take Nixon on. Anyone who waits beyond, say, November 15, is going to be second guy."

The staff was not so sure. The coming elections had to be considered. How would other politicians take to the offer of aid from a presidential candidate? Then there was the Reform Commission to think of. If McGovern announced in November, he would certainly have to resign his chairmanship, with much of the work still undone. Finally, an early announcement might lack the drama that had attended Robert Kennedy's late entry into the race. That point worried McGovern least; he wasn't Robert Kennedy. We have to go early, he kept pressing, and eventually he swung the staff around. They left Cedar Point intending to make a November 10 announcement.

Soon after McGovern returned to Washington it became apparent that the November date was out of the question. Hart and his staff simply needed more time to work out the logistics of a presidential campaign. The first thought was to delay a month, but that would put McGovern in the middle of the Christmas season, where the announcement, Stearns noted, was "likely to be buried under the Christmas carols." Thus, the date became January.

In the meantime, McGovern considered various ways of dramatizing his entry into the presidential race. Someone observed that just running was drama enough; no other candidate had announced that early since Andrew Jackson, who had declared a full four years in advance of the election. But McGovern was looking for more than a gimmick. He was searching for some means to convey that what he and his campaign stood for had its roots deep in American history, that his so-called radicalism was nothing more than fidelity to the principles of Jeffersonian democracy. The mention of Jefferson set historian Wade to thinking. Jefferson, he seemed to recall, had announced his candidacy in a series of handwritten letters to the newspaper editors of the country. Why not do the same, he suggested, and with the aid of a jet go Jefferson one better, and hand-deliver them? The idea caught McGovern's fancy, as it did everyone's, until someone mentioned that the Associated Press and the United Press International hadn't existed in Jefferson's day. As soon as McGovern dropped off his first letter, the wires would see to it that all the other editors in the country knew its contents within minutes. So much for letters to the editors.

But McGovern did not discard the idea of writing some kind of letter. He was determined to get away from the slick media campaign that so appalled him in McGinniss' *The Selling of the*

President and that Guggenheim* and others had been urging on
him. A letter somehow had an old-fashioned Populist ring, which
was precisely the kind of campaign image McGovern wanted to
convey. People felt that government was out of their control, he
told his staff; if his campaign did nothing else, he wanted it to
involve people, to give them a sense of participation. Gradually
the two ideas converged. The letter McGovern would write
would be not to the newspaper editors but to the people, or more
precisely to the 200,000 or so liberal voters and friends he had
assembled on a computerized mailing list. Included in the letter
announcing his candidacy would be an appeal for funds, their
initial means of participation. "Nobody's ever done this before,"
said McGovern. "I want to run a campaign financed by tens of
thousands of small contributions. That's how I want to build my
organizational base, not with a lot of money from a few big contributors."

While McGovern sat down to write, rewrite, and write again
his letter of candidacy, Morris Dees, a Birmingham-based direct-
mail wizard who made his first million in his twenties, was brought
in to advise on the fund-raising campaign. There was some
thought that McGovern's letter, which ran to seven typed pages
by the time he finished it, should be drastically edited for the sake
of his readers, but Dees told them not to cut a line. The most successful direct-mail solicitation in history, he noted, was a twenty-
two-page letter. A longer letter give people the impression that

---

* Guggenheim wanted to portray McGovern as the candidate of Middle
America. He urged in an August 1969 memo:

   The necessity to turn your concerns to the "forgotten man" in
America cannot be overemphasized. You have certainly earned and
have the respect of the young and thinking liberal. You may even
have the farm vote (whatever that may represent these days) but the
vast throng of hard-working urbanites, the fellow who pays most of
the taxes, reads the *Reader's Digest*, and is on the cutting edge of most
of today's social reforms, really doesn't know what to make of George
McGovern of South Dakota. You enter national politics with your
own coalition, but it does not include the people who won for Bobby
in Indiana, Nebraska, and South Dakota and defeated him in Oregon.
It does not include the people that Norman Rockwell painted. It does
not include those people you must have to win outside the glandular
and issue-oriented constituencies of the American seaboard.

the author cared about them. Dees did make one change, and that was to transform each of McGovern's sentences into a short paragraph. Tom Collins, a New York ad man, made a few minor fixes and the letter was put in the mail on Friday, January 15, so that it would arrive in most homes the very moment that McGovern was making his formal declaration in a statewide television address to the people of South Dakota.

McGovern's declaration of candidacy, delivered from the Sioux Falls studios of KELO-TV on the evening of January 18, 1971, was not the most inspiring or eloquent speech of his career. It had perhaps been rewritten a few too many times to have the spontaneity required of greatness. But it did get the message across:

I seek the presidency because I believe deeply in the American promise and can no longer accept the diminishing of that promise. Our country began with a declaration of man's right to "life, liberty, and the pursuit of happiness." . . . But today, our citizens no longer feel that they can shape their own lives in concert with their fellow citizens. Beyond that is the loss of confidence in the truthfulness and common sense of our leaders. The most painful new phrase in the American political vocabulary is "credibility gap"—the gap between rhetoric and reality. Put bluntly, it means that people no longer believe what their leaders tell them. . . . The kind of campaign I intend to run will rest on candor and reason. . . . I make one pledge above all others—to seek and speak the truth with all the resources of mind and spirit I command.

I believe the people of this country are tired of the old rhetoric, the unmet promise, the image makers, the practitioners of the expedient. The people are not centrist or liberal or conservative. Rather, they seek a way out of the wilderness. But if we who seek their trust, trust them, if we try to evoke the "better angels" of our nature, the people will find their own way. We are the children of those who built a great and free nation. And we are no less than that. We must decide whether our courage and imagination are equal to their talents. If they are, as I believe, then future generations will continue to love

America, not simply because it is theirs but for what it has become—for what, indeed, we have made it.

So now he was committed. Few people gave him a chance.
Time commended his courage for embarking on a "swift swim
against a strong tide" but predicted that he would eventually be
pulled under. *Time*'s fear was Muskie. Others worried about decency. *The Nation* wondered:

> Can a Good Man Win? Is it possible that Senator McGov-
> ern just might win the Democratic nomination and then go on
> to win the presidency? There is something rather terrifying in
> the prospect. Good men have made it to the White House so
> infrequently that the thought of George McGovern's becoming
> President is positively unnerving. We have had, of course,
> great Presidents, men of high intelligence, courage, vision, high
> character, and other admirable qualities, but genuine human
> decency has not been a common trait. George McGovern is
> one of the rare good men in national politics. It is difficult to
> imagine his being vindictive or inconsiderate or indifferent to
> human suffering. His decency as a human being, let it be con-
> fessed, is a distinct liability.

The "Durocher issue," as some came to call it, was real enough.
It was not, however, McGovern's biggest problem. That, quite
simply, was convincing people—himself foremost—that he was in
the race to win, that he wanted to win, and that given the right
combination of circumstances he could indeed do it. There were
times when even his friends wondered if McGovern was truly
serious. "Well, whatever happens," he remarked at an early campaign meeting, "we're going to have a lot of fun in the next
months." "Senator," snapped Joe Dolan, "I never want to hear
that kind of talk again. Unless you believe yourself that you are
going to win, you never will. You might as well stop right now."
Later, when his campaign staff, which had grown to six by the
time of the announcement and to twenty within a few months,
was designing a sign to hang outside the campaign headquarters,
McGovern dropped by to inspect the plans. The words "Thirty-
eighth President of the United States" made him blanch. "Gee,"

he said, "don't you think that's a little pretentious?" Of course it was, but McGovern had missed the obvious psychological point.

McGovern wanted power—there was no denying that. But his ambition was burdened by a heavy sense of fatalism. For all his years in Washington, he had not quite shaken the wonder that a preacher's kid from Avon had made it to the Senate and now was dicing for the biggest stakes of all.

After one particularly successful campaign trip he reflected to his staff:

> We have the greatest privilege that is open to any person in the world, and that is to run for the presidency without regard to whether we win or lose, but just to come to know the United States. There is no person in this country that is ever going to get to know it like a guy who runs for President, because what you're doing is imploring every guy in this country—from the lowliest bootblack to the president of the New York Stock Exchange—to listen to you while you try to figure out what is on his mind. . . . I think I am much more philosophical about the whole question of whether we actually get the most votes for the nomination, although, of course, I want to win. What I now see is a great opportunity to know this country as you can know it in no other way, and that is by going out to deal with the people in every nook and cranny of this country, and God, what an exciting country it is.

McGovern meant to see most of it, especially the primary states. Early on in the planning process, his advisers and staff (which now included Frank Mankiewicz, who had left his syndicated newspaper column to become "senior political adviser" with special responsibility for the press) had given each state a color and letter rating. The white or "f" states were those judged to be politically valueless or, for McGovern, politically hopeless. The candidate would husband most of his time and energies for the "a" and "b" states, some twenty-four in all, which included most but by no means all of the primary states. Ultimately, McGovern would enter as many as eighteen primaries, including some—notably, New Hampshire—in which he did not figure to do well but could hardly avoid. The strategy called for McGovern to do moderately but not overwhelmingly well in the "first half" of the primary season, which included states like New Hampshire, Florida, West Virginia, and Massachusetts. Midpoint in the campaign—and a crucial test of McGovern hopes—was Wisconsin. Here McGovern had to do more than well; he had to win—and convincingly—if he was to remain a credible candidate. "Let's put it this way," said one of his advisers. "If we don't win in Wisconsin, we better have a helluva good excuse."

On the face of it, McGovern's prospects seemed bright in the Dairy State. Wisconsin had a deep-rooted Populist tradition, a sizable liberal-intellectual community, and an encouragingly large farm population, which, McGovern figured, by rights would be his. On the darker side, there were all those people of Polish origin in Milwaukee just itching, it was presumed, to vote for Edmund Sixtus Muskie. And Wisconsin, for all its populism, had also given the nation the "bad" Senator McCarthy. To offset these disadvantages, McGovern's campaign staff assigned Wisconsin the largest share of its organizational and political resources, not the least of which was the frequent presence of the candidate himself. If McGovern survived Wisconsin, the remaining primaries would stack up far more favorably than those that had preceded them. In the vision of McGovern's planners, he would sweep through Nebraska, pick up his own state's twenty-six delegate votes, then, gaining momentum, blitz through Oregon for the finale in California, where winner would take all. With California under his belt, New York would be a cinch. Then on to Miami Beach, if not as the front runner then no worse than second man. There perhaps on the second or third ballot it would come down to a test of two men: the representative of the left (McGovern, naturally) and whoever the right wing of the party decided to put up —Jackson, Humphrey, or Muskie. Confronted with that choice, the convention would of course turn to McGovern. Such, at least, was the theory.

It all sounded so grand and so logical—almost too easy. Of course, it was none of these. No doubt there were far more reasonable scenarios, being drawn up that very moment in other campaign headquarters, that left McGovern out entirely. Theoretically, McGovern could have tinkered with the strategy he had chosen to follow. For one thing, he could have made some move toward the center, where, he kept telling a disbelieving staff, a not inconsiderable reservoir of support waited to be tapped. But such a ploy would not have been McGovern's style—and it would not have been McGovern. He was what he was, and despite minor concessions to image-making, like wider lapels, longer hair, and bushier sideburns,* he was both unwilling and unable to fundamentally change it. Whether or not the McGovern strategy for capturing the nomination made sense, he and those who went with him were prisoners to it. "There are some things both we and he can do," says Rick Stearns. "He can improve his performance, the way he handles himself with party people. But these are improvements of degree. Most of the rest of it is really out of his control."

McGovern the historian believed in 1972, as he had twenty years before, that some men, by force of will or intellect or chance, were able to "channel" history, to guide it in some measure to their advantage if not to their total end. This is what he set out to do in the winter of 1971. His approach this time was far

---

* The cosmetic and sartorial reconstruction of McGovern had its beginnings in 1968 during his short-lived campaign for the presidency. Arriving at a New York television studio for a talk show appearance, McGovern was as usual ill-dressed and pale. Worst of all, he was wearing socks that just barely cleared his ankles. When McGovern crossed his legs, a vast expanse of white shin was exposed to the cameras. Gloria Steinem solved that problem and set McGovern on the road to recovery by dashing to a local men's store and bringing back a pair of over-the-calf socks. She also introduced him to the benefits of an all-year tan courtesy of an electric sunlamp. When McGovern arrived in Chicago for the convention, a cadre of union tailors was commissioned to create in twenty-four hours a replacement for the "electric green" number he was wearing.

McGovern's wardrobe has gradually expanded from there, to the point that today, when his tie is right, he is one of the better dressed men on Capitol Hill—though some friends, like Schlesinger, complain that he is "almost too mod." McGovern has also let his hair grow long and now combs it over the front of his head in a vain effort to camouflage his baldness, which results partially from his bouts with hepatitis. A more radical solution—the wearing of a toupee—was discontinued after a few days of use in 1965. McGovern became the butt of many jokes among his colleagues for being a "big wig" and finally took it off when Bob Kennedy told him bluntly: "George, that thing looks terrible."

more paced, far less frenetic than it had been eighteen months or
even a year before. The campaign schedule that Hart, Mankiewicz, and Van Dyk devised was cyclical in nature: a few months
of heavy public appearances on the road, then a few months of
rest and regrouping, followed by yet another raid into the countryside, an ebb and flow of action and planning. It was not a flashy
tactic. Indeed, there was little more to it than the nuts and bolts of
the most basic political organizing—only done on a massive scale.
But it suited McGovern's personality perfectly. As one of his advisers described it: "He's doing nothing less than running the campaign he has always run in South Dakota, only in all the primary
states."

So, sometimes, it seemed. In dozens of small and middle-sized
towns and cities across the country—places like Tomah, Wisconsin; Laurel, Nebraska; Hollis, New Hampshire; Barrackville,
West Virginia—the routine was the same. A tall, balding middle-
aged man walking unnoticed down a main street until he summoned the nerve to stick out his hand at startled passers-by.
"Hello, I'm Senator McGovern." "Oh, hello, Governor," they'd
sometimes say, and that would be the start of it. "It's a nice town
you have here," McGovern would go on. "You come from
here?" Assured that they did, McGovern would continue. "You
know, I'm running for the presidency, and I'm going to be
coming out here often. Because I want to hear what's on people's minds. They're pretty concerned about the economy, aren't
they?" Invariably, they were, or about whatever else McGovern
mentioned: the war, taxes, the flight to the cities, farm problems,
and again and again belief in government. "Well," McGovern
would say, "I'm trying to do something about that. It's an important issue, and I think people want to hear about it, don't
you?" He wasn't giving a speech, he was asking a question, and
more remarkably he wanted to hear the answer. Usually, the
interchange went on for two or three minutes, often longer.
Then at precisely the right moment, McGovern would say:
"Thanks for visiting with me. I hope you can give me your support."

To reporters used to the surging crowds, which literally
ripped the shirt off a presidential candidate's back, the candidacy

of George McGovern presented an odd, even ludicrous aspect. Could so plain a man be serious about running for the presidency, especially when he spent ten minutes talking with the town barber instead of calling on the county chairman? They could only wonder and write about what seemed obvious: the lack of charisma, the failure to budge in the polls, the strong words about the war. A few, a very few, saw something else: the unseen but potentially powerful building of an organization at the grassroots, the almost imperceptible turning away from the Kennedy style of charisma, even, and this was rarest of all, the appeal of a quietly decent man. "George McGovern comes at you like one of those big Irish heavyweights in the 1930s," columnist Pete Hamill wrote, "a little slow, but with the chin shut hard against the chest, the jab reaching out, coming on, daring you to do your best. Like Jim Braddock, he might be beaten, but you will know he was there, he will not fold up on you, he will surrender no dignity, and you will come away speaking about him with respect. Sometimes, he will even win."

Hamill was one of the convinced. There were few others. Many journalists who might otherwise have looked on McGovern with a kindlier or more objective eye were unsettled by the undeniably large presence of former Kennedy men—like Mankiewicz, Salinger, and Schlesinger, to name but three of the more well known—either on McGovern's staff or at his ear. That other Kennedy hands were aiding Muskie or that "Bob Kennedy people are not necessarily Ted Kennedy people," as Gary Hart pointed out, or even that the large number of Kennedy hands in Democratic politics made it inevitable that a good portion of them would wind up working for McGovern, impressed the reporters little. McGovern, they insisted, was a "stalking horse" for Ted Kennedy. McGovern's own opinion of Kennedy seemed to count not at all. "Maybe he's not a conscious stalking horse," said a top executive for a major newsgathering organization, "but he's sure as hell at least an unwitting one." McGovern himself was certainly alive to the possibility. While personally convinced that Kennedy would never run, if only because of the possibility of assassination, he could not help looking over his shoulder from time to time. Once on the Senate floor a few months after his declaration of candidacy, at a time when the polls showed Kennedy even more popular than Muskie, McGovern remarked to Kennedy half-jokingly: "Well, it doesn't look like you are going to be able to stay out of this thing." Kennedy was dead serious. "I am out of it, George, and I am never getting back into it." Of course, events might prove otherwise; they had for another Kennedy who a year before the election had been just as stout in his denials. If that happened, McGovern admitted privately, the going would be tough. Some staff members would undoubtedly leave. The ones he counted on though, like Mankiewicz, would stay. "It will be painful for him," McGovern said of Mankiewicz, "but he'll stick."

McGovern, however, could never convince the press of that. In fact, the press and its image of him loomed as his most serious political problem. Whatever he did, he could not escape the inevitable identification in every news story as "mild-mannered George McGovern." The way to change his image, Mankiewicz kiddingly suggested, was to "get the rumor spread that someone at a cocktail party made a remark that you didn't like, and you gave him a quick karate chop that broke his arm." McGovern was not amused. "It galls the hell out of me," he said in exasperation, "that every time Pete McCloskey says something about the war, it's 'war hero Pete McCloskey.' Why don't they ever write about 'bomber pilot McGovern'?" The answer was only too obvious: handsome, jut-jawed Californian Pete McCloskey *seemed* like a war hero; the image of George McGovern dodging flak over Germany strained belief. McGovern wouldn't have minded being portrayed as Clark Kent if he could at least have shaken journalistic typecasting as a one-issue man. "The President's got to know about a lot of things," said one liberal political reporter. "And McGovern only knows about one: Vietnam." In fact, by the summer of 1971 McGovern was talking about Vietnam rarely, if at all. His speeches, instead, dwelled on the economy, the environment, the plight of the cities—on "reordering America's priorities," as he prosaically put it. But the reporters were not listening. They heard only the questions about Vietnam, and that was hardly news. Finally, in some desperation McGovern called a press conference in August 1971 to announce that he would no longer talk about Vietnam. "And," he added candidly, "I hope the press will see fit to report the other things I have to say." Whether it would remained open to serious question.

It was unfortunate that the press was not listening, because much of what McGovern was saying was fresh and new to the American political debate. He talked of cutting $30 billion or more from the defense budget, of naming a woman to the Supreme Court and several to the Cabinet, and of relieving much of the racial tension by offering everyone in the country a good job at a decent wage. The last proposal, he promised, would be his first priority as President. He would gather the agencies of government, the labor unions, and private industry and have them come up with the kind of "economic conversion" he had been talking about since 1963. And when the plans were laid, he would go to the people and say: "Look, everybody who wants to work is going to have a job. We don't know quite yet what you will be doing. You are going to have a good job. And the government is going to guarantee that kind of employment at decent wages. We'll put you to work rebuilding dilapidated housing, we'll clean up the parks or clean up the neighborhoods, we'll go to work on developing a low-cost transit system and traffic control systems, we'll train those who want to work as paramedical personnel, nurses, nurse's aides, day-care center supervisors. There is enough to do in this country. Everybody can have a chance to work."

McGovern saw nothing radical or revolutionary in his proposals. The government giving a man a job, he said, was "really a kind of intelligent modern application of the Puritan ethic. It's saying that we shouldn't waste labor, we shouldn't waste human life." The same was true about the other things he said, from ending the war to healing the divisions between young and old. The kind of America envisioned in his speeches was neither very radical nor even necessarily very liberal. Indeed, in the sense that it harkened back to an easier, simpler time, a mélange of Jeffersonian democracy and Wilsonian idealism (and it was no accident that those two Presidents were his heroes), it was an almost conservative philosophy. But none of the traditional political labels fit, neither radical, liberal, conservative, nor even

Populist, though in many ways that seemed to come closest. McGovern on occasion called himself a Populist, and he liked to be compared with other prairie radicals, especially Peter Norbeck of South Dakota and, more secretly, William Pettigrew, the Senator whose gradual radicalization finally ended in Marxism. "I think I feel more at home," McGovern said once, "when I read the Populists than any other group." But on the cities the great Populists like William Jennings Bryan were xenophobes, and McGovern was hardly for that. What was he then? In the set-piece speech he delivered across America perhaps lay the answer:

> Come home, America, from Saigon, where we are wasting young blood in support of a political regime that does not even have the respect of its own citizens. . . .
>
> From the evils of racism to the dignity of brotherhood, Come home, America. . . .
>
> From boasts of a silent majority to the higher ground of conscience and responsibility, Come home, America. . . .
>
> From political intimidation and conspiracy trials to the Constitution and the Bill of Rights, Come home, America. . . .
>
> From the hunger of little children, from the loneliness of the aging poor, from the despair of the homeless, the jobless, the uncared-for sick, to a society that cherishes the human spirit, Come home, America. . . .
>
> Come home, prodigal America, to the land of your fathers, where we can rebuild our cities, revitalize our farms and towns, reclaim our rivers and streams. . . .
>
> Come home, America, to that sense of community that opened the country and gave us nationhood. For what we need most of all is the assurance that each one of us is part of a nation where we care about each other. . . .
>
> That is the way home for America.

"Come Home, America" was not so much a speech as a sermon. To the professional wordsmiths, the rhetoric was almost embarrassingly old-fashioned. Even McGovern's friends sometimes cringed when he launched into the peroration. "He sounds like a minister saying that stuff," one of them winced, unconsciously putting the finger on the heart of McGovern's campaign. Because

McGovern, despite the political trappings, was preaching. The campaign was his "bully pulpit." There was nothing new in what McGovern was saying or in the way he was saying it. In fact, it was very, very old. What made it seem so extraordinary was that its likes had not been seen in a very long time.

12

The Politics of Belief

A PROFESSOR ONCE told McGovern that he would be a Congressman in the 1950s, a Senator in the 1960s, and President in the 1970s.

He may yet be proved right.

If the professor's prediction turns out to be wrong, it will not be because his pupil lacked the will or the ambition. An interviewer found that out when he asked McGovern if perhaps it didn't require some extraordinary sense of righteousness, almost a power neurosis, to seek the highest office in the land. McGovern didn't hesitate a moment. "I don't think it requires a power neurosis," he replied evenly. "As a matter of fact, I would say that anyone in a position to make a reasonable bid for the presidency, who has some reasonable understanding of what needs to be done [and] who backs away from it, that he is neurotic. Seeking the presidency may be facing reality, a willingness to do what is responsible and courageous. The greater danger of neurosis is on the side of those who drop out or back away from the opportunity to bring about change."

On another occasion a particularly persistent reporter in Green Bay, Wisconsin, challenged McGovern: "Are you a doubter?" "Doubt?" McGovern replied, as if he were just being introduced to the concept for the first time. "Doubt about what?" "About anything," the reporter pressed. "Just about life." Said McGovern: "No."

Anyone who has seen McGovern field questions from an audience will know what the reporter was getting at. The answer comes back as soon as the question is finished. There is never a pause, never a hesitation, and only rarely any qualification. The responses are chiseled in the plainest of words and they are refreshingly direct. The same is true of his position on the issues. McGovern is the most predictable—the most readily knowable—of all the candidates. He could be called an ideologue, except that the ideology he so faithfully follows is a patchwork of his own creation. A closer explanation is that he has developed a conceptual framework into which, as one friend puts it, "everything fits."

Because everything does fit, and so maddeningly well, McGovern at times comes off as almost too self-confident, even arrogant. McGovern himself admits that there is some of this in his personality. The best explanation, though, is the simplest: he is a man who knows himself.

This does not mean that he lets others know him. Even his friends, like Charles Guggenheim, who has studied him with a sensitive, critical eye, are hard put to easily characterize him. "It's difficult to use the usual shorthand to describe George," says Guggenheim. "The obvious images don't come to mind. He doesn't fit into a lot of recognizable political modes." "I don't think that anyone ever gets really close to McGovern," adds Gordon Weil, who perhaps knows him as well as anyone who works for him. "However close you think you get, there is that distance, that little cushion of reserve, that separates you from the man."

Like everyone else who works for McGovern, Weil rarely sees his boss outside the office; McGovern's personal and professional lives are kept carefully distinct. Though the people who vote for him wouldn't dream of calling him anything but "George," to the people who do his bidding in Washington he is always "Senator" —to his face or behind his back. In themselves these little touches are insignificant. But they portend something deeper in the man himself.

Unfortunately, few people have had the opportunity to see how deep that something goes. It is not that they don't try; it is that he doesn't let them. McGovern guards himself and his emotions well, probably too well. His is a complex defense mechanism that operates on two different levels. On the surface there is the image of a man who will answer almost any question, who seemingly is ready, almost eager, to provide the most intimate details of his personal and political failings. "It is quite an experience when he first lays it on you," says a reporter who has covered several of McGovern's campaigns. "I mean, he was just telling me everything. Some of the things were almost embarrassing. But it was a helluva good technique. Because when I came away from him, I couldn't write anything critical. How could I? George was my friend."

At the same time this man who is so ready to deliver up facts and opinions about himself, talking all the while in the same flat tone, is personally incapable, save in the rarest circumstances, of revealing real emotion. There are a good number of people, including many who claim to know him well, who say that they have never seen McGovern angry. In fact, McGovern gets angry as often as the next man, sometimes at what seem to be inconsequential mistakes. Where he fools his friends, and most of the press, is that he does not show his anger in the usual, expectable fashion. Instead, McGovern withdraws. The voice lowers, the words come a fraction slower, and the reproof says: "Gee, do you think we would have done it that way?" "What he really means," says someone who has been asked that question, "is 'Listen, you dumb son of a bitch, if you ever do that again, I'm going to fire your ass out of here.'"

McGovern laughs well and has a broad sense of humor that tends to storytelling rather than wit, but even here something is held back. What McGovern hides best, however, is pain and fear. It is not insignificant that his wife has seen him cry only once since she has known him. It will be even more remarkable if she sees him cry a second time.

Overt emotion is foreign to McGovern, not because he doesn't feel, but because he feels deeply. He has difficulty understanding people who express obvious emotion and plain distaste for those who succumb to it. Ironically, he seems to admire the trait, if only because it would make him more politically appealing. "I only wish," he says, with a trace of wistfulness in his voice, "that just once I'd be on some network television show and some newsman said something to really tee me off, and I got angry, pounded my fist on the desk. Then everyone could see how really angry I am." On a personal level McGovern reflects: "I suppose it would be good if I could let my feelings out more. It's not good to have things building up inside with no way to let them get out."

It is unlikely that McGovern will ever give in to the advice of his friends to "loosen up"—nor does he really want to. The controlled evenness of his disposition is not only one of his most valuable protections; it has also been, at least in the past, one of his greatest strengths. Certainly the Air Force must have thought so to put him, at the age of twenty-two, in command of a four-engine bomber with responsibility for eight other men's lives. It is also reasonable to suppose that some of McGovern's more "radical" ideas have gone down better in South Dakota than they would have coming from the mouth of a shrill demagogue. McGovern himself lists the "steadiness" of his temperament as one of his chief qualifications for President. "I don't explode under pressure," he boasts. "I'm the type of person whose best writing, best speaking, best performances, have always come at times of great challenge, and that's a good quality to have in the President of the United States."

Undoubtedly. Whether it is a good quality for a *candidate* for President of the United States is something else again. A freer, more emotional McGovern, the image makers contend, would make him more attractive as a person, less cold, somehow more human. McGovern himself says: "It would be nice, I suppose, to have a few more exciting personal qualities." As it is, McGovern must rely on bluntness to convey what emotion cannot. Thus, for instance, the "This chamber reeks of blood" speech. Thus also the description of the Nixon wage-price freeze as "economic madness" and "bunk." The point is not so much the language as the way it is used. As one of McGovern's friends admits: "When he gets angry, it sounds like he is whining."

The impression is unfortunate, because it contributes to the image that McGovern's mildness is actually a lack of strength. He suffers from a "nice guy" reputation. Gloria Steinem's first impression of McGovern is typical: "I thought he was too nice to be a Senator." The feeling derives principally from the way McGovern treats other people. Those who feel his scorn usually get an apology within the hour. He is more than commonly courteous, even to those for whom he has personal as well as political contempt, and he expects his staff to do the same. "What galls me above everything else," he complained to one interviewer, ". . . [are] just simple things like having the courtesy to follow up with a thoughtful personal note to somebody who has done you a favor. . . . I have a helluva time getting my staff people to do some of those simple little thoughtful things that are to me more helpful than where I ought to stand on Red China. I can figure that out for myself." "I think," says one of his friends, who wishes McGovern were a bit tougher, "that he is incapable of seriously hurting anyone."

That is certainly true of his staff, which for years was riddled with intellectually weak sisters. The less than complete competence of his staff was hardly a secret to McGovern. He often mentioned it—to anyone but the staff itself. Like FDR, he found it nearly impossible to call someone into his office for a face-to-face dismissal. Such sessions, he said, were "personally demeaning." Instead, McGovern permitted conditions to deteriorate, trusting that the law of natural selection would take over and the offender would eventually be forced to leave. In the end McGovern's method usually worked, though in some cases it took years. Even then, McGovern was reluctant to release some staffers whose departure would have done him good. There was a closeness, he said, in a campaign staff that was duplicated in few other places. The only thing McGovern could compare it to was the tight-knittedness of his bomber crew. He valued loyalty and sometimes placed a higher premium on it than competence. "Do you know," he would say to friends who were critical of any of his staff, "that they would jump off a cliff for me if I asked them to?" Sometimes it was a car they would lie down in front of, or a truck or a train, but the message was the same. His staff depended on him for more than ordinary sustenance. He was, to some of them, the psychological center of their lives. And that was the way he seemed to like it.

McGovern's critics were willing to allow him that role—though as one of them noted: "You never get loyalty like that for nothing; those people own a piece of him." But they wondered how he would deal with a White House staff, where the stakes were far higher than a few votes in South Dakota. Some suggested that staff was not the real issue, that McGovern's supposed weakness was, as one friend put it, "hating personal confrontation. He can't stand it. He will do anything to avoid it." That explained, some said, McGovern's failure to clean out the old party hacks in South Dakota, or face down Freeman over Food for Peace, or stand up to Jackson on the Indian Affairs Subcommittee, or nail a witness before the Committee on Nutrition and Human Needs, or any of a dozen similar incidents. Demanded one doubter: "I want to know what happens when the railroads go out on strike and McGovern has to bring those union guys into the White House and say: 'Look, son of a bitch, you have to do it my way —or else.' Or what happens when the Joint Chiefs of Staff start to make an end run. Will McGovern be there to stop them?" "The problems that confront this country," says a long-time associate of Robert Kennedy, "are not easy problems and they are not going to be solved with easy answers. You are going to have to be mean. You are going to have to be tough. You are going to have to be, if you will, ruthless."

The last word is a tipoff to the source of McGovern's difficulties. He is forced to compete, as Adam Walinsky puts it, "with images, shadows, and ghosts that grow only larger in death." McGovern's critics, and many of his supporters, want him to be nothing less than Robert Kennedy.

But Kennedy is only the personification of something far larger in American politics, something that might be called the "tough guy" school of the presidency. The theory began with the election of John Kennedy, continued through Lyndon Johnson's presidency, and reached its zenith in the spring of 1968 in the tragic odyssey of Robert Kennedy. The election of Richard Nixon may be looked on as a temporary aberration, an historical accident wrought by Sirhan Sirhan, though in the "tough guy" school—which includes not only the candidates but the people who elect candidates, others who give them shape, and still others who write about them—Nixon has his defenders. There are even those who would award honorary membership in the school to Eugene McCarthy, who is credited with being in his own fashion "unpredictable," even "dangerous," as evinced by his willingness to let party and principle go down the drain in 1968.

The cardinal virtue of this new theory of the presidency is "pragmatism." Its members are invariably described as "tough-minded realists" with a taste for power and getting things done. *Time* magazine once approvingly characterized the Kennedys, for instance, as having "an instinct for the jugular." Those blessed with such instincts always seem to be "lean and hungry," in a way not unlike Shakespeare's Cassius. The emphasis is heavy on the masculine virtues. Even the language of the "can-do" politicians and intellectuals reflects it. They do not solve poverty; they make "war" on it. They "jawbone" the economy into line. The news of their exploits is "managed." More elusive problems are handled by men in their own image. It is no accident that the Green Beret training school in Fort Bragg, North Carolina, is named after John F. Kennedy.

George McGovern does not fit well into this milieu. The high-noon showdowns that Lyndon Johnson use to revel in are not his style. (One likely exception will be the Joint Chiefs of Staff. "I've been watching those guys make mistakes for the last twenty-five years," says McGovern, with a glint in his eye. "I can't wait to have a crack at them.") He rejected the advice of friends who wanted him to be "on the next plane for Saigon," as one of them urged, when Nguyen Cao Ky threatened to personally kick him out of Vietnam. He also disregarded Frank Mankiewicz' initial counsel, which was to address the workers at Lockheed and explain why he was voting against a $250 million loan for the ailing aerospace giant. Bob Kennedy probably would have done both. But McGovern is not Kennedy. Nor does he have Kennedy's "killer instinct," and what is more he wants no part of it. "I think we need precisely the opposite in politics today," McGovern says. "We need someone who places high values on humanity, on human relationships, on the dignity of the person. I think one of the things that has been wrong with American politics in recent years is that we've had too much of the killer instinct and too much tendency to disregard simple, old-fashioned human relationships."

Those are not the expected words of a presidential candidate. And quite frankly they have cost McGovern. The toll has been particularly high among the press, which has been conditioned—and has itself conditioned its readers—to the gut-cutting style of presidential politics. Partially as a result, McGovern has found it difficult to receive objective, much less sympathetic treatment at the hands of the country's opinion makers. His statements, when reported, are routinely relegated to the back columns of the major media, while the comings and goings of unannounced and less credible candidates are given prominent display. One example was McGovern's announcement for the presidency. Most major papers tucked the news away on the inner pages. When New York Mayor John Lindsay decided to become a Democrat, by contrast, thirty camera crews were on hand to record his words, which were played on page one of every newspaper from coast to coast.

The editors will explain the difference in terms of charisma. Charisma is news. Lindsay has it; McGovern does not. That is not charisma, though, as the Greeks defined it. The way the term has come into popular use, and the sense in which the editors use it, it is not leadership but the ability to arouse emotion. That McGovern does not do; in fact, does not choose to do. McGovern will edify an audience, sometimes inspire it. He will seldom incite it. One of the few times he did was in March 1971 when he spoke to 5,000 University of Wisconsin students crammed into the Madison Stock Pavilion. The antiwar message McGovern delivered that night was interrupted more than a dozen times by stormy, emotional applause. One could sense McGovern building with it, like a swimmer riding the crest of a giant wave. Then suddenly he pulled back, relaxed, and let the crowd calm down. "I could have turned that audience into a frenzy," he said later. "There was so much electricity in the air that I could have just literally stampeded the audience." Most politicians, given the opportunity, would have leaped at it. But not McGovern. "It's possible to dazzle a crowd if you really work at it," he says. "But that is no qualification for leadership. Hitler was a master at crowds."

McGovern will never be. Emotionalism in public is just as abhorrent to him as it is in private. Frenzy, he thinks, helped kill Bobby Kennedy. He does not want it to kill anyone else. Thus he recoils from it or any behavior even suggesting violence. To one newsmagazine this makes him "the Wally Cox of the campaign." A jab like that wounds McGovern. He broods, far too much for his own good, about what people think of him—not only the press or his colleagues in the Senate but the man he meets on the street who won't shake his hand. But he has learned to live with it, and so inevitably will he learn to live with the "Mr. Peepers" image, unfair as that characterization may seem for a former war hero who has risked his political life not once but a number of times. One thing is sure: he will not give in to the public mood. Not on the issue of violence.

That is not to say that McGovern is completely guileless or unwilling to make the minor adjustments—of which the change in appearance is only the most obvious—that he feels are necessary to win the nomination. He has already limited his statements on Vietnam in the interests of electability and, in a remarkably candid admission in *Playboy*, has announced that he might well be "more circumspect about the kind of groups with which I am associated," meaning that he may be seeing Sandy Gottlieb and Cora Weiss a little less. While some of McGovern's liberal friends may find such statements startling, political realism is nothing new to his personality. McGovern has always been an uncommonly good politician. A Democrat has to be to get elected in South Dakota. "One of the things that people miss about George," says a veteran political analyst in his home state, "is that he is a helluva good politician. Smooth, really cagey. And tough. Tough as a son of a bitch. But not on people. George is tough on issues."

There are other things that people miss, and some of them are vital to understanding the man. He is in the most general sense, and far more than most public men, the product of his past. A crucial element of that past is the place of his rearing. Unlike Nixon, the rootless, anonymous Californian, McGovern springs from an historically definable time and place. The Plains on which he was born and grew to manhood have a fabric, texture, and system of values all their own. To an extent not usually guessed at, the collective experience of the Plains, and McGovern's own particular memories of a boyhood spent on them, are at work in his person—shaping his attitudes, conditioning his reactions—even today.

Some of the traits of course are obvious: the lack of social sophistication, the Wedgewood cufflinks that in Gloria Steinem's words "drag on the floor," the fascination with "glittery people" like Shirley MacLaine or even more improbably the Supremes (for whom he once hosted a reception in Washington attended by more public relations people than guests), the nasal twang that a New York elocutionist has so far been unable to correct, the inability to distinguish a clam from an oyster, the slow and deliberate pattern of speech, even the plain words.

But these are merely marks of caricature. Where being a "Plainsman" truly reveals itself is in McGovern's regard for the land and the people who live on it. The attachment, says someone who has known him intimately for the last twenty years, "is an emotionalism that approaches religion."

Truly it seems that way. What faith McGovern has is grounded in the land. He trusts it. He believes in its ability to recover from whatever plagues befall it if not this season then the next or surely the one after that. By necessity he is an optimist, like all who work the land. And like them too he takes the longer view, both of hardship and of plenty. To the extent that his vision of life is bounded by certain, immutable values—the importance of family, the dependence on nature, the strength of community, the worth of living things—he is a conservative. He seeks not so much to change America as to restore it, to return it to the earliest days of the Republic, which he believes, naïvely or not, were fundamentally decent, humane, and just. Like the Populists, he is willing to gamble with radical means to accomplish his end. There remains in him, though, as it remained in the Populists, a lingering distrust of government, a suspicion of bigness in all its forms.

He is a man of the people, not in the sense that he panders to their whims—quite obviously, he does not—but in that he trusts their ultimate judgment. He talks with them and he listens, sometimes perhaps too much. Because he assigns their opinions more or less equal rank, he can be indiscriminate in taking advice, not on major concerns, but on matters of procedure and even more especially on how he regards himself. "Political advice from someone like Jack Gilligan," notes one member of his staff, "is more important than what you heard from a guy you just bumped into in the hotel lobby. But sometimes you have a tough time convincing McGovern of that."

There are others who complain that McGovern spends too much time talking with ordinary people he meets along the campaign trail. Smart politics, they contend, and perhaps correctly, calls for a quick touch of the hand, a fleeting "Good to see you," and a lightning move to the next voter. What they fail to realize once again is that the Kennedy style is not the McGovern style. More to the point, it is not the style of a former teacher who still seeks to teach.

Teaching has been McGovern's overriding ambition since he was a sophomore in high school, and despite apparent detours into religion and politics it has remained so ever since. What has changed is the mode. What has enlarged is the classroom. The impulse remains the same. And it is not just anything that McGovern is teaching. It is history, a record of events in which he sees himself as an integral part—turning the nation away from Vietnam, arousing the public's conscience about hunger, restructuring the country's political institutions, and (in many ways the achievement of which he is most proud) offering a political option to the people of his state. It is not surprising that of all the accolades and compliments he has received McGovern treasures most deeply the remark of another South Dakota professor, who explained how the same state could elect a Karl Mundt and a George McGovern. "Mundt," said the professor, "tells us what we want to hear. McGovern shows us what we should be."

If he does so in an often moralistic, preachy way, it is only because he is the son of a minister and a former minister himself. That heritage is never far from him. It betrays itself most evidently in the manner of his campaign, in the almost Jesuitical scorn he reserves for those who challenge his word, in his habit of casting issues in moral terms. Philosophically as well as politically, he considers himself one of the elect. Such people are not easy to know or even like. There is a righteousness in their demeanor that puts off more fallible men. So it is with McGovern, a man for whom respect comes easier than love.

The respect McGovern commands has been won the hard way, by being "tough on issues," as his friend puts it, "not on people." On China, on Vietnam, on the whole specter of militarism in American life, he has, as one journalistic observer notes, "seen over the horizon" better than anyone else. And he has guarded that vision with fierce tenacity, even in the face of opposition that could well have cost him his political career. Today, having been proved right on nearly all his predictions, he is proud of that record, even a little arrogant about it. He tends to congratulate himself in speeches about "being courageous" and "taking the tough stand" a shade more than is seemly. Somehow these qualities should be evident. McGovern seems to want to ensure that no one misses the point. No one does, though the force of it is diminished, if ever so slightly, by having come from the man himself. McGovern will also remind reporters—off the record—that Ed Muskie was "nowhere" when the Senate doves needed help on the "transcendent" issue of the war.

Neither was Hubert Humphrey, but McGovern forgives him his sins. In fact, it is Humphrey more than any opponent, McCarthy and Kennedy included, for whom McGovern has the most respect. The reason is simple: "Hubert always believed in what he said." It is that quality McGovern values most keenly in others. Not coincidentally, it is also his greatest strength.

Belief—sheer credibility—is the key to McGovern. More than any single factor it explains the phenomenon of his success in conservative South Dakota. Planning, intelligent organization, and a string of uncommonly inept opponents certainly helped, but poll after poll has confirmed that when everything else is said and done South Dakotans vote for him for one reason: they trust him. In his early days on the Hill, McGovern, like most Congressmen, used to conduct mail surveys of constituent attitudes on various

issues. He discontinued the practice after some of the leaflets came
back with the scrawled notation: "Do what you think is best. We
trust you." They have continued to trust him through the years,
even though more often than not they have violently opposed
much of what he stood for. One had only to look at the battered
bumpers of the pick-up trucks on the back country roads of South
Dakota in 1968 to see the source of McGovern's strength. There,
stuck incongruously next to the advertisements for the "Courageous Prairie Statesman," were exhortations to "Stand Up for
America: Wallace for President!" The sentiments were not contradictory. Both men in their way were battlers. Both men in their
way had the power of belief.

Today McGovern is trying to transfer that faith from a single
rural state smaller than San Diego to a complex, troubled nation
of 200 million. Vietnam, the economy, urbanism, and law and
order gnaw at people's minds, he says, but at the root of their
uneasiness is something far more basic: "They have lost faith in
their government."

It is that which McGovern seeks to reclaim, not by any complex formula of social engineering, but by a single campaign
promise: "to seek and speak the truth." That is his issue, in many
ways his only issue. Out of the cataclysm of 1968 the Democratic
candidates—with the exception of Jackson and, from moment to
moment, Muskie—have coalesced on the great concerns. There is
no disagreement that the economy is a mess, that the cities are fast
becoming unlivable, that the races are more polarized than ever,
that there is a gap between generations, that the air and the water
must be made pure, that priorities need reordering, or that the
boys must be brought home not later but now. Even Hubert
Humphrey supports the McGovern-Hatfield amendment. The
differences are of degree rather than kind. Thus, ultimately, the
choice must devolve on one consideration: Which man is to be
believed?

On the answer to that single question McGovern staked his
hopes for the presidency. When he talked of the "credibility gap,"
of "deceit and dishonesty at the highest levels of government,"
he was touching an exposed nerve. His denunciations of the war

might have aroused college kids to follow him, but when he spoke of "belief" and "trust" and "truth" he was moving an audience that knew no boundaries. "That is the major issue in this campaign today," he declared, "the simple necessity for government to begin telling the truth." As the applause welled up, McGovern would go on: "You try telling mothers who have lost their sons, as the government is telling them today, that the war is winding down. You try telling men standing in unemployment lines, as the government is telling them today, that the economy is turning up. You try telling blacks living in the slums, as the government is telling them today, that it is a time for benign neglect and lowering their voices. It is too bad that this administration won't tell the people the truth. Because it is a hard truth, and the people know it is hard."

McGovern has been pointing out the hard truths since the end of World War II. When he said them, they were usually not listened to, not at first and not by many. By the 1970s, he was convinced, the ideas he had been talking about for the last twenty-five years had at last won majority acceptance. In the interval he had built a public career on a willingness to be oddly out of kilter with his time. Now, he felt, had come the moment to act on what he had been warning about. There was a sense of finality, of apocalypse, in some of his statements. The liberal delaying tactics he himself had been such a master at in the Senate no longer were enough. He doubted frankly that the people would go on trusting. Their patience had been used up. "Nineteen seventy-two," he said in all seriousness, "may be the last turnaround we will have. If we continue on this present course . . . under the kind of leadership we've had in recent years, it's an open question whether this society can survive."

Nineteen seventy-two was in many ways the last chance also for George McGovern. Nineteen sixty-eight had already passed him by. There would be no 1976, as far as he was concerned. "This is the last time I am running," he said. McGovern was not about to become the Harold Stassen of the Democratic party. So, quite literally, it was now or never.

Which it would be depended on the country's perception of

itself. In their relatively brief history, Americans had chosen a variety of men to lead them, both the brave and the weak, the knight and the knave. Not often had they chosen a quietly decent man who offered nothing so much as the promise of belief.

Index

Abel, I. W., 247, 249
Aberdeen American News, 121, 122–123
ABM, 133, 141, 168
Adams, Sam, 40, 46, 47
Adderson, George, 227
Adderson, Mary, 227
AFL–CIO, 94–95, 143*n*. *See also* CIO
Agricultural surpluses. *See* Surplus commodities
Agriculture, 89–90, 115, 221
  House Committee, 86, 100, 106
  Senate Committee, 128, 134, 224
  See also U.S. Department of Agriculture
Aid to Dependent Children Act, 141
Aiken, George, 176, 177
Air Force, U.S., 39–40, 42, 45, 133, 141, 281
Alioto, Joseph, 204
Americans for Democratic Action, 5, 139
Andersen, Harl, xiii, 72, 80, 86
Andersen, Sigurd, 121
Anderson, Clinton, 177
Anderson, Jack, 239
Anti-Catholicism, 95
Anti-Communism, 59, 64, 69,

Anti-Communism (*continued*)
  81–83, 97–98, 114
Antiwar demonstrations, 161, 169–174, 184, 185, 250
Argentina, 107, 108
Arms spending. *See* Military appropriations
Ashlock, William, xiii, 41, 42, 43, 44, 47–48

Baldwin, Hanson, 157–158
Bangs, Archie, xiii, 195
Barnet, Richard, xiii, 4–5, 129, 138
Bayh, Birch, 248
Beale, David, xiii, 168, 171, 243, 244, 261, 262
Beck, Dave, 90
Beltran, Pedro, 109
Benson, Ezra Taft, 80–81, 88, 89
Bickel, Alexander, 254
Billington, Ray Allen, xiii, 61–62, 63
Bode, Ken, 248
Bond, Julian, 206
Bottum, Joe, 121, 123–125
Brady, Mildred McGovern, xiii, 17, 23, 25, 36, 50
Brazil, 108–109
Briles, Olive McGovern, xiii, 17, 25, 50

Brown, J. Marshall, 249
Brown, Joseph, 226–227
Brown, Sam, 169, 171, 172, 175
Bryan, William Jennings, 276
Bryant, Rosalee, 228
Bunker, Ellsworth, 184
Burgess, Karl, 197

California
  convention delegates, 10, 204–207
  federal food distribution, 236
Calley, William, 182
Cambodia, ix, 134, 141, 176, 235, 263
Camus, Albert, 170, 242
CARE, 102, 120
Case, Francis, 75, 101, 116–118, 121
Castro, Fidel, 128–129
Cather, Willa, 20
Central Intelligence Agency (CIA), 162
Chayes, Abe, 101
Chiang Kai-shek, 60
Chicago convention. *See* Democratic party
China
  and Food for Peace, 106–107, 114
  McGovern on, 65, 81, 126, 158, 183n, 282, 289
Choate, Robert, 223, 224
Church, Frank, 4, 8, 133, 157, 159–160, 165, 176, 177
CIO, 34, 57. *See also* AFL–CIO
Citizens Board of Inquiry, 219–220, 222, 223
Civil disobedience, 181n
Civil rights, 115, 141, 143
Clark, Blair, xiii, 259
Clark, Joseph, 165, 204, 219, 223
Clark, Ward, 66–67, 70
Clark, William, 204
Clifford, Clark, 177

Coffin, William Sloane, 171
Cold War, 51, 58, 62, 109
Collingwood, Charles, 157
Collins, Leroy, 247
Collins, Tom, 267
Communism
  in Henry Wallace campaign, 60–61
  McGovern on, 90, 104, 109, 124n, 129, 161
  See also Anti-Communism; China; Soviet Union
Conlon, Margaret, xiii, 18
Connally, John, 199
Cook, Marlow, 227, 233
Cooper, John Sherman, 176, 177
Cooper-Church amendment, 176, 177
Cotton, Norris, 138n
Cranston, Alan, 169, 175, 176
Cuba, 115, 128–129, 151
Cunningham, George, xiii, 77–78, 125, 127–128, 171, 200, 202, 243, 259, 264

Dairy industry, 240
Dakota Queen (aircraft), 41–43, 44–45
Dakota Story, A (film), 126
Dakota territory, 12–15, 20
Dakota Wesleyan University, 31, 32–33, 50, 63–65, 66, 82, 126, 146, 147
Daley, Richard, 10, 170–171, 203, 212, 213, 214, 250, 251
Davis, Rennie, 173
Davis, Will, 247
Dees, Morris, 266–267
Defense spending. *See* Military appropriations
de Gaulle, Charles, 153
Dellinger, David, 170
Democratic party, 66–67, 68–75
  Chicago convention, 2, 197–212, 250, 251–252

Democratic party (*continued*)
  in Mississippi, 201
  National Committee, 249, 255,
    256*n*, 264
  Platform Committee, 166
  Reform Commission, 245–256,
    262, 264–265
  South Dakota, 6, 27, 32, 64,
    69, 74, 84, 116–118, 119, 122,
    123–124, 147, 212
Dent, Harry, 239
Depression, 19, 24–25, 31–32, 69,
  223
Diem, Ngo Dinh. *See* Ngo Dinh
  Diem
Dirksen, Everett, 160, 204
Disarmament, 82, 149–151
Discrimination, 236, 251–256.
  See also Civil rights; Racism
Distinguished Flying Cross
  awarded McGovern, 45, 89,
    235
  returned by veterans, 179
Docking, Robert, 100
Dolan, Joe, 192, 244, 268
Dole, Robert, 138*n*, 238–239
Donley, Owen, xiii, 87, 152, 197,
  208
Donovan, Pat, xi, 105–106, 112,
  113, 126, 264
Dougherty, William, xiii, 6, 117,
  189, 192, 193, 196–197, 200
Douglas, John, xiii, 59
Douglas, Paul, 59, 151
Dunn, Francis, 76
Dutton, Fred, 247, 254, 259, 261–
  262

Eagleton, Thomas, 177
Ecker, Peder, xiii, 6, 69, 75, 117
Economic conversion, 131–132,
  138, 275
Edelman, Peter, 223
Edenfield, Frederick, 228
Education, 140

Eisenhower, Dwight D., 68, 80,
  88, 102, 103, 110, 134, 153
"Eisenhower Doctrine," 86
Elections. *See* McGovern,
  George; Primary elections
Ellender, Allen, 134, 136, 221–
  222, 227, 228, 233, 241
Ellington, Buford, 250
Ellsberg, Daniel, 181, 182
Ellsworth Air Force Base
  (S.D.), 134
Environmental legislation, 142
Excess profits tax, proposed, 137

Fall, Bernard, 152, 156
Famine. *See* Hunger
Farm problems, 86, 88, 89–90,
  122
  See also Agriculture
Farmers Union, 100
FBI, 64, 214
Federal Housing Authority,
  239–240, 241
Feldman, Myer, xiii, 101, 105,
  113, 115, 117, 259
Field Foundation, xii, 219
Finch, Robert, 229, 230, 232
Fisher, Roger, 175
Fitzgerald, Ray, 95
Florida, hunger in, 224–227, 242
Floyd, Joe, xiii, 161, 162
Food for Peace, xii, 9, 101–116,
  117, 122, 136, 139, 218, 223
Food stamp program, 139, 176,
  218, 220, 229, 231–234, 236,
  238, 242
Foreign aid appropriations, 133–
  134
Foss, Joe, 87–90, 121
Fraser, Donald, 256*n*
Freeman, Orville, 96, 100–101,
  113, 114, 135, 215, 221, 238,
  283
Frondizi, Arturo, 108
Fulbright, J. William, 4, 8, 151

Galbraith, J. Kenneth, 115, 147
Gandhi, Mohandas K., 52, 185
Gans, Curtis, 260
Garland, Hamlin, 14–15, 20
Garrett Theological Seminary, 53, 57
Gavin, James, 3, 133, 156
Geneva agreements, 151, 155
Giants in the Earth (Rölvaag), xii, 13–14
Gilligan, Jack, 196, 288
Goldwater, Barry, 153
Goodell, Charles, 169, 172, 174–175, 176, 184
Goodwin, Richard, 194
Gottlieb, Sanford, xiii, 129, 130, 133, 134, 214, 286
Gravel, Mike, 182, 184
Greening of America (Reich), 146n
Gruening, Ernest, 3, 8, 134, 152, 181, 184
Gubbrud, Archie, 121, 127, 212
Guggenheim, Charles, xiii, 117, 126, 214, 266, 279
Gulf of Tonkin resolution, 152–153
Gun control, 142, 214

Hamer, Fannie Lou, 204
Hamill, Pete, 273
Hardin, Clifford, 229, 230, 232
Harriman, Averell, 120, 168
Harris, Fred, 140–141, 245, 246, 249
Harrison, David, 198, 200
Hart, Gary, xiii, 263–264, 265, 272
Hart, Philip, 138
Hartke, Vance, 169
Hatfield, Mark, 141, 175, 176
Hawk, David, 169
Hayden, Tom, 174
Health care, 140
Henry, Aaron, 247

Heroin traffic, 179
Herseth, Ralph, 95
Higgins, Ken, 40
Hilburn, Samuel, 64–65
Hilsman, Roger, 157, 158
Hitchcock, Herbert, 67
Ho Chi Minh, 151, 155, 165
Hoff, Philip, 196
Hoffa, James, 90, 94, 241
Hoffman, Abbie, 174
Hofner, Rose, 28
Holum, John, xiii, 2, 136, 138, 139, 175, 176, 178, 183
Holum, Ken, 75
Hooker, John, 247
Hoover, J. Edgar, 97–98
Hospital construction, 140
Hot dogs, fat content of, 240
House Agriculture Committee, 86, 100, 106, 221
Housing, 140, 239–240, 275
Howe, Oscar, 18
Hughes, Harold, 169, 175, 196, 197, 245, 246, 247, 250, 253, 264
Hughes, Richard, 245, 247, 253
Humphrey, Hubert, 9–10, 28, 95, 112, 120, 130, 228
  as candidate, 194, 197, 198, 204, 205–206, 210, 216n, 245, 260, 270
  McGovern and, 85–86, 188, 190, 202–203, 210–211, 289
  and party reform, 247–248, 250
  on Vietnam war, 85–86, 154, 290
Humphrey, Muriel, 85
Hunger, 103, 122, 218–219, 222–239, 241–242
Hunger USA, 220–222

Immokalee, Florida, 225–227, 242
India, 102, 111

Indian affairs, 144–145, 283
Indochina. *See* Cambodia; Laos; Vietnam
Institute for Policy Studies, 5, 130
International cooperation, 51, 52–53
Italy, 39–40, 46, 223

Jackson, Henry, 144, 270, 283, 290
Jackson, Jesse, 201, 239
Janke, George, xiii, 30
Javits, Jacob, 177, 227, 228, 229, 233
Jobs, legislation on, 140, 275
John XXIII, Pope, 112
Johnson, Haynes, 262
Johnson, Lyndon, 284
    administration, 132, 136, 193, 238
    challenge to, 2, 4, 250
    and party reform, 247
    supporters of, 204, 206
    as Vice President, 106
    war policy, 85–86, 155–156, 157, 159–160, 164, 165–166, 168, 186, 198, 203, 215
Joint Chiefs of Staff, 283, 284
Jordan, Len, 177
Juliao, Francisco, 109

Kahin, George, 129
Kendall, Art, 25
Kennedy, Edward M., 145, 210, 244, 250, 256
    McGovern and, 169, 187, 191, 257, 258, 260–261
    as possible presidential candidate, 196, 199, 207–208, 259, 273–274
Kennedy, Ethel, 125
Kennedy, John A., 97–98
Kennedy, John F., x, 2, 9, 74, 90, 91, 120, 124*n*, 133, 152, 190, 228, 283

Kennedy, John F. (*continued*)
    and Food for Peace, 103–104, 112–113, 114–115, 218
    McGovern and, 95–96, 98, 99–101, 122, 128
Kennedy, Robert F., 2–4, 90–91, 96, 98, 167, 235, 241, 283–284
    assassination of, 9, 142, 285
    on hunger, 219, 223, 226
    McGovern and, 8–9, 105, 142–143, 147, 187–188, 189, 190–191, 217
    as presidential candidate, 191, 199, 217*n*, 245, 263, 265, 283
Kennedy-Ives labor reform bill, 90
Khrushchev, Nikita, 122, 129
Kimmelman, Henry, xiii, 147, 257–258*n*, 259
Kirk, Claude, 228, 229
Klein, Herbert, 229
Kleindienst, Richard, 171, 172
Kopechne, Mary Jo, 200
Korean War, 65, 102, 158
Kotz, Nick, xii, 218–219, 238
    See also *Let Them Eat Promises*
Ky, Nguyen Cao. *See* Nguyen Cao Ky

Labor, organized, 94–95, 114, 249
    legislation on, 90–91, 142
    McGovern and, 34, 57, 124*n*, 143
Lansdale, Edward, 162
Laos, 115, 141, 168, 176, 178
Latin America, 107–110, 128–129, 225
Lawler Café, 18, 126
LeMay, Curtis, 159
Leone, Richard, xiii, 245, 258, 259, 260, 261, 262–263
Let Them Eat Promises (Kotz), xii, 218, 230–231

Liberalism, 57
McGovern and, 61, 139–140, 202, 215, 242
Lindley, John, 118, 119
Lindsay, John V., 264, 285
Link, Arthur, xii, xiii, 61, 62, 85
Lockheed Aircraft Corporation, 284
Lodge, Henry Cabot, 161
Lon Nol, 134
Loveless, Herschel, 96, 100
Lovre, Harold, 75–76, 77, 79, 80–81, 83, 84–85
Lowenstein, Allard, xiii, 2–4, 5–9, 186, 198, 259
Lucey, Patrick, 194, 196
Ludlow Massacre, xii, 57

McAfee, William, xiii, 40, 41
McAnich, Don, 50
McCarthy, Eugene, 8, 139, 166, 235, 245, 284
McGovern and, 175, 189–190, 192–193, 202, 205, 250
as presidential candidate, 9, 10, 169, 187, 188, 191–192, 194, 197–198, 204–205
McCarthy, Joseph, 2, 270
McCloskey, Paul ("Pete"), 274
McDermott, Ed, 201–202
McDougal, Curtis, 59
McGee, Gale, 157
McGinniss, Joe, 265
McGovern, Ann (daughter), 50, 145
McGovern, Eleanor Stegeberg (wife), x, 9, 31–32, 33–34, 35, 36, 98, 250
in campaigns, 83, 116n, 125
marriage and family life, 37–38, 43, 50, 53, 54, 65, 72, 145, 146, 197
on McGovern's career, 51, 56, 67
McGovern, Frances McLean (mother), 17, 19, 20, 50, 55

McGovern, George Stanley
advisers, 129–130, 152, 259–260, 288
on American values, 52, 146n
and athletics, 16
beliefs, 284–287
birth and childhood, 17, 19–20, 23, 25–26
as campaigner, 74, 79–80, 272–273, 288, 289–290
character, x–xi, 3, 19–20, 29–30, 268, 279–281, 287
children, 50, 53, 63, 65
choice of career, 24, 34, 51, 55–56, 66n, 70–71
as Congressman, 8–9, 59, 85–87, 103
contributors to campaigns, 78–79, 95, 197, 200, 257n
as debater, 10, 27–32, 35, 51, 96–97
decision to run for President, ix–x, 192–199
decision to run for Senate, 92
driving habits, 77–78n
election campaigns, 75–85, 88–90, 93–98, 116, 122–126, 215–216
endorsement of Henry Wallace, 59–60
entry into politics, 64, 67, 70, 74
family life, 79, 145–147, 195, 196
fatalism, 46–47, 101, 269
flying career, 5, 36, 37–38, 40–48, 158–159, 274
fundamentalist upbringing, 20, 22, 50, 63
as graduate student, 55, 56, 61–63
homes, 19–20, 23, 54, 56, 145, 146, 147
illness with hepatitis, 112–113, 116n, 125, 271n
lack of flamboyance, x, 29–30,

McGovern, George (*continued*)
229, 235, 241, 273, 281–282,
285–286
marriage, 37–38
as moviegoer, 21, 146
naming of, 15
opposition to Vietnam war, 3,
7, 10, 85, 149–185, 186, 199,
211–212, 215, 242, 263, 274–
275, 289, 290–291
as party organizer, 67, 70–75
on party reform, 245–256
as peace orator, 34–35
political instincts, 5, 7, 8, 10,
67, 142, 144, 153, 262
presidential ambitions, 4–6,
256–257, 261–262, 278
as presidential candidate, 199–
210, 243–246, 264–277, 284–
292
reading, 20, 146
relations with staff, 282–283
as Senator, 77*n*–78*n*, 128–148,
149–185, 190, 222–242
speaking fees, 244
speeches, 34–35, 52–53, 128–
131, 267–268, 276
as student minister, 53–55
studies, 43–44, 50
as teacher, 64, 70, 288
trips to Vietnam, 161–162,
183–184
voting record, 139–143
on women, 275
in World War II, 35–36, 40–
48, 50, 51, 126, 223, 274
writings, xii, 102, 104, 136, 152
See also Communism; Farm
problems; Food for Peace;
Gun control; Housing;
Hunger; Labor, organized;
"Overkill"; Racism; Wel-
fare
McGovern, Joseph (father), 15–
17, 19–20, 21, 23–24, 36, 55–
56, 63

McGovern, Joseph (*continued*)
death, 41, 49
McGovern, Larry (brother),
17, 25–26, 50
McGovern, Mary (daughter),
85
McGovern, Steven (son), 65,
145
McGovern, Susan (daughter),
53, 145
McGovern, Terry (daughter),
195, 196, 197, 217, 257
McGovern-Hatfield amend-
ment, 139, 175–179, 290
McGrory, Mary, 169
MacLaine, Shirley, 287
McNair, Robert, 249
Maddox, Lester, 250
Magness, Jim, 93, 118
Malaria, campaign against, 102,
111
Mankiewicz, Frank, xiii, 183,
192, 198, 200, 203, 210–211,
269, 272, 273, 274, 284
Mansfield, Mike, 169, 176, 258
Marijuana, 140, 195–196
Martin, Yancey, xiii, 264
Martz, Glenn, 88–89
Mass transit, 140, 141
Mater et Magistra (Pope John
XXIII), 112
Mayday movement, 173
Mayer, Jean, 231
Meany, George, 143*n*, 249
Melman, Seymour, 129, 130
Metcalf, Lee, 8, 188
Methodism, 15, 16–17, 24, 50,
66*n*
Middle America, McGovern on,
26–27
Middle East, 86, 153
Migrant workers, 226
Militarism, 133–134, 289. *See
also* Military appropria-
tions; "Overkill"

Military appropriations, 130–132, 133–134, 141–142, 150
Military draft, 140, 141
Milk, 100, 227, 228, 235
  and Food for Peace, 109, 111
  school programs, 220, 237
Minority rights, and convention delegations, 251–256. *See also* Civil rights; Racism
Missile systems. *See* ABM
Mississippi, xii, 236
  convention delegates, 201, 204
  hunger in, 218–219
Mitchell, George, 255
Mitchell, South Dakota, 17–19, 26–27, 96, 104
Mitchell *Daily Republic*, 59–60, 65, 66
Mixner, David, 169, 247, 250, 259
Mizel, Edmund, 30, 32, 35
Mobilization to End the War, 170–172, 173, 184, 208, 263
Mondale, Walter, 227, 228, 229
Moore, Dan, 210
Moratorium, 169–170, 171, 263
Morse, Wayne, 3, 4, 8, 133, 134, 152, 154, 165, 181, 184, 243
Moss, Frank, 251
Moynihan, Daniel, 230, 231
Mundt, Karl, 4, 9, 28, 64, 75, 88, 89, 116, 140
  McGovern and, 92–94, 96–98, 124n, 129n, 138n, 288
Mundt-Nixon bill, 59, 92
Murphy, Katie Dell, 227
Muskie, Edmund, 10, 138, 161, 170, 172, 244, 248, 250
  as presidential candidate, 263, 268, 270, 290
  voting record, 141–142
  on war issue, 289
My Lai massacre, 182

Nader, Ralph, 240

Napolitan, Joe, 123n–124n
NASA. *See* Space program
Nation, The, 268
National Council of Churches, 35, 219
National Council on Hunger and Malnutrition, 231
National Environmental Policy Act, 142
National Forensic Society, 28, 98
National Milk Producers Federation, 100
National Nutrition Survey, 224, 229, 231, 234, 236–237
National Right to Work Committee, 142
Nelson, Gaylord, xiii, 8, 181, 184, 240
Nelson, Robert, xiii, 81, 97, 248, 253
New Democratic Coalition, 248
New Hampshire primary, 4, 188, 269–270
"New Mobe." *See* Mobilization
New Republic, 234–235
New York Times, 157, 181, 225
Newton, Huey, 174
Ngo Dinh Diem, 151, 152
Ngo Dinh Nhu, 152
Nguyen Cao Ky, ix, 166, 179, 284
Nguyen Van Thieu, 166, 180, 184
Nichol, Fred, xiii, 71–72, 84
Nixon, Richard M., 9, 98, 140, 167, 178, 180, 211, 225, 264
  and hunger, 229–233, 235, 237
  wage freeze, 137
  war policy, McGovern and, 168–169
Norbeck, Peter, 70, 116, 276
Northwestern University, 53, 55, 56, 57–58
Nuclear Test Ban Treaty, 130, 132, 151

Nuclear weapons, 149, 159. *See
    also* ABM; "Overkill"

O'Brien, Don, xiii, 200
O'Brien, Lawrence, 124*n*, 255,
    256
O'Connell, Bob, 41
Office of Economic Opportu-
    nity, 140
Operation Breadbasket, 201
"Overkill," 130–131, 149, 232

Paarlberg, Don, 103
Pacification, 165
Pearson, Robert, xiii, 28–29, 31,
    34, 35, 67
    attack on McGovern, 82–83
Peck, Sidney, 209
Pell, Claiborne, 196
Pennington, Ila Stegeberg, xiii,
    31, 33, 54, 61
Pennington, Robert, xiii, 54–55,
    56, 60, 64, 67
Pentagon Papers, 181–182
Percy, Charles, 177, 233, 239
Peru, 108–109
Pettigrew, Richard, 70, 276
Phillips, Channing, 201, 207, 210
Phillips, Kevin, 145*n*
Playboy magazine, 180, 286
Poage, Robert, 106, 221, 233
Police brutality, 209*n*, 213–214
Polls, 2, 76, 83, 96, 164, 172, 177–
    178, 213, 215*n*, 263, 289
Populist tradition, 68–69, 70,
    256, 270, 276, 287
Post, Nelson, xiii, 105, 109, 110,
    112, 115, 116
Poverty, 25, 219–223
Primary elections, 74–75, 253–
    255
    presidential, 191, 197, 251,
    269–270. *See also* New
    Hampshire primary

Progressive party, 58, 60–61
Proxmire, William, 138, 141

Quadros, Janio, 108

Racism, 143*n*, 199, 206, 276
Radicalism, 170–174, 275
Randolph, Jennings, 177
Raskin, Marcus, 4–5, 129
Rauh, Joseph, 5
Rauschenbusch, Walter, 51
Ray, Norman, 35, 38
Red-baiting. *See* Anti-Commu-
    nism
Reich, Charles, 146*n*
Republican party, 68, 69, 80, 84,
    88
    McGovern and, 73–74, 75, 197
    in South Dakota, 120, 121–122,
    195–196, 212
Reuter, Richard W., 120
Ribicoff, Abraham, 141, 203,
    210, 259
Rölvaag, O. E., xii, 13–14, 27
Roosevelt, Franklin D., 68
Rounds, Bill, 40, 44
Rowan, James, 145
Rubin, Jerry, 174
Rusk, Dean, 128

Salinger, Pierre, 200, 208, 273
SANE, 129, 175
Saxbe, William, 177
Schaefer, Arnold E., 225, 234,
    236–237
Schlesinger, Arthur M., xii, xiii,
    4, 99, 100, 120, 147, 273
    and Food for Peace, 103, 107,
    108, 112
Schlesinger, Steve, 260
School lunch programs, 102,
    109, 111–112, 136, 139, 141,
    237, 242

Segal, Eli, xiii, 246, 247, 248, 253
Select Committee on Nutrition and Human Needs, xii, 143, 224–228, 234, 238, 239–242, 246, 262, 283
Selective Service Act, 141, 180
Shapiro, Sam, 247
Siegal, Isadore, 41
Sioux Falls Argus-Leader, 83, 94, 97, 98, 119, 129n, 164
Sioux Indians, 144, 216
Smith, Bill, 223, 224, 232, 239
Smith, Jeff, xiii, 216n
Smith, Matt, Jr., 35
Smith, Matt, Sr., xiii, 35
Smith, Preston, 249
Son of the Middle Border (Garland), 14–15
Sorensen, Theodore, 132–133, 187, 194
South America. *See* Latin America
South Dakota, 12–15, 90
politics, 3, 5, 6, 59, 68–70, 76–77, 80, 189–191, 288
Soviet Union, 60, 65, 149
wheat shipments to, 114, 143n
Space program, 140, 141, 239
Stacey, Lionel, 82
Stacks, John, xiii, 137, 243, 261, 262
Starvation, 108. *See also* Hunger
Stavrianos, Lefton, xiii, 61, 62–63
Stearns, Richard, xiii, 264, 271
Stegeberg, Earl, 32, 34
Steinem, Gloria, xiii, 147, 200, 209, 259, 271n, 282, 287
Stennis, John, 138n, 179
Stevenson, Adlai, 65, 264
Stoner, Bruce, xiii, 66, 69
Stong, Ben, xiii, 136–137, 223–224
Strikes, 57
Supersonic transport (SST), 142
Supreme Court, U.S., 86, 275

Surplus commodities, 102–103, 104, 109, 110, 218
Symington, James, xiii, 105, 106, 107, 110–111, 113–114, 115, 124n

Taft-Hartley Act, 142
Talmadge, Herman, 134, 241
Taxes, 137, 141
Taylor, Maxwell, 133
Thieu, Nguyen Van. *See* Nguyen Van Thieu
Thomas, Norman, 60
Thompson, Frank, 188
Thousand Days, A (Schlesinger), xii, 103
Thurmond, Strom, 221
Time magazine, x, 137, 243, 268, 284
A Time of War, A Time of Peace (McGovern), xii, 152
Tonkin, Gulf of. *See* Gulf of Tonkin
Towner, Lawrence, xiii, 58
Truman, Harry S, 58, 60
Tydings, Joseph, 259

Udall, Morris, 259
Udall, Stewart, 75, 188, 258n, 259
United Auto Workers, 219
United Nations, 51, 81, 115, 156
U.S. Agency for International Development (AID), 114, 156
U.S. Air Force, 39–40, 42, 45, 133, 141, 281
U.S. Department of Agriculture, 99, 100–101, 103, 104, 218, 222, 233
U.S. Department of Health, Education and Welfare, 229
U.S. Public Health Service, 225

U.S. Senate
  Agriculture Committee, 128,
    134, 221, 224
  Appropriations Committee,
    131
  Rules Committee, 224, 239
  South Dakota members, 70
  See also Select Committee
    on Nutrition and Human
    Needs
United World Federalists, 156*n*
University of Iowa, 65–66
Unruh, Jesse, xiii, 192, 194, 196,
    198, 207
Urban renewal, 240

Valko, Michael J., 41
Van Dyk, Ted, xiii, 260, 272
Vanocur, Sander, xiii, 137
Vietnam war, ix, x, 115, 141, 150
  bombing, 155, 157, 158–159,
    160, 166
  enclave strategy, 156, 160, 167
  legislative efforts, 174–179
  troop withdrawals, 167–168
  veterans, 178, 179
  See also Humphrey, Hubert;
    Johnson,   Lyndon;   Mc-
    Govern, George
"Vietnamization" program, 175
Viorst, Milton, 180

Wade, Richard, xiii, 203, 264
Walinsky, Adam, xiii, 167–168,
    192
Wallace, Henry, 58–61, 65
  McGovern and, 81, 82, 126
War Against Want (McGov-
    ern), xii, 102, 104, 136
War on Poverty, 140–141
Washington *Post*, 181*n*, 232, 238

Washington *Star*, 128, 169, 180,
    262
Wechsler, James, 5
Weil, Gordon, xi–xii, 183, 274
Weiss, Cora, xiii, 171, 286
Welfare   legislation,   140–141,
    222, 224, 232–234, 237–238,
    239
Wendt, William, xiii, 27
Westmoreland, William, 165
Wheat
  federal subsidy on, 135
  shipments   under   Food   for
    Peace, 106, 111, 114, 143*n*
White,   Theodore   H.   ("Ted-
    dy"), 2, 9–10, 209
White, William S., 249
White House Conference on
    Hunger, 235, 238
Whitten, Jamie, 233
Williams, John Bell, 249
Wilson, Woodrow, 61, 62, 190,
    275
Women, 68, 259, 275
  in   convention   delegations,
    251–252
Women's Strike for Peace, 171
Woonsocket, South Dakota, 31
World Council of Churches, 75,
    194
World War II, 34, 35, 38–39, 137
Wrisley, Stanley, 226
Wyman, Eugene, 204

Xuan Thuy, 183

Young, Alfred, xiii, 57
Young, Bradley, 67
Young, Stephen, 8
Yugoslavia, 65